Faith and Piety in
Early Judaism

Faith and Piety
in Early Judaism

Texts and Documents

GEORGE W. E. NICKELSBURG and MICHAEL E. STONE

Trinity Press International
Philadelphia

First Trinity Press Edition 1991

Trinity Press International
3725 Chestnut Street
Philadelphia, PA 19104

Cover design by Steven Zellers

Library of Congress Cataloging-in-Publication Data

Faith and piety in early Judaism : texts and documents / [compiled
by] George W.E. Nickelsburg and Michael E. Stone.
    p.   cm.
    Reprint. Originally published: Philadelphia : Fortress Press,
© 1983.
    Includes bibliographies and index.
    ISBN 1-56338-012-9 :
    1. Judaism – History – Post-exilic period, 586 B.C-210 A.D.–
Sources. 2. Judaism – Doctrines – History – Sources.
I. Nickelsburg, George W.E., 1934- . II. Stone, Michael E., 1938-
[BM176.F34 1991]
296'.09'014 – dc20   91-12033
                                                                CIP

Printed in the United States of America

92   93   94   95   96   6   5   4   3   2

For Krister Stendahl

Contents

Preface

This reader was compiled in order to present some aspects of early Judaism unencumbered by the apparatus of technical scholarship. We have gathered the material in this way so that it is readily accessible to students and the broader public, as well as to colleagues who are not specialists in the area of early postbiblical Judaism.

The book was completed in 1980–81, when the authors were Fellows-in-Residence of the Netherlands Institute for Advanced Study at Wassenaar. Chapters 1, 3, and 6 were first prepared by Michael Stone, and Chapters 2, 4, and 5 by George Nickelsburg. In its present form, however, the whole book is the product of both authors. We are indebted to the staff of N.I.A.S., who facilitated our work in many ways, and particularly to Katherine Murphy and Marina Voerman, who typed the manuscript. Editorial assistance was provided by the University of Iowa, the University of Pennsylvania, and the Hebrew University. Proofs were read by James Peterson and Philip Frank of the University of Iowa. To our families we owe very special thanks for their patience and support.

From the very beginning of the project, we have received the hearty support and encouragement of Norman Hjelm, the Director of Fortress Press. The task of editing a complex manuscript and designing a readable book from it was executed with great skill and creativity by Edward A. Cooperrider, Peggy Hoover, and Phyllis Carson.

Wherever possible, we have used extant translations of the texts, which are cited in the chapter bibliographies. Where no such source is cited, the translations are our own.

We dedicate this book to our teacher, friend, and colleague, Krister Stendahl, whose charity, perceptiveness, and intellectual honesty have been, for three decades, a stimulus toward mutual understanding and respect between Jews and Christians—heirs of a common tradition.

Acknowledgments

Basil Blackwell
A. Dupont-Sommer, ed., *The Essene Writings from Qumran*. Cleveland: Meridian, 1961. Reprinted by permission of Basil Blackwell Publisher, Limited, Oxford, England.

Bobbs-Merrill Co.
Frederick C. Grant, *Hellenistic Religions*. New York: Bobbs-Merrill Co., 1953. Copyright © 1953 by Bobbs-Merrill Company. Reprinted by permission.

Walter de Gruyter & Co.
John MacDonald, *The Samaritan Chronicle II*. Berlin: W. de Gruyter, 1969. Reprinted by permission.

Doubleday & Co.
Theodor H. Gaster, *The Dead Sea Scriptures*, 3d ed. New York: Anchor, 1967. Copyright © 1956, 1964, 1976 by Theodor H. Gaster. Reprinted by permission of Doubleday & Company, Inc.

Frank Moore Cross, Jr., *The Ancient Library of Qumran and Modern Biblical Studies*. New York: Doubleday & Co., 1958. Copyright © 1958 by Frank Moore Cross, Jr. Reprinted by permission of Doubleday & Company, Inc., and Frank Moore Cross, Jr.

Harvard University Press
Loeb Classical Library, *Diodorus of Sicily* (XII); *Josephus* (I, II, III, VI, VII, IX); and *Philo* (II, V, IX). Reprinted by permission.

National Council of the Churches of Christ in the U.S.A.
Revised Standard Version of the Bible, copyrighted 1946, 1952, © 1971, 1973 by the Division of Christian Education of the National Council of the Churches of Christ in the U.S.A. Reprinted by permis-

sion. Special permission granted to use, in this publication, the you-your-yours form of personal pronoun in the address to God.

Oxford University Press
Herbert Danby, *The Mishnah*. London: Oxford University Press, 1933. Reprinted by permission.

J. A. Sanders, *The Dead Sea Psalms Scroll*. Ithaca, N.Y.: Cornell University Press, 1967. Copyright © 1967 by Oxford University Press. Reprinted by Permission of Oxford University Press, Oxford, England.

Penguin Books Ltd.
G. Vermes, *Dead Sea Scrolls in English*, 2d ed. London: Penguin Books, 1975. Reprinted by permission.

Scholars Press
Joseph A. Fitzmyer, "Further Light on Melchizedek from Qumran Cave 11," in idem, *Essays on the Semitic Background of the New Testament*, SBLSBS 5. Missoula: Society of Biblical Literature, 1974. Reprinted by permission of Joseph A. Fitzmyer.

Michael E. Stone, *The Testament of Abraham*. Missoula: Society of Biblical Literature, 1972. Reprinted by permission of Scholars Press, Chico, Calif.

The Society for Promoting Christian Knowledge
S. Gaselee, The Testament of Isaac and the Testament of Jacob, in G. H. Box, *The Testament of Abraham*. London: SPCK, 1927. Reprinted by permission.

Soncino Press
I. Epstein, *The Babylonian Talmud: Seder Zera'im*. London: Soncino Press, 1948. Reprinted by permission.

Yale University Press
William G. Braude, Commentary on Psalm 43, in idem, *The Midrash on Psalms*, Yale Judaica Series 13:2. New Haven: Yale University Press, 1959. Reprinted by permission.

The Fathers According to Rabbi Nathan, in Judah Goldin, *The Fathers According to Rabbi Nathan*, Yale Judaica Series 10. New Haven: Yale University Press, 1955. Reprinted by permission.

Abbreviations and Symbols

Add Esth	Additions to Esther
Ant.	Josephus, The Jewish Antiquities
Apoc. Abr.	Apocalypse of Abraham
APOT	R. H. Charles, ed. *Apocrypha and Pseudepigrapha of the Old Testament*. 2 vols. Oxford: Clarendon, 1913.
b.	*ben* (Hebrew for "son of")
Bar	Baruch
B.C.E.	Before the Common Era (= B.C.)
C.E.	Common Era (= A.D.)
1, 2 Cor	1, 2 Corinthians
Dan	Daniel
Deut	Deuteronomy
DJD(J)	*Discoveries in the Judaean Desert (of Jordan)*. Oxford: Clarendon, 1955–
Exod	Exodus
Ezek	Ezekiel
Gen	Genesis
Gk	Greek
Hab	Habakkuk
Hag	Haggai
Heb	Hebrew, Hebrews
HTR	*Harvard Theological Review*
IDB	G. A. Buttrick, ed. *Interpreter's Dictionary of the Bible*. 4 vols. Nashville: Abingdon, 1962.
IDB Sup	Keith Crim, ed. Supplementary Volume to *IDB*.
Isa	Isaiah
Jas	James
JBL	*Journal of Biblical Literature*
Jer	Jeremiah
JJS	*Journal of Jewish Studies*
Josh	Joshua

Jub.	Jubilees
Judg	Judges
1 Kgs	1 Kings
LCL	Loeb Classical Library
Lev	Leviticus
LXX	Septuagint, Greek translation of the Hebrew Bible
M.	Mishnah
1, 2, 3, 4 Macc	1, 2, 3, 4 Maccabees
Mal	Malachi
Matt	Matthew
Mic	Micah
Num	Numbers
Obad	Obadiah
Phil	Philippians
Prov	Proverbs
Ps	Psalm(s)
Ps. Sol.	Psalms of Solomon
1QH	Hymn Scroll. Published by E. Sukenik. *The Dead Sea Scrolls of the Hebrew University.* Jerusalem: Magnes, 1955. Translation by Vermes, *Scrolls,* 149–201.
4QpNah	Nahum Commentary. Published by J. Allegro. *DJDJ* 5:37–42. Translation by Vermes, *Scrolls,* 231–35.
11QPs[a]	Psalms Scroll. Published by J. A. Sanders. *The Dead Sea Psalms Scroll.* Ithaca, N.Y.: Cornell University Press, 1967.
1QS	Rule of the Community (Manual of Discipline). Published by M. Burrows. *The Dead Sea Scrolls of St. Mark's Monastery 2.* New Haven: American Schools of Oriental Research, 1951. Translation by Vermes, *Scrolls,* 71–94.
1QSb	Manual of Blessings. Published by J. T. Milik. *DJD* 1:118–29. Translation by Vermes, *Scrolls,* 231–35.
4QTest	Testimonia. See pp. 176–77.
4QT Levi[a]	Aramaic Testament of Levi. Published by J. T. Milik. *The Books of Enoch.* Oxford: Clarendon Press, 1976. Pp. 23–24.
RB	*Revue Biblique*
RelSRev	*Religious Studies Review*
Rev	Revelation
Rom	Romans
RSV	Revised Standard Version of the Bible
1, 2 Sam	1, 2 Samuel

SBLSBS	Society of Biblical Literature Sources for Biblical Study
SBLSCS	Society of Biblical Literature Septuagint and Cognate Studies
Sib. Or.	Sibylline Oracles
Sir	The Wisdom of Jesus the Son of Sirach (or Ecclesiasticus)
T.	Testament of
Abr.	Abraham
Benj.	Benjamin
Iss.	Issachar
Mos.	Moses
Napht.	Naphtali
Reub.	Reuben
TDNT	G. Kittel and G. Friedrich, eds. *Theological Dictionary of the New Testament*. English translation. Grand Rapids: Eerdmans, 1964–74.
1 Thess	1 Thessalonians
Tob	Tobit
Vermes, *Scrolls*	Geza Vermes. *The Dead Sea Scrolls in English*. Second edition. Harmondsworth: Penguin, 1975.
War	Josephus, The Jewish War
Wis	Wisdom of Solomon
Zech	Zechariah
( )	Parentheses indicate that the words are supplied by a modern editor to clarify the meaning of the ancient text.
[ ]	Brackets indicate that the words are supplied by a modern editor to fill a physical lacuna in the ancient manuscript, or by the present editors to summarize portions of the ancient text not here reprinted.
⟨ ⟩	Angle brackets indicate that the words are supplied by a modern editor who assumes that they were erroneously omitted from the ancient text.

Introduction

The present volume is designed to illustrate certain salient points about Judaism as it developed in the last two centuries B.C.E. and in the century after the birth of Jesus. In this crucial period the patterns were set in which Judaism grew and developed for the next two millennia and in which Christianity arose and took on its enduring form.

Because this period was so crucial for the development of the two faiths, both Jews and Christians have tended to see the Judaism from which they issued in an oversimplified fashion. Jews have generally seen the religion of this age merely as a forerunner of the rabbinic Judaism which became dominant; Christianity has tended to interpret it in light of the attitudes toward Judaism found in the New Testament—many of which were generated in the heat of Jewish-Christian polemic. In fact, both these assessments underestimate the great variety of religious belief, expression, and practice which existed in early postbiblical Judaism.

Indeed, what is most remarkable about Judaism before the destruction of the temple is the wealth of its spiritual and conceptual world. Not only were there many Jewish groups, but these groups generated a broad range of religious thinking and expression. One major concern was the attempt to work out the implications of living according to the will of God and of interpreting his relationship to Israel as expressed in the covenant on Sinai and in all that flowed from it. Ideas developed about the fate of man, the providence and justice of God, the purpose of history, and other issues lying at the heart of human concern. Indeed, the Jewish texts of this age foreshadow most of the answers that were later given to the basic problems of humanity, its relationship to God and its life in the world.

The piety and spirituality of Jews in this age had many faces. One

1

aspect was reverence for the temple and its service; a second was a devotion to God that led people to join a "monastic" community in the desert such as that of the Essenes; a third was practical and sensible instruction that reflects the desire to conduct oneself and one's daily life in a fashion pleasing to God and acceptable to one's fellows. By seeking insight into these aspects and others, we can perceive something of the attitudes that permeated the Judaism of that time.

Because we direct this work to nonexperts, we have eschewed the technicalities of the scholarly debate and have presented certain essential concerns and concepts as these are found in the ancient texts themselves. To facilitate this presentation, we have selected half a dozen vitally important topics and have assembled texts and documents that illustrate these topics graphically and clearly. It is from the study of the ancient texts themselves that we gain an insight into the literary, religious, and social variety of the Judaism of the age. Moreover, when we assemble from different sources texts focused around a single theme, the diversity of perceptions, as well as the commonality of certain underlying assumptions, stand out clearly. The six topics we have chosen illustrate different modalities of Jewish religious thinking and life of the period, they embody important creative thought, and the conceptions they set forth have had a profound influence on later Jewish and Christian thinking.

Chapter 1 deals with the variety of Jewish life in the large number of sects and parties that existed in this period. These different groups comprised the social reality in which beliefs were developed and piety was practiced, for Judaism was basically a religion of the community, not of the individualist living on his own. We have discussed only the most important of these many groups. It is extremely important to realize, moreover, that our knowledge of them derives from biased sources—whether the bias be that of partial documents of the group concerned or of tendentious attacks by its opponents. The truth about the groups, of course, lies somewhere in between. Insight into these groups provides a "road map" for tracing the location of the religious ideas. Thus it is crucial for understanding the social and religious history of the period.

In this age, Judaism was a religion of the temple; at its heart stood the sanctuary on Mount Zion in Jerusalem (Chapter 2). This temple was a center of sacrificial worship of God. Here Jews came to express their joy in God, their contrition before him, and their awe at his work of creation. Much of the Book of Psalms is the prayer book of the temple. The temple was a central economic, spiritual, and legal institution of Judaism. Jews today find it difficult to appreciate that at the center of the spiritual life of their ancestors stood an institution in which animal sacrifices and other priestly actions were thought to have real sacred efficacy. Judaism today has much less of this sense of what Christians might call a sacrament. Christians too, and Protestant Christians in particular, have found it difficult to comprehend or to sympathize with the idea of temple. They tend to identify their faith with that of the prophets; and the prophets, like Jesus after them, attacked the abuse of temple worship uncompromisingly. Yet if we are to understand ancient Judaism, it is absolutely essential to recognize the importance of the temple and its cult. Thus our selection of texts and our exposition of them present some aspects both of the material institution of the temple and of its spiritual importance and character. At the same time, we have traced traditions that reflect a critique of the temple and hopes for a new and better temple.

Piety, however, was not expressed only in worship at the temple. Human action generally is central to the way Judaism showed its fervent desire to conform to the will of God. This doing took on many forms, but it was—and it remains—the central aspect of Jewish religious life. As a means of presenting some of the varieties of Jewish religiousness, we have chosen, in Chapter 3, exhortations to the religious life. Some of these call on people to follow the path of upright and just action, devotion, love of God, and righteousness toward their fellows. Others summon the individual to a monastic life in a desert community with strict rules, habits, and customs. Still other texts set up the sage, the wise teacher and expounder of the Torah, as the ideal pattern. It is important to view these and other Jewish religious ideals over against the stereotype often perpetuated in studies of early Judaism that present Judaism as a dry, legalistic, external faith obsessed with the idea that God kept an account of one's deeds in a balance book. The fervor of some of the texts also reminds us that modern Jewish presentations of the religion of this ancient period have too often been typified by an overintellectualization of the ancient patterns.

At the root of much Jewish thinking is the belief in God's justice. This is not simply the idea that God rewards one somehow for good or evil deeds, but also the belief that the just and righteous God will vindicate his faithful in times of crisis. This belief—which enfolds the basic urge to show forth the righteousness of the Deity—was a primary motive in the development of the expectation of judgment at the end of days. This is the subject matter of Chapter 4. In that judgment, then, the justice of God would be apparent in the vindication of the righteous and their deliverance from their enemies. Belief in God's justice and judgment, which took on its enduring forms in this age, became a basic part of both Judaism and Christianity. For the New Testament, and Christianity after it, God's act of vindication par excellence was the resurrection of Jesus. The last judgment has also played an important role in Christian thought, although Reformation polemics have obscured for Protestant Christians the thrust of New Testament texts that speak of a judgment on the basis of one's deeds. The hope and expectation of divine vindication rooted in the justice of God sustained the Jewish people through the vicissitudes suffered during the two thousand years of their exile.

In some Jewish texts God is depicted as the executor of judgment. More often, however, judgment and vindication were expected to come by means of an agent. It was not that *the* Jews, as a single dogmatic group, awaited *the* Messiah. The variety of Judaism is reflected in a spectrum of beliefs as to who would be God's agent (Chapter 5). The Messiah, the son of David, the future king of Israel, is perhaps the best known of these. But there were others. Some texts speak of two Messiahs—a priest and a king. Others anticipate a future supernatural judge and redeemer, created before the world and enthroned with God. Sometimes this figure is entitled "Son of Man"; elsewhere he is called Melchizedek. Other texts speak of a tribunal in which Abel, the son of Adam and the first righteous man, will judge the souls of the dead. Appreciation of this variety of figures is crucial for understanding the message of Jesus and the responses to him in the Jewish community. Moreover, the different expectations provided a variety of instruments by which Christianity could understand and interpret the special personality and role of Jesus. Because the person and work of Jesus are central to Christianity, we have illustrated the spectrum of New Testament belief by means of a relatively large number of texts. The belief in divine deliverance and the expectation of a messianic deliverer at the end of days has also been crucial to Jewish thought over the centuries, and indeed, these ideas comprise one of the major contributions of second temple Judaism to the ongoing thought of Israel.

In our final chapter, "Lady Wisdom and Israel," we trace the development of wisdom from practical teaching to a semi-mythological figure, depicted as female. She becomes the wisdom of God, a personality separate from God and acting along with him in the world, particularly in the drama of creation and redemption. Behind this development may lie older mythological patterns. The teachings of proverbial wisdom books were infused with these patterns, and then mythologized wisdom was identified with the Torah. Thus the Torah itself took on a cosmic role. In the growth of the idea of wisdom, we perceive the development of conceptual structures that intersected and cross-fertilized one another, shaping early Christian thought and modifying the Judaism contemporary to it. For the rabbis it became self-evident that wisdom is the Torah, by which the world is constituted. Early Christianity, on the other hand, used the language and terminology of wisdom to express and interpret the person and activity of Jesus. He was wisdom which became incarnate in order to redeem the creation.

Our presentation of these texts and our commentary on them are designed, then, to provide a better appreciation of the varieties of Jewish belief and practice at the turn of the era. This period is crucial for an understanding of the history of Judaism and the rise and development of Christianity, for at this time the types of Jewish religion were many, and the social settings in which they developed and received formulation were complex. The literature of this period allows us to perceive this richness and diversity. The subsequent course of political events led to the destruction of the temple (70 C.E.), with the loss of national independence and the exile of many Jews. This in turn brought about a certain withdrawal, consolidation, and conscious delimitation of variety, and as a result, many of the types of Jewish thought and piety that were earlier vital and living disappeared.

Since our purpose is to illustrate Judaism of the second temple period, particularly from the second century B.C.E. on, we have presented the texts in their own right and we have interpreted them in their historical contexts. We do not view them, nor do we present them, as mere adjuncts to the study of the New Testament or as examples of an early form of rabbinic Judaism. Admittedly that type

of Judaism existed in this period, and we have adduced texts belonging to it. Nonetheless, it was not the sole form of Judaism, nor, we
maintain, a normative one. For this reason, our presentation is not
weighted in favor of those forms of Judaism that later became dominant. It would be foolish, of course, to deny that both Christianity
and rabbinic Judaism grew out of this age and that from the study of
it a great deal can be learned about the predecessors of the rabbis
and about the ground from which Christianity sprang. For this reason, we have concluded each chapter with rabbinic and early Christian texts that illustrate the further developments of the faith and
piety that characterized the early Judaism with which this volume is
primarily concerned.

The ancient texts illustrate the multiplicity of forms of Jewish
religious expression. Nonetheless, at the present state of knowledge, they cannot tell us very much about the actual social relationships between their authors and proponents. Some insight into this
may be gained from the texts dealing with sects and parties (Chapter
1); however, the sort of historical evidence at our disposal does not
enable us to make decisive and final statements. And if we could
describe the actual situation at a given point in the second temple
period, even that might be misleading for the understanding of later
realities. So, for example, what must have been a minor group
during this period—the early Christian community—became wide-
spread and extremely important in the coming centuries. So did
another of the streams of Judaism that was inherited by the rabbis.

In our discussion we have adduced a number of parallels from
Greco-Roman religion. These show that Judaism did not live in a
vacuum, but was influenced and affected by the religious currents of
the broader world, although it modified and contained them according to its own particular character.

The format of the book was designed to provide a balance between the texts and some necessary interpretation. The emphasis is
on the texts. Accordingly, we have kept as brief as possible our
introductions to the chapters and to the individual texts so that the
reader encounters the texts themselves as quickly as possible.
Nonetheless, texts always require explanation for the readers of a
later age and a different culture. We have provided such explanation, in brief form, through titling, notes, and summary expositions.
It should be emphasized that we intend the introductions, texts, and
summary expositions to be read as a continuous whole. That is, each

chapter is a selective treatment of a particular aspect of the religion of early postbiblical Judaism.

For practical reasons, we have limited the number of topics to be treated. The study of other topics would provide a broader and more holistic view of early Judaism, better insight into the wealth of its religious expression, and a greater sensitivity to its complexities. Such additional topics would include: the interpretation and exposition of Scripture; the view of the world and humanity; personal religious experience; individual and communal prayer and devotion; regulations and law to guide one to the righteous life; magic and astrology; and speculations about the nature of the world, the geography of heaven and earth, and their human and superhuman forces. Although we have not dealt with these topics, the material that has been selected offers the reader a firsthand encounter with exciting and unusual religious thinking and with documents that are highly significant for the development of biblical religion and religious thought.

BIBLIOGRAPHY

Companion Books

The topical approach of this reader is complementary to two recent books by the authors:

Michael E. Stone, *Scriptures, Sects, and Visions: A Profile of Judaism from Ezra to the Jewish Revolts* (Philadelphia: Fortress, 1980).

George W. E. Nickelsburg, *Jewish Literature Between the Bible and the Mishnah: A Historical and Literary Introduction* (Philadelphia: Fortress, 1981).

Scriptures, Sects, and Visions discusses a number of aspects of Jewish religion as these are understood by modern scholars. Thus it deals especially with the impact of recent discoveries on our understanding of the development of Judaism. The book has a brief "Key to Ancient Writings" as well as an index which, as far as the modern discussion of the history of the religion of Judaism is concerned, will help the reader find material that illustrates, expands, and supplements what is presented here.

Jewish Literature Between the Bible and the Mishnah is a detailed exposition of the various literary works produced in this period, understood in the historical context in which they were created, and set within the tradition of biblical literature, both of the Hebrew Scriptures and the New Testament. A detailed topical index provides further access to documents and references that illustrate the subjects discussed in the texts printed in the present volume.

General Bibliography

Each chapter of this book concludes with a bibliography of sources quoted and of selected works for further study. Normally texts from the Jewish Pseudepigrapha have been taken from the translations in the collection of R. H. Charles, *The Apocrypha and Pseudepigrapha of the Old Testament* (Oxford: Clarendon, 1913), vol. 2, or they have been translated anew by the authors. One may also consult the new translation of 1 Enoch by Michael A. Knibb, *The Ethiopic Book of Enoch* (Oxford: Clarendon, 1978), vol. 2, and for the whole Pseudepigrapha the new collection edited by James H. Charlesworth, *The Old Testament Pseudepigrapha* (Garden City, N.Y.: Doubleday, forthcoming).

In addition to the secondary literature cited in the chapter bibliographies, a number of works of general reference may be mentioned. Articles from these works have generally not been cited in our bibliographies.

Encyclopedia Judaica, 14 vols. (New York: Macmillan, 1971).

Interpreter's Dictionary of the Bible, 4 vols. (Nashville: Abingdon, 1962).

Interpreter's Dictionary of the Bible, Supplementary Volume (Nashville: Abingdon, 1976). Expands and updates the earlier four-volume work.

Otto Eissfeldt, *The Old Testament: An Introduction* (New York: Harper & Row, 1965). Technical introduction to the Hebrew Scriptures, the Apocrypha, Pseudepigrapha, and Dead Sea Scrolls. Dated in some respects.

Martin Hengel, *Judaism and Hellenism,* 2 vols. (Philadelphia: Fortress, 1974). Detailed study with excellent bibliography.

Shmuel Safrai and Menaham Stern, eds., *The Jewish People in the First Century,* Compendia Rerum Iudaicarum ad Novum Testamentum, 1:1–2 (Assen: Van Gorcum, 1974, 1976). Numerous studies—in

English—of aspects of the social, economic, and religious history of the Jews at this time. The forthcoming volumes of this series will deal with the literature.

Emil Schürer, *History of the Jewish People at the Time of Jesus Christ,* rev. ed. by Geza Vermes and Fergus Millar (Edinburgh: Clark, 1973, 1979). Revision of an old classic; two volumes have appeared so far. Good survey of the sources and the history of the time. Includes an introduction to the Dead Sea Scrolls.

Geza Vermes, *The Dead Sea Scrolls* (Philadelphia: Fortress, 1981). The most up-to-date discussion of the Scrolls.

Joseph A. Fitzmyer, *The Dead Sea Scrolls: Major Publications and Tools for Study,* SBLSBS 8 (Missoula: Scholars Press, 1975). Basic bibliography for the study of the Scrolls.

James H. Charlesworth, *The Pseudepigrapha and Modern Research,* SBLSCS 7S, rev. ed. (Chico, Calif.: Scholars Press, 1981). Bibliography for the study of the Pseudepigrapha.

1
Sects
and Parties

Judaism of the last two centuries B.C.E. and the first century C.E. saw a rich, variegated development of groups, sects, and parties, and tendencies, points of view, and concepts. In this chapter we shall present certain of these groupings, both as they saw themselves and as others saw them. Pharisees and Sadducees, Hasideans and Essenes, Therapeutae, and others will come to our attention. The diversity is not of name alone, but also of belief and practice, order of life and customary conduct. The diversity raises certain dominant questions: Where did this diversity come from? What were the predominating characteristics of Judaism of that age, or were there such? Was there a Judaism or were there many Judaisms? How do rabbinic Judaism and early Christianity emerge from it or them?

The question of origins takes us back into the unknown. The religious and social history of Judaism in the latter part of the Persian era and in the Ptolemaic age (the fourth and third centuries B.C.E.) is little documented. The Persian province of Judah was a temple state ruled by a high-priestly aristocracy. Although the later parts of the Bible were gathered together in this age, the age itself remains largely unknown.

Some scholars have tried to reconstruct the history of this period by working back from the conflict between Hellenism and Judaism which broke into open revolt in the early second century. With the conquests of Alexander the Great (if not somewhat earlier), the vital and powerful culture of the Greeks and the age-old cultures of the Near East entered upon a process of contact and conflict, synthesis and self-definition. The Jews in the land of Israel, and even more so in the dispersion, were deeply involved in this process.

In the third century, and particularly in the early second century, the danger arose that parts of the Jewish population and of Judaism would be completely assimilated to Hellenistic culture, values, and practices. This would have meant the loss of the distinctively Jewish heritage, a threat which undoubtedly caused tensions and polarization within the Jewish community. In the 60s of the second century open conflict broke out in Judea between the Seleucid kings and their Hellenizing backers on the one hand and their opponents on the other. After this Maccabean revolt, the danger of the assimilation of Judaism into Hellenism passed. In the third century, however, the danger was already present, and it seems reasonable to assume that the groups of the pious—who later formed the backbone of the Maccabean guerrillas—were already coming into being.

But they were not alone, and from the early second century on we hear of many different groups and sects. To evaluate the relationship of these groups to one another we have no public opinion polls or census figures. We do know that, despite conflict, rivalry, and occasional mutual persecution, Pharisees, Sadducees, and some others functioned in the temple of Jerusalem and sat together in the national council, the *gerousia* or Sanhedrin. Josephus presents a picture of the growing dominance of the Pharisees during the last century B.C.E. and first century C.E., and his picture is apparently based on fact. Certain other groups were clearly sects, cut off from the community of Israel not so much by doctrine and dogma as by practice and observance. It was generally by divergent practice rather than by holding differing theological views that one cut oneself off from the general community of Israel. The Essenes were one such sect; they rejected the legitimacy of the temple—the great common institution of all Jewry—and of its high priest. They observed a different calendar. Well before the Essenes, probably by the third century at the latest, another sect in this sense arose—the Samaritans.

Thus there was a great variety of groups, tendencies, and points of view, held together by certain common practices and allegiances. The temple and the Sabbath, monotheism and the rejection of images, and reverence for the Torah of Moses and circumcision were some of the things they had in common.

The Hellenistic period in general was an age of great religious experimentation and variety. Under the impact of the Oriental cultures and religions that they encountered, the Greeks formulated and developed many and varied forms of religious expression. Of Judaism in the Hellenistic world, alas, we know relatively little. The writings that have survived exhibit a range of synthesis with Hellenism: from the Platonizing Stoicism of the exegetical (interpretative) writings of Philo of Alexandria (25 B.C.E.–50 C.E.) to the prayers and religious poems written in Greek in a style and form totally influenced by the Hebrew Bible; from the *diatribe* of Fourth Maccabees' discourse *The Rule of Reason over Passions* to the greatly reputed Jewish magicians of that period.

Three forms of postbiblical Judaism survive today: rabbinic Judaism, the heir of Pharisaism, from which all modern forms of Judaism descend; Christianity; and Samaritanism. The explanation of how these particular forms survived and dominated is a story for elsewhere. Here we can try only to penetrate back before this dominance was exclusive, and to do this we shall examine the better-documented groups and sects of that age.

THE SAMARITANS

Early in the period of the second temple, soon after the return from the Babylonian Exile, conflict erupted between the returning Judeans and the inhabitants of Samaria, the area north of Judea. Samaria had historically been part of David's kingdom and had become the separate kingdom of Israel after Solomon's death in the tenth century B.C.E. The Judeans had their center in Jerusalem, where their temple was; the Samaritans had theirs on Mount Gerizim by the city of Shechem. Both groups claimed to be the true people of Israel, each accusing the other of being apostate and a falsifier of Scripture. Scripture for the Samaritans meant only the Five Books of Moses; for the Jews (as the Judeans were later called) it was the broader body of writing which was developing into the Bible at this time. So the rift between Jews and Samaritans was ancient and deep; it touched on basic issues, the temple and the scope and authority of Scripture.

It is impossible to tell just when the split between the Jews and the Samaritans became irreparable. Some place it as far back as the conflicts at the time of Ezra and Nehemiah (the latter part of the fifth century B.C.E.). Others, stressing the documented ongoing contacts between the two communities, date it later and say that the conquest of Shechem by the Hasmonean monarch John Hyrcanus I (128 B.C.E.) precipitated the final split between the two groups. It is certain that by the latter part of the second century B.C.E. the two groups were quite separate.

The Samaritans differed from the Jews in many matters of faith and practice, but the two groups also had much in common. Samaria and Judea were both temple states whose chief authorities, down to the Roman period, were hereditary high priests. They shared the Torah as the most sacred Scripture, as well as a common history and language. Moreover, in the fourth and third centuries there were considerable contacts between the priestly aristocracies of Jerusalem and Shechem.

The Samaritans clung to the strict interpretation of the Pentateuch, which was the focus and most sacred object of their faith. Their life was centered around their temple, and priests played a predominant role in the community life. The direct line of the high priesthood was preserved continuously down to the seventeenth century, and even today the high priest (from another branch of the Aaronid family) is the head of the tiny surviving Samaritan community. The first text we present is drawn from an early twentieth-century Samaritan chronicle compiled from ancient sources. It relates the foundation of the Samaritan community as they understand it and depicts the Jews as schismatics. A second text, drawn from the biblical Book of Kings, gives a very different, Judahite version of the same event. The third, drawn from the Jewish historian Josephus, recounts an event later in the life of the Samaritans.

A Samaritan Story of the Formation of the Judahite (Jewish) Sect

The Samaritan Chronicle II, J–L

J [I*]When the high priest Uzzi[a] took up the high priesthood in succession to his fathers, there was a man named Eli the son of Jephunneh, of the descendants of Ithamar son of Aaron the priest, as overseer of the House of Ithamar.

K [A*]This Eli sacrificed on the altar of stones, and under his control was the entire revenue of the Israelites' tithe which they offered to the Lord. [B*]He was a prince over the whole tribe of Levi, under the command of the high priest Uzzi. [C*]Now this Uzzi was but a youth, and Eli the son of Jephunneh was well advanced in age. [D*]Eli yearned to take over the position of the high priest Uzzi. . . . And the people of Israel again did, at that time, what was evil in the sight of the Lord;[b] [G*]and furthermore Eli the son of Jephunneh was possessed of evil designs, with the result that many of the Israelites turned from the way of truth.[c] [H*]He seduced them, and they took after idols, formed marriage alliances with Gentiles, and even gave their daughters to them; [I*]and they took the daughters of Gentiles as wives for themselves. . . .

L [A*]Now Eli was ambitious, and he let it be known that he wanted to take over the position of high priest. . . . (E*)Eli won over to himself many of the Israelites by saying to them, "Is it right that I should minister to a youth? (F*)I do not want such a status for myself, and I expect you to share my opinion and follow me." (G*)Eli went on to write to all the cities in the neighborhood of Mount Gerizim Bethel, and he addressed the above words to them. (H*)These all gathered to his side and they addressed him as follows: "We accept what you have said; we will not disobey your orders. Everything you command us we will do." (I*)They made a covenant with him accordingly. . . .

(O*)At that particular time the Israelites who dwelt in the cities of Shechem, the cities of Philistia, and the cities of Jebus were divided in two. (P*)One side followed the high priest Uzzi the son of Bahqi, and the other followed Eli the son of Jephunneh. (Q*)The latter became evil-minded, and they all followed their own inclinations. . . . (T*)The Josephites followed the high priest Uzzi the son of Bahqi, and the Judahites followed Eli the son of Jephunneh. (U*)The Ephraimites and Manassites drove out Eli and his community from the chosen place Mount Gerizim Bethel.

(V*)Eli and his community, with their families and cattle, departed to sojourn in the territory of the tribe of Judah at Shiloh. (W*)Eli dwelt there in that place, and he made himself an ark of gold based on the structure of the ark of the testimony. (X*)He made himself also a mercy seat, cherubs, a table, a lampstand, and altars just like those of the sanctuary of Moses, which is to be found in the chosen place Mount Gerizim Bethel.

(Y*)Eli wrote letters, sending them to the chiefs of the Israelites addressing them as follows: (Z*)"Let whoever desires to see signs and wonders come to me at Shiloh, for the ark of the testimony containing the tablets is in my hands." (AA*)He put into the ark the books of the law which were the version of Ithamar[d] the son of Eleazar son of Aaron the priest, peace be upon him. (BB*)A good many Israelites gathered to him, and he built at Shiloh a tent based on the design of the tent of meeting.[e] (CC*)This Eli did not change a single word of the holy law, but he revised the order of words. (DD*)Eli went on sacrificing the offerings on the altars which he had made. (EE*)Every one of his festivals was in accordance with the commandments of the holy law.[f]

a. According to Samaritan views, Uzzi was high priest in the true line of descent from Phineas, son of Eleazar, son of Aaron. His role is predominant: "They have charge of the holy things, and they have the supremacy and the final decision. The king of Israel comes and goes at their command. . . . He is the one who is priest above every priest" (J:B*–C*, G*).

b. = Judg 13:1.

c. Term often found in Samaritan sources.

d. A Samaritan reference to the Judahite version of the Torah.

e. Here the tabernacle at Shiloh is viewed as a false imitation of the true Tent of Meeting, which of course belonged to the Samaritans.

f. Compare with the opinion of the rabbinic sages that "every commandment which the Cutheans (i.e., the Samaritans) observed, they observed more punctiliously than Israel" (Babylonian Talmud, *Berakot* 47b).

This is the Samaritan view of the story. They preserved the true tradition, the true high priesthood, the true holy place.

The Judahites (Jews) on the Origins of the Samaritans

2 Kings 17

1 In the twelfth year of Ahaz king of Judah, Hoshea the son of Elah began to reign in Samaria over Israel, and he reigned nine years. [2]And he did what was evil in the sight of the Lord, yet not as the kings of Israel who were before him. . . . [6]In the ninth year of Hoshea, the king of Assyria[a] captured Samaria, and he carried the Israelites away to Assyria and placed them in Halah, and on the Habor, the river of Gozan, and in the cities of Medes.[b]

[7]And this was so because the people of Israel had sinned against the Lord their God, who had brought them up out of the land of Egypt from under the hand of Pharaoh king of Egypt, and had feared other gods [8]and walked in the customs of the nations whom the Lord drove out before the people of Israel, and in the customs which the kings of Israel had introduced. [9]And the people of Israel did secretly against the Lord their God things that were not right. They built for themselves high places at all their towns, from watchtower to fortified city; [10]they set up for themselves pillars and Asherim on every high hill and under every green tree; [11]and there they burned incense on all the high places, as the nations did whom the Lord carried away before them. And they did wicked things, provoking the Lord to anger, [12]and they served idols, of which the Lord had said to them, "You shall not do this." [13]Yet the Lord warned Israel and Judah by every prophet and every seer, saying, "Turn from your evil ways and keep my commandments and my statutes, in accordance with all the law which I commanded your fathers and which I sent to you by my servants the prophets." [14]But they would not listen, but were stubborn, as their fathers had been, who did not believe in the Lord their God. [15]They despised his statutes and his covenant that he made with their fathers and the warnings which he gave them. They went after false idols and became false, and they followed the nations that were round about them, concerning whom the Lord had commanded them that they should not do like them. [16]And they forsook all the commandments of the Lord their God and made for themselves molten

images of two calves; and they made an Asherah and worshiped all the host of heaven and served Baal. [17]And they burned their sons and their daughters as offerings[c] and used divination and sorcery, and sold themselves to do evil in the sight of the Lord, provoking him to anger. [18]Therefore the Lord was very angry with Israel and removed them out of his sight; none was left but the tribe of Judah only.

[19]Judah also did not keep the commandments of the Lord their God, but walked in the customs which Israel had introduced. [20]And the Lord rejected all the descendants of Israel, and afflicted them and gave them into the hand of spoilers until he had cast them out of his sight.

[21]When he had torn Israel from the house of David, they made Jeroboam the son of Nebat king. And Jeroboam drove Israel from following the Lord and made them commit great sin. [22]The people of Israel walked in all the sins which Jeroboam did; they did not depart from them [23]until the Lord removed Israel out of his sight, as he had spoken by all his servants the prophets. So Israel was exiled from their own land to Assyria until this day.

[24]And the king of Assyria brought people from Babylon, Cuthah, Avva, Hamath, and Sepharvaim and placed them in the cities of Samaria instead of the people of Israel; and they took possession of Samaria and dwelt in its cities. [25]And at the beginning of their dwelling there, they did not fear the Lord; therefore the Lord sent lions among them, which killed some of them. [26]So the king of Assyria was told, "The nations which you have carried away and placed in the cities of Samaria do not know the law of the god of the land; therefore he has sent lions among them, and behold, they are killing them, because they do not know the law of the god of the land." [27]Then the king of Assyria commanded, "Send there one of the priests whom you carried away thence; and let him[d] go and dwell there and teach them the law of the god of the land." [28]So one of the priests whom they had carried away from Samaria came and dwelt in Bethel and taught them how they should fear the Lord.

[29]But every nation still made gods of its own and put them in the shrines of the high places which the Samaritans had made, every nation in the cities in which they dwelt;[e] [30]the men of Babylon made Succothbenoth, the men of Cuth made Nergal, the men of Hamath made Ashima, [31]and the Avvites made Nibhaz and Tartak; and the Sepharvites burned their children in the fire to Adrammelech and Anammelech, the gods of Sepharvaim. [32]They also feared the Lord, and appointed from among themselves all sorts of people as priests of the high places, who sacrificed for them in the shrines of the high places. [33]So they feared the Lord but also served their own gods, after the manner of the nations from among whom they had been carried away. [34]To this day they do according to the former manner.

They do not fear the Lord, and they do not follow the statutes or the ordinances or the law or the commandment which the Lord commanded the children of Jacob, whom he named Israel. [35]The Lord made a covenant with them and commanded them, "You shall not fear other gods or bow yourselves to them or serve them or sacrifice to them; [36]but you shall fear the Lord, who brought you out of the land of Egypt with great power and with an outstretched arm; you shall bow yourselves to him, and to him you shall sacrifice. [37]And the statutes and the ordinances and the law and the commandment which he wrote for you, you shall always be careful to do. You shall not fear other gods, [38]and you shall not forget the covenant that I have made with you. You shall not fear other gods, [39]but you shall fear the Lord your God, and he will deliver you out of the hand of all your enemies." [40]However they would not listen, but they did according to their former manner.

[41]So these nations feared the Lord and also served their graven images; their children likewise, and their children's children—as their fathers did, so they do to this day.

a. Shalmanezer V, 727–722 B.C.E.
b. Sargon II captured Samaria in 721 and exiled 27,290 inhabitants.
c. Or "made their sons and their daughters pass through the fire."
d. Syriac Latin; Heb "them."
e. From this point the term "Samaritans" is used.

According to this Judahite version of the story, the Samaritans were descendants of the forced Gentile settlers whose conversion to the faith of Israel was under duress. They were the heirs of the idolatrous and faithless kingdom of Israel, and their own religious practice was syncretistic and faithless.

Samaritan and Judean Relations

This event in the latter part of the fourth century B.C.E. indicates a close relationship between the priesthoods of Jerusalem and Gerizim at that time, as well as conflicts within the Jerusalemite community.

Josephus, Antiquities 11:306–12

306 Now the elders of Jerusalem, resenting the fact that the brother of the high priest Jaddus was sharing the high priesthood while married to a foreigner,[a] rose up against him, [307]for they considered this marriage to be a stepping-stone for those who might wish to transgress the laws about taking wives and that this would be the beginning of intercourse with foreigners.[b] [308]They believed, moreover, that their former captivity and misfortunes had been caused by some who had erred in marrying

and taking wives who were not of their own country. They therefore told Manasses either to divorce his wife or not to approach the altar. [309]And, as the high priest shared the indignation of the people and kept his brother from the altar, Manasses went to his father-in-law Sanaballetes[c] and said that while he loved his daughter Nikaso, nevertheless the priestly office was the highest in the nation and had always belonged to his family, and that therefore he did not wish to be deprived of it on her account. [310]But Sanaballetes promised not only to preserve the priesthood for him but also to procure for him the power and office of high priest and to appoint him governor of all the places over which he ruled, if he were willing to live with his daughter; and he said that he would build a temple similar to that in Jerusalem on Mount Garizein—this is the highest of the mountains near Samaria—and undertook to do these things with the consent of King Darius.[d] [311]Elated by these promises, Manasses stayed with Sanaballetes, believing that he would obtain the high priesthood as the gift of Darius, for Sanaballetes, as it happened, was now an old man. [312]But, as many priests and Israelites were involved in such marriages, great was the confusion which seized the people of Jerusalem. For all these deserted to Manasses, and Sanaballetes supplied them with money and with land for cultivation and assigned them places wherein to dwell, in every way seeking to win favor for his son-in-law.

a. I.e., the daughter of Sanaballetes.

b. The Judahites so regarded the Samaritans.

c. A dynastic name of the governors of Samaria, as is now clear from the Wadi Daliyeh papyri; see F. M. Cross, Jr., "A Reconstruction of the Judean Restoration," *JBL* 94 (1975) 4–18.

d. This story, then, places the foundation of the Gerizim temple in the fourth century.

THE HASIDEANS

Our direct information concerning the Hasidean group is sparse. First and Second Maccabees give certain details, particularly of how the Hasideans joined the Maccabean revolt at its inception and how they abandoned it after the priesthood of Alcimus was established. Probably this group had not suddenly sprung up at the time of the revolt, but developed from pietistic tendencies that grew within Judaism during the Hellenization of the Ptolemaic age.

As well as being the name of a particular group, *ḥasid* means "pious," so when a source like the Book of Psalms talks of *ḥasidim*, it does not necessarily refer to this group but may just denote "pious ones." Nonetheless, some scholars see "the community of the pious" mentioned in Psalm 149:1 as a possible reflection of an early stage in the development of the Hasidean community. The relevant verse reads:

> Praise the Lord,
>> sing to the Lord a new song,
>> his praise in the assembly of the pious.

A well-preserved Psalms scroll from Cave 11 at Qumran, called 11QPsᵃ by scholars, contains a number of apocryphal compositions in addition to parts of the canonical Psalter. These apocryphal psalms were not the creation of the Qumran sectaries (some of them we know from other sources), although they resemble the sectarian compositions in some respects. One of these psalms, some have speculated, may come from Hasidean circles. The psalm is a praise of Wisdom (on which see below, "Wisdom," pp. 210–11), but the verses cited here show the attitude of the author toward his own community.

Apocryphal Psalms, col. 18

1 [With a loud voice glorify God;
　　in the congregation of the many proclaim his majesty.
²In the multitude of the upright glorify his name
　　and with the faithful recount his greatness.]
³[Bind] your souls with the good ones
　　and with the pure ones to glorify the Most High.
⁴Form an assembly to proclaim his salvation,
　　and be not lax in making known his might
　　and his majesty to all simple folk. . . .
¹²From the gates of the righteous is heard her (i.e., Wisdom's) voice
　　and from the assembly of the pious her song.
¹³When they eat with satiety she is cited,
　　also when they drink in community together,
¹⁴Their meditation is on the law of the Most High,
　　their words on making known his might.
¹⁵How far from the wicked is her word,
　　from all haughty men to know her.

It is not certain that the community from which this psalm sprang was that of the Hasideans, but it is not out of character with what we know of them.

Passive Resistance

The First Book of Maccabees relates how the revolt against the

Greeks broke out. Mattathias rose up, raised the banner of revolt in the country town of Modein, and was joined by his sons and fled to the hills, followed by many of the faithful (1 Macc 2:29). There are two descriptions of events of passive resistance by the faithful. It is not stated explicitly that these "passive resisters" were Hasideans, but this is very possible.

1 Maccabees 1:62–64

62 But many in Israel stood firm and were resolved in their hearts not to eat unclean food.[a] [63]They chose to die rather than to be defiled by food or to profane the holy covenant; and they did die. [64]And very great wrath came upon Israel.

a. The Seleucids, as part of their policy of repression of Judaism, attempted to force Jews to eat forbidden foods.

1 Maccabees 2:29–38

29 Then many who were seeking righteousness and justice went down to the wilderness to dwell there, [30]they, their sons, their wives, and their cattle, because evils pressed heavily upon them. [31]And it was reported to the king's officers, and to the troops in Jerusalem the city of David, that men who had rejected the king's command had gone down to the hiding places in the wilderness. [32]Many pursued them and overtook them; they encamped opposite them and prepared for battle against them on the Sabbath day. [33]And they said to them, "Enough of this! Come out and do what the king commands, and you will live." [34]But they said, "We will not come out, nor will we do what the king commands and so profane the Sabbath day."[a] [35]Then the enemy hastened to attack them. [36]But they did not answer them or hurl a stone at them or block up their hiding places, [37]for they said, "Let us all die in our innocence; heaven and earth testify for us that you are killing us unjustly." [38]So they attacked them on the Sabbath, and they died, with their wives and children and cattle, to the number of a thousand persons.[b]

a. Compare the attitude of Mattathias and his sons, who decide to fight on the Sabbath (vv. 39–41).
b. Compare T. Mos. 8–10, and below, pp. 127–30.

The context makes it clear that the people described in this second text are not the same as Matthias and his sons. The atmosphere of rigorous observance of the Torah and devotion to its injunctions, particularly the Sabbath, and to God as its author is typical of pious circles of the time. If these were not the Hasideans themselves, they were groups of the same type. Later rabbinic traditions refer to the zeal of the "former Hasidim" for Sabbath observance.

The Hasideans Join the Armed Resistance

The most certain references to the Hasideans also occur in the Books of Maccabees. The first of them refers to the outbreak of the revolt.

1 Maccabees 2:42–44

42 Then there united with them[a] a company of Hasideans,[b] mighty warriors of Israel, everyone who offered himself willingly for the law.[c] [43]And all who became fugitives to escape their troubles joined them and reinforced them. [44]They organized an army and struck down sinners in their anger and lawless men in their wrath; the survivors fled to the Gentiles for safety.

   a. Mattathias and his sons.
   b. I.e., "community of the pious"; cf. Ps 149:1 and 11QPs[a] 18:12, quoted above (p. 20).
   c. Compare the term in 1QS 1:7.

Here the Hasideans move to activism and organize an army of "mighty warriors." Their first action is against the Hellenizing apostates. Somewhat later, when Alcimus was intriguing to get the high priesthood, he reported to the Seleucid authorities, according to 2 Maccabees 14:6, that "those of the Jews who are called Hasideans, whose leader is Judas Maccabeus, are keeping up war and stirring up sedition and will not let the kingdom attain tranquillity." Whatever be the accuracy of the report, it clearly shows both the association of the Hasideans with the revolt and their repute for military prowess.

The Hasideans Abandon the Revolt

In 161 B.C.E., Alcimus succeeded in getting himself appointed high priest. At that time he was approached by a group of Jews, apparently the Hasideans, who sued for terms and with whom he dealt most treacherously. He killed sixty of them. This is the last text dealing explicitly with them.

1 Maccabees 7:12–18

12 Then a group of scribes[a] appeared in a body before Alcimus and Bacchides[b] to ask for just terms. [13]The Hasideans were the first among

the sons of Israel to seek peace from them, [14]for they said, "A priest of the line of Aaron has come with the army and he will not harm us." [15]And he spoke peaceable words to them and swore this oath to them: "We will not seek to injure you or your friends." [16]So they trusted him, but he seized sixty of them and killed them in one day, in accordance with the word which was written, [17]"The flesh of your saints and their blood they poured out round about Jerusalem, and there was none to bury them."[c] [18]The fear and dread of them fell upon all the people, for they said, "There is no truth or justice in them, for they have violated the agreement and the oath which they swore."

a. The Hasideans are here represented as part of a "group of scribes" (1 Macc 7:12). The term "scribe" is a difficult one; it starts as a designation of the wise court official in the old wisdom tradition. Perhaps a special application of this term was responsible for Ezra's title as "scribe of the Torah of Moses" (Ezra 7:6); later ben Sira refers to himself as a scribe (Sir 38:24); Enoch is the prototypical scribe of heavenly wisdom (Jub. 4:17–20); the New Testament on a number of occasions refers to "the scribes and the Pharisees" (note esp. Matt 23 par.) or "the scribes of the Pharisees" (Mark 2:16; cf. Luke 5:30). In the present text, perhaps, the reference is not to a specific group but to a particular learned class which could have included the Hasideans.

b. Seleucid general.

c. Ps 79:2–3.

The reason the Hasideans gave for their misplaced trust in Alcimus was that "a priest of the line of Aaron has come." They regarded the proper character of the priesthood as particularly important; and apparently, with the accession of Alcimus, they considered the true line of the priesthood to have been restored.

Two further pieces of information may help illustrate this little-known group. First, a number of rabbinic sources (edited in the second to fifth centuries C.E.) refer to "the former Hasidim" or "the Hasidim and the men of action." These groups were characterized by a particularly rigorous approach to the spirit and practice of the *halakha* (Jewish religious law). Their views on Sabbath observance, for example, were stricter than those of others. They emphasized devoutness in prayer, charity, and the redemption of slaves as prime religious obligations. The possible connections between these Hasidim and the Hasideans mentioned by the Books of Maccabees have been discussed (see above, p. 19). Second, some scholars have suggested that the Psalms of Solomon, which were written in the middle of the first century B.C.E., may reflect the ideas of groups which continue the tradition of the earlier Hasideans (see the term "the community of pious" in Ps. Sol. 17:18). This we do not know.

Certain recent authors have attributed to the Hasideans a number of apocalyptic writings which stem from the time of the Maccabean revolt and deal with the problems arising from the persecution of the righteous. These writings include the Book of Daniel and the "Dream Visions" of 1 Enoch. Although these writings are, on the whole, not dissonant with what can be perceived about the Hasideans from the sources which refer directly to them, there is in fact no indication that they were the creation of the Hasidean community. There may have been other, not dissimilar pious groups at that time whose very name has perished.[1]

So for all the great interest which inheres in the study of the oldest discernible such group known by name, the paucity of the assured information will permit us to gain only the barest insight into their character, and nothing at all is known of their size, influence, or organization.[2]

PHARISEES, SADDUCEES, AND ESSENES

The most important report on the Jewish parties is that of the historian Flavius Josephus. Himself of priestly descent and an avowed Pharisee, Josephus wrote two histories: The Jewish War, composed soon after the conclusion of the great revolt against the Romans in the year 70 C.E., and the Jewish Antiquities, published in Rome a quarter of a century later. Both histories preserve passages characterizing the chief Jewish groups of the age. Although they were written at a great remove in time from the origins of the groups they discuss, Josephus's reports are still the best historical information at our disposal. They were written for inclusion in historical works of quite distinct purposes. Josephus wished to show that the Jews were not alone responsible for the great revolt but that great blame also devolved on the corrupt and venal procuratorial government. Moreover, he maintained that the Pharisees, who emerged after the revolt as the predominant group, were in fact dominant in the preceding period. In addition, Josephus was writing for a cultured, pagan audience, so he tended to reformulate in the conceptual terminology of the Greeks the views and doctrines of the groups he discussed.

Josephus distinguishes four parties (he calls them "philosophies") among the Jews: the Pharisees, the Sadducees, the Essenes, and the Zealots (we leave this last group apart for the moment, for it does not seem to have roots going back as far as the others). His reports on the Pharisees and the Sadducees are quite brief. Those on the third group, the Essenes, are much more extensive. The Pharisees and Sadducees were both religious groups functioning within the broader community, while the Essenes were a separatist sect. As such they were probably less known to Josephus's readers and excited even more interest, especially in a Greek world which was greatly fascinated by reports about ascetic Oriental saints and communities.[3] These descriptions of the Essenes have been supplemented by the discovery of the Dead Sea Scrolls, which were the library of an Essene community.

In addition to Josephus's information on the Pharisees, some interesting reports of them, and to a lesser extent of the Sadducees, occur in the New Testament. Moreover, the Qumran Commentary on Nahum gives us some insight into how the Essenes viewed the other two groups. The direction and thrust of this sadly fragmentary document are quite clear. Significantly, it preserves some information, however meager, about the Sadducees, the least known sect of all. We possess not one word assuredly written by a Sadducee, only things written about them by their opponents.

The Pharisees

The Pharisees and the Essenes both have been regarded as offshoots of the Hasideans. While we cannot determine this on the basis of the preserved evidence, it is not implausible that both these groups arose from that wing of Judaism to which the Hasideans also belonged.

Josephus, Antiquities 18:12–15

THE DOCTRINES AND ROLE
OF THE PHARISEES

12 The Pharisees simplify their standard of living, making no concession to luxury.[a] They follow the guidance of that which their doctrine has selected and transmitted as good, attaching the chief importance to the observance of those commandments which it has seen fit to dictate to them.[b] They show respect and deference to their elders, nor do they rashly presume to contradict their proposals.

13 Though they postulate that everything is brought about by fate, still they do not deprive the human will of the pursuit of what is in man's power, since it was God's pleasure that there should be a fusion and that the will of man with his virtue and vice should be admitted to the

council-chamber of fate.[c] [14]They believe that souls have power to survive death and that there are rewards and punishments under the earth for those who have led lives of virtue or vice: eternal imprisonment is the lot of evil souls, while the good souls receive an easy passage to a new life.[d]

[15]Because of these views they are, as a matter of fact, extremely influential among the townsfolk; and all prayers and sacred rites of divine worship are performed according to their exposition.[e] This is the great tribute that the inhabitants of the cities, by practicing the highest ideals both in their way of living and in their discourse, have paid to the excellence of the Pharisees.

a. Some have seen in this an indication that the Pharisees came from the more modest and popular classes.

b. Josephus alludes to the respect that the Pharisees showed to the traditions of their teachers. This is related to their chief characteristic according to para. 15 below and other sources, i.e., their tradition and modes of exegesis.

c. Compare the rabbinic saying "All is foreseen, yet freedom of choice is given" (M. Abot 3:19). The paradox implicit here is basic to the Pharisaic and later rabbinic view on free will and divine omniscience. Compare briefly War 2:162 below and Ant. 13:172, "As for the Pharisees, they say that certain things are the work of Fate, but not all; as to other events, it depends upon ourselves whether they shall take place or not." An earlier formulation of this problem is Sir 33:7–15.

d. Here Josephus appears to formulate the idea of resurrection in terms readily comprehensible to his Greek readers.

e. The popular role of the Pharisees is emphasized. The people, particularly those of the towns, follow their expositions.

Josephus, Jewish War 2:162–63

THE PHARISEES' VIEW OF FATE

162 Of the two first-named schools, the Pharisees, who are considered the most accurate interpreters of the laws[a] and hold the position of the leading sect, attribute everything to Fate and to God; [163]they hold that to act rightly or otherwise rests, indeed, for the most part with men, but that in each action Fate cooperates. Every soul, they maintain, is imperishable, but the soul of the good alone passes into another body,[b] while the souls of the wicked suffer eternal punishment.

a. Here the particular characteristic of the Pharisees as interpreters of the laws is emphasized.

b. The reincarnation of the righteous is attributed to the Pharisees by this passage; see also War 3:374. This is unusual and is perhaps a Hellenizing formulation.

Elsewhere Josephus, relating events of the time of John Hyrcanus I (135–105 B.C.E.), has occasion to set the views of the Pharisees and the Sadducees in contrast with one another.

Josephus, Antiquities 13:297–98

THE PHARISEES AND THE SADDUCEES

297 For the present I wish merely to explain that the Pharisees had passed on to the people certain regulations handed down by former generations and not recorded in the laws of Moses,[a] for which reason they are rejected by the Sadducean group, who hold that only those regulations should be considered valid which were written down (in Scripture), and that those which had been handed down by former generations need not be observed. [298]And concerning these matters the two parties came to have controversies and serious differences, the Sadducees having the confidence of the wealthy alone but no following among the populace, while the Pharisees have the support of the masses.[b]

a. Note Josephus's clear statement that the Pharisaic tradition of exegesis was originally independent of the written "laws of Moses." Again this feature of the Pharisees is to the fore, and the authority of their traditional exegesis is one of the points at which they are contrasted with the Sadducees.

b. This is one of the clearest statements of the differing social contexts of these two groups and of the overwhelming predominance of the Pharisees, which Josephus emphasizes repeatedly; cf. Ant. 13:288: "And so great is their influence with the masses that even when they speak against a king or high priest, they immediately gain credence."

The general picture Josephus gives of the Pharisees is borne out by the attitudes toward them expressed by groups or individuals who were not in agreement with them. They were the transmitters of a legal tradition and above all exegetes of the Torah of Moses. They accorded great authority to their received legal tradition. Certainly by the end of the second temple period, if not somewhat earlier, the majority of the people followed their views. The commentary on the Book of Nahum from Cave 4 at Qumran (4QpNah) is, alas, rather fragmentary, but some segments of it deal with the Sadducees and the Pharisees.

Nahum Commentary on 2:12 (col. 1:4–8)

JANNAI CRUCIFIES THE PHARISEES

". . . And filled his caves with prey, and his abodes (dens) with torn flesh." [This refers to] the Young Lion[a] who [wrought venge]ance on them "that sought smooth things," in that he proceeded to hang them up alive.[b] [Such a thing had never] before [been done] in Israel, for the Scripture designates a man hung up alive as ["a reproach unto God"].

a. Alexander Jannai, a Hasmonean (Maccabean) king.

b. Compare Ant. 13:380. The "seekers after smooth things," or "smooth exegetes," are the Pharisees. The Essenes clearly do not approve of them.

Nahum Commentary on 3:1–4 (col. 2:1–10)

THE RULE AND FALSE TEACHING
OF THE PHARISEES

2 [1]"Woe to the bloody city! It is all full of fraud and rapine." This alludes to the city of Ephraim[a]—to those "seekers after smooth things" who, in the latter days, will walk in fraud and lies.

"The prey departs not, nor do the crack of the whip, the whir of wheels, the prancing horses, the bounding chariots, the charging horsemen, the flashing [sword], the glittering spear, the multitude of slain, the great heap of carcasses. No end is there to the bodies; men stumble over those bodies." This alludes to the period when the "seekers after smooth things" hold sway. [5]Never will the sword of the Gentiles depart from the midst of their community, nor yet captivity, spoliation, and internecine strife, nor exile through fear of an enemy. Many a guilty corpse shall fall in their days, and there shall indeed be no end to the slain. Moreover, through the guilty counsel (policy) of these men, men will indeed stumble in the body of their own flesh.

"Because of the manifold whoredoms of the well-favored whore, that mistress of witchery, who sells whole nations through her whoredom, and whole families through her wit[cher]y." This alludes to those of Ephraim who will go astray,[b] those by whose false teaching, lying tongue, and guileful lips many shall indeed be led astray—kings, princes, priests, laymen, and affiliated strangers[c]—and through whose counsel (policy) their cities and families shall go to ruin, and through whose tongues nobles and rulers will fall.

a. Our rendering follows D. Flusser's interpretation: "city of Ephraim" is Jerusalem; "Ephraim" is the Pharisees; "Manasseh," below, is the Sadducees. This is typological exegesis in the Qumran style.

b. Gaster: "those who will go leading Ephraim astray." Note the emphasis on the false teaching and exegesis of the Pharisees.

c. This is external corroboration of Josephus's observation that most of the people followed the Pharisees.

Nahum Commentary on 3:6–7 (col. 3:1–8)

THE PEOPLE WILL ABANDON THE PHARISEES

3 [1]"And I will cast abominable filth upon you and make you vile and render you loathsome. And it shall come to pass that all who see you shall flee from you." This alludes to the "seekers after smooth things" whose evil works will, at the end of the present epoch, become manifest to all Israel. Many will then discern these people's iniquity and come to hate them and to hold them loathsome on account of their guilty arrogance. Moreover, when (eventually) the glory of Judah suffers dishonor, [5]those in Ephraim who have hitherto been duped will flee from the midst of those men's congregation and, renouncing them that led them astray, attach themselves (once more) to (the true) Israel.[a]

"And they will say, Nineveh is ravaged, (but) who bemoans her? Whence can I seek any who will condole with you?" This alludes to the "seekers after smooth things" whose counsel (policy) will come to naught and whose synagogue will be dispersed. No longer will they lead the congregation astray, and those who were previously duped will no longer hold to their counsel.

a. The author's expectation is that at the end of days the false teaching of the Pharisees will be uncovered and that many will turn from their congregation to the true Israel, i.e., the sect of the Essenes.

Nahum Commentary on 3:8 (col. 3:8–9)

THE SADDUCEES

3 [8]"Are you better than ⟨Nô⟩ Amon, that was situated by the rivers?" The allusion in the term "Amon" is to Manasseh. The "rivers" are the grandees of Manasseh, the nobles of . . . who . . . the. . . .

"Water was all around her; her rampart was the sea; water also formed her walls." The allusion is to the men of her army, her warriors. . . .[a]

a. Notice the terms "grandees," "nobles," "men of army"—all fitting for the aristocratic background of the Sadducees.

Nahum Commentary on 3:9b–11 (col. 3:12—4:8)

FURTHER HISTORY OF THE PHARISEES AND SADDUCEES

3 [12]"Put and Lubim are among her supporters." 4 [1]This alludes to the wicked men of . . . , that divisive group who ally themselves with Manasseh.

"She too is gone into exile, into captivity; her babes are dashed in pieces at the top of every street; over her nobles men cast lots, and her grandees are bound in chains." This alludes to Manasseh in the final era, when its kingdom will be brought low at [the hand of]. . . . Its womenfolk, babes, and infants will go into captivity; while its warriors and its honored men [will fall] by the sword.

"[You too shall become drunken], [5]become all beclouded." This alludes to the wicked men of Ephraim whose cup (of doom) will follow that of Manasseh, and who will become. . . .

The scroll breaks off at this point.

There are numerous references to the Pharisees in the New Testament. The reference in Acts 23:6–10, touching on doctrinal matters, is cited below. The famous attack on the "scribes and Pharisees" as hypocrites in Matthew 23 is paralleled by a very difficult passage in The Fathers According to Rabbi Nathan, A 37; this is also an attack on seven types of hypocritical Pharisees. The picture of the Pharisees in the New Testament is distorted by the heat of Jewish-Christian polemics. This is part of the same misapprehension that has made a proper understanding of the role of law in Judaism so rare (see Chapter 3, below). Nonetheless, the fact that there does exist some rabbinic criticism of the Pharisees for hypocrisy points to some basis in reality.

The Sadducees

Josephus provides certain details about the Sadducees.

Josephus, Antiquities 18:16–17

CHARACTER OF THE SADDUCEES

16 The Sadducees hold that the soul perishes along with the body. They own no observance of any sort apart from the laws:[a] in fact, they reckon it a virtue to dispute with the teachers of the path of wisdom that they pursue.[b] [17]There are but few men to whom this doctrine has been made known, but these are men of the highest standing.[c] They accomplish practically nothing, however. For whenever they assume some office, though they submit unwillingly and perforce, yet submit they do to the formulas of the Pharisees, since otherwise the masses would not tolerate them.

a. Here the Sadducean attitude to the oral law of the Pharisees is reflected. See also Josephus's comments at Ant. 13:297, quoted above. They seem to hold that there is no afterlife.

b. Surely the Sadducees did not just follow the literal word of Scripture with no exegesis. The difference with the Pharisees must have related to the extent of the development of the exegetical tradition and to the measure of authority attributed to it. It is questionable whether this Sadducean argumentativeness is what lies behind Josephus's comment in War 2:166 that they are "even among themselves, rather boorish in their behavior, and in their intercourse with their peers as rude as to aliens" (contrast the comment in LCL).

c. This seems to refer to the Sadducees having a doctrine revealed only to a few men of very high standing. It is not clear whether this implies that they had a secret teaching or whether their limited numbers are here reflected. This latter interpretation is supported by the following sentences.

Josephus, Jewish War 2:164–66

SADDUCEAN DOCTRINES

164 The Sadducees, the second of the orders, do away with Fate altogether, and remove God beyond, not merely the commission but the very sight of evil. [165]They maintain that man has the free choice of good or evil and that it rests with each man's will whether he follows the one or the other.[a] As for the persistence of the soul after death, penalties in the underworld, and rewards, they will have none of them.

[166]The Pharisees are affectionate to each other and cultivate harmonious relations with the community. The Sadducees, on the contrary, are, even among themselves, rather boorish in their behavior, and in their intercourse with their peers are as rude as to aliens. Such is what I have to say on the Jewish philosophical schools.

a. As in the passage on the Pharisees (162), the question of Providence is raised: The Sadducees have a radical attitude to free will, claiming that man's choice is completely free and denying post-mortem sanctions.

Acts 23:6–10

That the resurrection of the dead and the existence of angels were central points of difference between the Pharisees and the Sadducees is clear from two texts in the New Testament. Matthew 22:23 par. mentions that the Sadducees deny the resurrection of the dead and relates an incident in which the Sadducees attempt to prove this from Scripture. In Acts 23:6–10 Paul, standing before the tribunal of the Sanhedrin, uses the well-known disagreement of the two groups in these matters as part of his forensic approach. These texts corroborate the observations made by Josephus.

ANGELS AND RESURRECTION

6 But when Paul perceived that one part were Sadducees and the other Pharisees, he cried out in the council, "Brethren, I am a Pharisee, a son of Pharisees; with respect to the hope and the resurrection of the dead I am on trial." [7]And when he had said this, a dissension arose between the Pharisees and the Sadducees; and the assembly was divided. [8]For the Sadducees say that there is no resurrection, nor angel, nor spirit; but the Pharisees acknowledge them all. [9]Then a great clamor arose; and some of the scribes of the Pharisees' party stood up and contended, "We find nothing wrong in this man. What if a spirit or an angel spoke to him?" [10]And when the dissension became violent, the tribune, afraid that Paul would be torn in pieces by them, commanded the soldiers to go down

and take him by force from among them and bring him into the barracks.

The Fathers According to Rabbi Nathan, A 5

A clearly apocryphal story of the formation of two sects, the Sadducees and the Boethusians, is presented in The Fathers According to Rabbi Nathan. They disagreed over a saying of Antigonus of Soko, who stands in the chain of tradition in Mishnah *Abot* (Ethics of the Fathers) 1:3 between Simeon the Righteous and the first of the "pairs." His dictum touches on the motives for moral action, and in this context the question of the future life arises. Here, apparently, the term "Pharisees" implies a measure of ascesis. Of the Boethusians little is known. The sect is perhaps to be connected with Simon ben Boethus, who was appointed high priest by Herod in 24 B.C.E.

THE FORMATION OF TWO SECTS

Antigonus of Soko took over from Simeon the Righteous. He used to say: "Be not like slaves that serve their master for the sake of compensation; be rather like slaves who serve their master with no thought of compensation. And let the fear of heaven be upon you, so that your reward may be doubled in the age to come."

Antigonus of Soko had two disciples who used to study his words. They taught them to their disciples, and their disciples to their disciples. These proceeded to examine the words closely and demanded: "Why did our ancestors see fit to say this thing? Is it possible that a laborer should do his work all day and not take his reward in the evening? If our ancestors, forsooth, had known that there is another world and that there will be a resurrection of the dead, they would not have spoken in this manner."

So they arose and withdrew from the Torah and split into two sects, the Sadducees and the Boethusians: Sadducees named after Zadok, Boethusians after Boethus. And they used silver vessels and gold vessels all their lives—not because they were ostentatious; but the Sadducees said, "It is a tradition amongst the Pharisees to afflict themselves in this world; yet in the world to come they will have nothing."

The Essenes

The Dead Sea Scrolls now provide the chief sources for our knowledge of the Essenes and their doctrine. There are also extensive accounts of this sect in the works of Josephus and Philo.[4]

Josephus, Antiquities 18:18–22

THE DOCTRINES AND LIFE OF THE ESSENES

18 The doctrine of the Essenes is wont to leave everything in the hands of God.[a] They regard the soul as immortal and believe that they ought to strive especially to draw near to righteousness.[b]

[19]They send votive offerings to the temple but perform their sacrifices employing a different ritual of purification.[c] For this reason they are barred from those precincts of the temple that are frequented by all the people and perform their rites by themselves. Otherwise they are of the highest character, devoting themselves solely to agricultural labor. . . .

[20]Moreover, they hold their possessions in common,[d] and the wealthy man receives no more enjoyment from his property than the man who possesses nothing. The men who practice this way of life number more than four thousand. [21]They neither bring wives into the community, nor do they own slaves, since they believe that the latter practice contributes to injustice and that the former opens the way to a source of dissension. Instead they live by themselves and perform menial tasks for one another. [22]They elect by show of hands good men to receive their revenues and the produce of earth and priests to prepare bread and other food.[e]

a. Here the Essene attitude to divine Providence is given. Their belief in determinism is borne out by the Qumran texts.

b. The Qumran texts do not contradict this claim. They nowhere refer, e.g., to the resurrection of the body.

c. Here the particular attitudes of the Essenes to the temple and their strict views of ritual purity are expressed.

d. The principles of communal life and its regulation are spelled out in much greater detail in The Rule of the Community and the Damascus Document.

e. Here the special role of the priests, particularly with respect to the bread of the communal meal, is mentioned; compare also the Manual of Blessings (lQSb).

Josephus, Jewish War 2:119–61

This passage opens with a general account of the sanctity of the Essenes, their celibacy, community of goods, feeling of brotherhood, and simplicity of deportment (paras. 119–27).

THE ESSENE DAILY ORDER OF LIFE

128 Their piety toward the Deity takes a peculiar form. Before the sun is up they utter no word on mundane matters, but offer in his direction[a] certain prayers, which have been handed down from their forefathers, as though entreating him to rise. [129]They are then dismissed by their superiors to the various crafts in which they are severally proficient and are strenuously employed until the fifth hour, when they again assemble in one place and, after girding their loins with linen cloths, bathe their

bodies in cold water. After this purification, they assemble in a private apartment which none of the uninitiated is permitted to enter; pure now themselves, they repair to the refectory, as to some sacred shrine. [130]When they have taken their seats in silence, the baker serves out the loaves to them in order, and the cook sets before each one plate with a single course. [131]Before meat the priest says a grace, and none may partake until after the prayer. When breakfast is ended, he pronounces a further grace; thus at the beginning and at the close they do homage to God as the bountiful giver of life. Then laying aside their raiment, as holy vestments, they again betake themselves to their labors until the evening. [132]On their return they sup in like manner, and any guests who may have arrived sit down with them. No clamor or disturbance ever pollutes their dwelling; they speak in turn, each making way for his neighbor. [133]To persons outside, the silence of those within appears like some awful mystery; it is in fact due to their invariable sobriety and to the limitation of their allotted portions of meat and drink to the demands of nature.

The following sections (134–36) stress the Essenes' charity and mutual self-help, moderation of character, and avoidance of oaths. Josephus continues: "They display an extraordinary interest in the writings of the ancients, singling out in particular those which make for the welfare of soul and body; with the help of these, and with a view to the treatment of diseases, they make investigations into medicinal roots and the properties of stones." Next Josephus describes their rules of admission to the sect in a fashion not dissimilar to The Rule of the Community 8:14–23 (paras. 137–42). Particular note is taken of their oaths to preserve secretly "the books of the sect and the names of the angels" (142). Then follows a description of their legal practice and various other aspects of their way of life (143–49); the four grades of members as well as their fortitude under Roman persecution conclude this section (150–53).

THE IMMORTALITY OF THE SOUL

[154]For it is a fixed belief of theirs that the body is corruptible and its constituent matter impermanent, but that the soul is immortal and imperishable. Emanating from the finest ether, these souls become entangled, as it were, in the prisonhouse of the body, to which they are dragged down by a sort of natural spell;[b] [155]but when once they are released from the bonds of the flesh, then, as though liberated from a long servitude, they rejoice and are borne aloft. Sharing the belief of the sons of Greece, they maintain that for virtuous souls there is reserved an

abode beyond the ocean, a place which is not oppressed by rain or snow or heat but is refreshed by the ever gentle breath of the west wind coming in from the ocean, while they relegate base souls to a murky and tempestuous dungeon, big with never-ending punishments.[c]

ESSENE FORTUNETELLERS

[159]There are some among them who profess to foretell the future, being versed from their early years in holy books, various forms of purification, and apothegms of prophets; and seldom, if ever, do they err in their predictions.[d]

OTHER ESSENE GROUPS

[160]There is yet another order of Essenes, which, while at one with the rest in its mode of life, customs, and regulations, differs from them in its views on marriage. They think that those who decline to marry cut off the chief function of life, the propagation of the race, and, what is more, that were all to adopt the same view the whole race would very quickly die out.[e] [161]They give their wives, however, a three years' probation, and only marry them after they have by three periods of purification given proof of fecundity. They have no intercourse with them during pregnancy, thus showing that their motive in marrying is not self-indulgence but the procreation of children. In the bath the women wear a dress, the men a loincloth. Such are the usages of this order.

a. Here the interpretation of John Strugnell ("Flavius Josephus and the Essenes: *Antiquities* 18:18–22," *JBL* 77 [1958] 111–13) is followed. Contrast LCL: "to him."

b. In this passage Essene determinism is formulated in terms of the Greek body-soul contrast. On the Essene attitudes in these matters, see the illuminating paper of D. Flusser, "The Dead Sea Sect and Pre-Pauline Christianity," *Scripta Hierosolymitana* 4 (1958) 215–66.

c. Here Essene views of the fate of the soul after death are most probably reinterpreted in terms of Greek eschatology.

d. Josephus mentions such predictions; see War 1:78; 2:113; Ant. 15:373ff. Cf. also Ant. 13:311.

e. It is clear that there were differing groups of Essenes. Those described in the main section live in villages and towns (124); a similar situation is implied by the Damascus Document. The Rule of the Community, however, prescribes for a group living at a single communal center.

ESSENE TEACHING ON THE TWO SPIRITS

The Rule of the Community 3:13—4:23

The Rule of the Community was discovered in a number of copies in the Qumran caves. Probably written in the early first century B.C.E., it contains instruction and regulations for a sectarian community life. Here we reproduce the major part of a lengthy theological exposition of the views of the sect. This exposition is notable as being the first—perhaps the only—systematic attempt before the Middle Ages to set forth a Jewish theological stance.

INTRODUCTION

3 [13]The Master[a] shall instruct all the sons of light and shall teach them the nature of all the children of men according to the kind of spirit which they possess, the signs identifying their works during their lifetime, their visitation for chastisement, [15]and the time of their reward.

GENERAL PRINCIPLES

From the God of Knowledge comes all that is and shall be. Before ever they existed he established their whole design, and when, as ordained for them, they come into being, it is in accord with his glorious design that they accomplish their task without change.[b] The laws of all things are in his hand, and he provides them with all their needs.

He has created man to govern the world[c] and has appointed for him two spirits in which to walk until the time of his visitation: the spirits of truth and falsehood. Those born of truth spring from a fountain of light, but those born of falsehood spring from a source of darkness. [20]All the children of righteousness are ruled by the Prince of Light and walk in the ways of light, but all the children of falsehood are ruled by the Angel of Darkness and walk in the ways of darkness.[d]

The Angel of Darkness leads all the children of righteousness astray, and until his end, all their sin, iniquities, wickedness, and all their unlawful deeds are caused by his dominion in accordance with the mysteries of God. Every one of their chastisements, and every one of the seasons of their distress, shall be brought about by the rule of his persecution; for all his allotted spirits seek the overthrow of the sons of light.[e]

But the God of Israel and his Angel of Truth will succor all [25]the sons of light, for it is he who created the spirits of light and darkness and founded every action upon them and established every deed [upon] their [ways]. And he loves the one **4** [1]everlastingly and delights in its works forever; but the counsel of the other he loathes and forever hates its ways.[f]

THE WAYS OF THE TWO SPIRITS

These are their ways: (the way of the spirit of truth)[g] in the world for the enlightenment of the heart of man, and that all the paths of true righteousness may be made straight before him, and that fear of the laws of God may be instilled in his heart: a spirit of humility, patience, abundant charity, unending goodness, understanding, and intelligence;

(a spirit of) mighty wisdom which trusts in all the deeds of God and leans on his great lovingkindness; a spirit of discernment in every purpose, of zeal for just laws, of holy [5]intent with steadfastness of heart, of great charity toward all the sons of truth, of admirable purity which detests all unclean idols, of humble conduct sprung from an understanding of all things, and of faithful concealment of the mysteries of God. These are the counsels of the spirit to the sons of truth in this world.

And as for the visitation of all who walk in this spirit, it shall be healing, great peace in a long life, and fruitfulness, together with every everlasting blessing and eternal joy in life without end, a crown of glory and a garment of majesty in unending light.

But the ways of the spirit of falsehood are these: greed, and slackness in the search for righteousness, wickedness and lies, haughtiness and pride, falseness and deceit, cruelty [10]and abundant evil, ill-temper and much folly and brazen insolence, abominable deeds (committed) in a spirit of lust, and ways of lewdness in the service of uncleanness, a blaspheming tongue, blindness of eye and dullness of ear, stiffness of neck and heaviness of heart, so that man walks in all the ways of darkness and guile.

And the visitation of all who walk in this spirit shall be a multitude of plagues by the hand of all the destroying angels, everlasting damnation by the avenging wrath of the fury of God, eternal torment, and endless disgrace together with shameful extinction in the fire of the dark regions. The times of all their generations shall be spent in sorrowful mourning and in bitter misery and in calamities of darkness until they are destroyed without remnant or survivor.

THE COURSE OF HISTORY

[15]The nature of all the children of men is ruled by these (two spirits), and during their life all the hosts of men have a portion in their divisions and walk in (both) their ways. And the whole reward for their deeds shall be, for everlasting ages, according to whether each man's portion in their two divisions is great or small. For God has established the spirits in equal measure until the final age and has set everlasting hatred between their divisions. Truth abhors the works of falsehood, and falsehood hates all the ways of truth. And their struggle is fierce in all their arguments, for they do not walk together.[h]

But in the mysteries of his understanding, and in his glorious wisdom, God has ordained an end for falsehood, and at the time of the visitation he will destroy it forever. Then truth, which has wallowed in the ways of wickedness during the dominion of falsehood until [20]the appointed time of judgment, shall arise in the world forever. God will then purify every deed of man with his truth; he will refine for himself the human frame by rooting out all spirit of falsehood from the bounds of his flesh. He will cleanse him of all wicked deeds with the spirit of holiness; like purifying waters he will shed upon him the spirit of truth (to cleanse him) of all abomination and falsehood. And he shall be plunged into the spirit of purification that he may instruct the upright in the knowledge of the Most High and teach the wisdom of the sons of heaven to the perfect of way. For God has chosen them for an everlasting covenant, and all the glory of Adam shall be theirs. There shall be no more lies, and all the works of falsehood shall be put to shame.[i]

a. A member of the community responsible for teaching its laws and doctrines.

b. God created everything; all is predetermined according to his will.

c. A common idea going back to Gen 1:28.

d. From the time of their creation, men are divided into two groups over each of which an angelic spirit is appointed.

e. This paragraph explains why the sons of light commit sins.

f. Here the involvement of God, not just of the Prince of Light, on behalf of the righteous is mentioned. This hints at a certain lack of symmetry in the dualism of the sect.

g. Some such phrase must have been lost. This section sets forth the characteristics of the sons of light and darkness and the visitations upon them.

h. No details of the reward are given here.

i. The course of history, including the period of the rule of the spirit of falsehood, is foreordained. The language of purification of the flesh and immersion in the spirit of purification are to be noted. The final aim is the teaching of the true and perfect way.

THE HISTORY OF THE SECT

Damascus Document 1:1–13

THE EXHORTATION

1 [1]Hear now, all you who know righteousness, and consider the works of God, for he has a dispute with all flesh and will condemn all those who despise him.

THE BABYLONIAN EXILE

For when they were unfaithful and forsook him, he hid his face from Israel and his sanctuary and delivered them up to the sword. But remembering the covenant of the forefathers, he left a remnant to [5]Israel and did not deliver it up to be destroyed. And in the age of wrath, three hundred and ninety years after he had given them into the hand of King Nebuchadnezzar of Babylon,[a] he visited them, and he caused a root of planting[b] to spring from Israel and Aaron to inherit his land and to prosper on the good things of his earth. And they perceived their iniquity and recognized that they were guilty men, yet [10]for twenty years they were like blind men groping for the way.[c]

THE RIGHTEOUS TEACHER

And God observed their deeds, that they sought him with a whole heart, and he raised for them a Teacher of Righteousness to guide them in the way of his heart.[d] And he made known to the latter generations that which God had done to the latter generation, the congregation of traitors, to those who departed from the way.

a. According to this view, the Restoration never took place, and consequently the temple was never rebuilt. This might have been written by a group which did not participate in the Return or, alternatively, one which denied that the Return was important in the sacred history. If taken seriously, the dates bring us down to the earlier part of the second century.

b. A term found repeatedly in sectarian documents. Drawing on Isa 60:21, it is most systematically developed in the fine poem in the Thanksgiving Hymns (1QH 8:4–37). It refers to the sect in this age.

c. The group that repented is seen by some to be the Hasideans. The twenty years then represent the time between the outbreak of the Maccabean revolt and the foundation of the Essene sect.

d. The priestly founder of the sect; the continuation of the passage refers, apparently, to the specific revelations made by the Righteous Teacher. Some have suggested that the latter was the author of the Thanksgiving Hymns (best preserved in 1QH), others that he instituted the sect's particular form of eschatological exegesis of prophetic texts called the *pesher*. An example of a *pesher* is the Nahum Commentary.

The Essene community settled at Qumran, on the northwestern coast of the Dead Sea late in the second century B.C.E., abandoned the site during the events of the first revolt against the Romans in 68–70 C.E., leaving their scrolls behind them. Nothing is known of their fate.

THE ZEALOTS

Josephus refers to this group as the "Fourth Philosophy" after the Pharisees, Sadducees, and Essenes; he calls them "bandits." The Zealots apparently originated with Judah the Gaulanite about 6 C.E., but subsequently nothing is heard of them until 66 C.E. At that time Judah's sons, Jacob, Simon, and Menahem, were active in the revolt. Another of the irredentist leaders, Eleazar ben Yair, was also of this family. They seem to have been characterized by their activist political and military policy in opposing Roman rule. In other respects they may not have differed greatly from the Pharisees (see Ant. 18:23). Josephus is violently opposed to the Zealots, "for so these miscreants called themselves, as though they were zealous in the cause of virtue and not for vice in its basest and most extravagant form" (War 4:161; see also 7:268–70).

Judah the Gaulanite

The context of the passage is the registration of Jewish properties by the Romans after Archelaus was deposed (6/7 C.E.).

Josephus, Antiquities 18:4–6, 9–10

4 But a certain Judas,[a] a Gaulanite[b] from a city named Gamala, who had enlisted the aid of Saddok, a Pharisee, threw himself into the cause of rebellion. They said that the assessment carried with it a status amounting to downright slavery, no less, and appealed to the nation to make a bid for independence. [5]They urged that in case of success the Jews would have laid the foundation of prosperity, while if they failed to obtain any such boon they would win honor and renown for their lofty aim; and that Heaven would be their zealous helper to no lesser end than the furthering of their enterprise until it succeeded—all the more if with high devotion in their hearts they stood firm and did not shrink from the bloodshed that might be necessary. [6]Since the populace, when they heard their appeals, responded gladly, the plot to strike boldly made serious progress; and so these men sowed the seed of every kind of misery, which so afflicted the nation that words are inadequate. . . .

[9]Here is a lesson that an innovation and reform in ancestral traditions weighs heavily in the scale in leading to the destruction of the congregation of the people. In this case certainly, Judas and Saddok started among us an intrusive fourth school of philosophy;[c] and when they had won an abundance of devotees, they filled the body politic immediately with tumult, also planting the seeds of those troubles which subsequently overtook it, all because of the novelty of this hitherto unknown philosophy that I shall now describe. [10]My reason for giving this brief account of it is chiefly that the zeal which Judas and Saddok inspired in the younger element meant the ruin of our cause.

a. The founder of the "Fourth Philosophy": War 2:118; Ant. 18:23; cf. Acts 5:37. War 2:118 states of him: "This man was a sophist who founded a sect of his own, having nothing in common with the others."
 b. Alternatively "Galilean"; cf. War 2:118.
 c. So Josephus attacks this group, which he does at every possible juncture.

Josephus, Jewish War 7:418–19

THE COURAGE OF THE ZEALOTS

418 For under every form of torture and laceration of body, devised for the sole object of making them acknowledge Caesar as lord, not one submitted nor was brought to the verge of utterance;[a] but all kept their resolve, triumphant over constraint, meeting the tortures and the fire with bodies that seemed insensible of pain and souls that well-nigh exulted in it. [419]But most of all were the spectators struck by the children

of tender age, not one of whom could be prevailed upon to call Caesar lord. So far did the strength of courage rise superior to the weakness of their frames.

a. This, in fact, together with an activist policy, seems to be the chief characteristic of the Zealots; the latter are the subject of the statement here. See the next passage.

Josephus, Antiquities 18:23–24
THE FOURTH PHILOSOPHY

23 As for the fourth of the philosophies, Judas the Galilean set himself up as leader of it. This school agrees in all other respects with the opinions of the Pharisees, except that they have a passion for liberty that is almost unconquerable, since they are convinced that God alone is their leader and master.[a] They think little of submitting to death in unusual forms and permitting vengeance to fall on kinsmen and friends if only they may avoid calling any man master. [24]Inasmuch as most people have seen the steadfastness of their resolution amid such circumstances, I may forgo any further account, for I have no fear that anything reported of them will be considered incredible. The danger is, rather, that report may minimize the indifference with which they accept the grinding misery of pain.

a. Feldman points out that Josephus nowhere makes the direct identification between the "Fourth Philosophy" and the Zealots, but from the characterization of them it seems likely.

Mishnah *Sanhedrin* 9:6
ZEALOT RETRIBUTION

He who steals the libation vessel; he who invokes curses by means of a magician; he who has intercourse with a pagan woman—the Zealots smite him.

This rabbinic text may also refer to the same Zealots. The practices mentioned here as incurring the wrath of the Zealots are affronts of basic religious sensibilities of the Jews.

THE THERAPEUTAE

In his treatise On the Contemplative Life, Philo describes a Jewish sect which settled on the shores of the Mareotic Lake in Egypt. His report is the only information we have about this group which has been regarded as an important indication of pre-Christian monastic tendencies in Egypt. Some have suggested that there are connections between the Therapeutae and the Essenes. The two passages from Philo's extensive account that are given here provide a general indication of the character of this group and illustrate one of their peculiar practices—ecstatic choral song and dance.

The Daily Life of the Therapeutae
Philo, On the Contemplative Life 24–33

THEIR DWELLINGS

24 The houses of the society thus collected are exceedingly simple, providing protection against two of the most pressing dangers, the fiery heat of the sun and the icy cold of the air. They are neither near together as in towns, since living at close quarters is troublesome and displeasing to people who are seeking to satisfy their desire for solitude, nor yet at a great distance, because of the sense of fellowship which they cherish, and to render help to each other if robbers attack them. [25]In each house there is a consecrated room which is called a sanctuary or closet, and closeted in this they are initiated into the mysteries of the sanctified life. They take nothing into it, either drink or food or any other of the things necessary for the needs of the body, but laws and oracles delivered through the mouth of prophets, and psalms, and anything else which fosters and perfects knowledge and piety. [26]They keep the memory of God alive and never forget it, so that even in their dreams the picture is nothing else but the loveliness of divine excellences and powers. Indeed, many when asleep and dreaming give utterance to the glorious verities of their holy philosophy.

DAILY ROUTINE

[27]Twice every day they pray, at dawn and at eventide; at sunrise they pray for a fine bright day, fine and bright in the true sense of the heavenly daylight which they pray may fill their minds. At sunset they ask that the soul may be wholly relieved from the press of the senses and the objects of sense and sitting where she is consistory and council chamber to herself pursue the quest of truth. [28]The interval between early morning and evening is spent entirely in spiritual exercise. They read the Holy Scriptures and seek wisdom from their ancestral philosophy by taking it as an allegory, since they think that the words of the literal text are symbols of something whose hidden nature is revealed by studying the underlying meaning.

THEIR WRITINGS

[29]They have also writings of men of old, the founders of their way of thinking, who left many memorials of the form used in allegorical interpretation, and these they take as a kind of archetype and imitate the method in which this principle is carried out. And so they do not confine

themselves to contemplation but also compose hymns and psalms to God in all sorts of meters and melodies which they write down with the rhythms necessarily made more solemn.

SABBATH OBSERVANCE AND CEREMONY

[30]For six days they seek wisdom by themselves in solitude in the closets mentioned above, never passing the outside door of the house or even getting a distant view of it. But every seventh day they meet together as for a general assembly and sit in order according to their age in the proper attitude, with their hands inside the robe, the right hand between the breast and the chin, and the left withdrawn along the flank. [31]Then the senior among them who also has the fullest knowledge of the doctrines which they profess comes forward and with visage and voice alike quiet and composed gives a well-reasoned and wise discourse. He does not make an exhibition of clever rhetoric like the orators or sophists of today, but follows careful examination by careful expression of the exact meaning of the thoughts, and this does not lodge just outside the ears of the audience but passes through the hearing into the soul and there stays securely. All the others sit still and listen, showing their approval merely by their looks or nods.

SABBATH SANCTUARY

[32]This common sanctuary in which they meet every seventh day is a double enclosure, one portion set apart for the use of the men, the other for the women, for women, too, regularly make part of the audience with the same ardor and the same sense of their calling. [33]The wall between the two chambers rises up from the ground to three or four cubits built in the form of a breastwork, while the space above up to the roof is left open. This arrangement serves two purposes; the modesty becoming to the female sex is preserved, while the women sitting within earshot can easily follow what is said, since there is nothing to obstruct the voice of the speaker.

The Dance and the Chorus

Philo, On the
Contemplative Life 83–85, 88–89

In this section, in the course of describing the more festal symposia of the Therapeutae, Philo relates the following:

83 After the supper they hold the sacred vigil which is conducted in the following way. They rise up all together and standing in the middle of the refectory form themselves first into two choirs, one of men and one of

women, the leader and precentor chosen for each being the most honored among them and also the most musical. [84]Then they sing hymns to
God composed of many measures and set to many melodies, sometimes
chanting together, sometimes taking up the harmony antiphonally,
hands and feet keeping time in accompaniment, and rapt with enthusi-
asm reproduce sometimes the lyrics of the procession, sometimes of the
halt and of the wheeling and counter-wheeling of a choric dance. [85]Then
when each choir has separately done its own part in the feast, having
drunk as in the Bacchic rites of the strong wine of God's love, they mix
and both together become a single choir, a copy of the choir set up of old
beside the Red Sea in honor of the wonders there wrought. . . .

[88]It is on this model above all that the choir of the Therapeutae of
either sex, note in response to note and voice to voice, the treble of the
women blending with the bass of the men, create a harmonious concent,
music in the truest sense. Lovely are the thoughts, lovely the words, and
worthy of reverence the choristers, and the end and aim of thoughts,
words, and choristers alike is piety. [89]Thus they continue till dawn,
drunk with this drunkenness in which there is no shame, then not with
heavy heads or drowsy eyes but more alert and wakeful than when they
came to the banquet, they stand with their faces and whole body turned
to the east, and when they see the sun rising they stretch their hands up
to heaven and pray for bright days and knowledge of the truth and the
power of keen-sighted thinking. And after the prayers they depart each
to his private sanctuary once more to ply the trade and till the field of
their wonted philosophy.

THE JEWS IN
THE EYES OF THE PAGANS

Two short passages illustrate how contemporary, educated pagans
looked at the Jews. Attitudes to the Jews ranged from highly positive
to rabidly anti-Semitic.

Hecataeus of Abdera, History of Egypt
(in Diodorus Siculus, Library of History 40, 3)

Hecataeus (ca. 300 B.C.E.) writes about the Jews as a people expelled
from Egypt. He indicates no anti-Jewish feeling and apparently also
used a Jewish source.[5]

1 When in ancient times a pestilence arose in Egypt, the common people
ascribed their troubles to the working of a divine agency, for indeed with

many strangers of all sorts dwelling in their midst and practicing different rites of religion and sacrifice, their own traditional observances in honor of the gods had fallen into disuse.

[2]Hence the natives of the land surmised that unless they removed the foreigners their troubles would never be resolved. At once, therefore, the aliens were driven from the country, and the most outstanding and active among them banded together and, as some say, were cast ashore in Greece and certain other regions; their leaders were notable men, chief among them being Danaus and Cadmus. But the greater number were driven into what is now called Judaea, which is not far distant from Egypt and was at that time utterly uninhabited.

[3]The colony was headed by a man called Moses, outstanding both for his wisdom and for his courage. On taking possession of the land he founded, besides other cities, one that is now the most renowned of all, called Jerusalem. In addition he established the temple that they hold in chief veneration, instituted their forms of worship and ritual, drew up their laws, and ordered their political institutions. He also divided them into twelve tribes, since this is regarded as the most perfect number and corresponds to the number of months that make up a year.

[4]But he had no images whatsoever of the gods made for them, being of the opinion that God is not in human form; rather the heaven that surrounds the earth is alone divine and rules the universe. The sacrifices that he established differ from those of other nations, as does their way of living, for as a result of their own expulsion from Egypt he introduced an unsocial and intolerant mode of life. He picked out the men of most refinement and with the greatest ability to head the entire nation and appointed them priests; and he ordained that they should occupy themselves with the temple and the honors and sacrifices offered to their God.

[5]These same men he appointed to be judges in all major disputes, and entrusted to them the guardianship of the laws and customs. For this reason the Jews never have a king, and authority over the people is regularly vested in whichever priest is regarded as superior to his colleagues in wisdom and virtue. They call this man the high priest and believe that he acts as a messenger to them of God's commandments.

[6]It is he, we are told, who in their assemblies and other gatherings announces what is ordained, and the Jews are so docile in such matters that straightway they fall to the ground and do reverence to the high priest when he expounds the commandments to them. And at the end of their laws there is even appended the statement "These are the words that Moses heard from God and declares unto the Jews." Their lawgiver was careful also to make provision for warfare and required the young

men to cultivate manliness, steadfastness, and generally the endurance of every hardship.

[7]He led out military expeditions against the neighboring tribes, and after annexing much land apportioned it out, assigning equal allotments to private citizens and greater ones to the priests, in order that they, by virtue of receiving more ample revenues, might be undistracted and apply themselves continually to the worship of God. The common citizens were forbidden to sell their individual plots, lest there be some who for their own advantage should buy them up, and by oppressing the poorer classes bring on a scarcity of manpower.

[8]He required those who dwelt in the land to rear their children, and since offspring could be cared for at little cost, the Jews were from the start a populous nation. As to marriage and the burial of the dead, he saw to it that their customs should differ widely from those of other men. But later, when they became subject to foreign rule, as a result of their mingling with men of other nations (both under Persian rule and under that of the Macedonians who overthrew the Persians), many of their traditional practices were disturbed. Such is the account of Hecataeus of Abdera in regard to the Jews.

Apollonius Molon, On the Jews

(in Josephus, Against Apion 2:79–80, 89, 91–96)

Apollonius Molon was a rhetor, originally from Caria, who lived in the first century B.C.E. According to Josephus he was a rabid anti-Semite; his views are typical of much Hellenistic and Roman anti-Jewish prejudice.

79 I am no less amazed at the proceedings of the authors who supplied him with his materials, I mean Posidonius and Apollonius Molon. On the one hand, they charge us with not worshiping the same gods as other people; on the other, they tell lies and invent absurd calumnies about our temple without showing any consciousness of impiety. Yet to high-minded men nothing is more disgraceful than a lie, of any description, but above all on the subject of a temple of worldwide fame and commanding sanctity.

[80]Within this sanctuary Apion has the effrontery to assert that the Jews kept an ass's head, worshiping that animal and deeming it worthy of the deepest reverence; the fact was disclosed, he maintains, on the occasion of the spoliation of the temple by Antiochus Epiphanes, when the head, made of gold and worth a high price, was discovered. . . .

[89]He adds a second story, about Greeks, which is a malicious slander

upon us from beginning to end. . . . [91]He asserts that Antiochus found in the temple a couch on which a man was reclining with a table before him laden with a banquet of fish of the sea, beasts of the earth, and birds of the air, at which the poor fellow was gazing in stupefaction.

[92]The king's entry was instantly hailed by him with adoration, as about to procure him profound relief; falling at the king's knees, he stretched out his right hand and implored him to set him free. The king reassured him and bade him tell who he was, why he was living there, what was the meaning of his abundant fare. Thereupon, with sighs and tears, the man, in a pitiful tone, told the tale of his distress.

[93]He said, Apion continues, that he was a Greek and that while traveling about the province for a livelihood he was suddenly kidnapped by men of a foreign race and conveyed to the temple; there he was shut up and seen by nobody, but was fattened on feasts of the most lavish description. [94]At first these unlooked-for attentions deceived him and caused him pleasure; suspicion followed, then consternation. Finally, on consulting the attendants who waited upon him, he heard of the unutterable law of the Jews, for the sake of which he was being fed. The practice was repeated annually at a fixed season. [95]They would kidnap a Greek foreigner, fatten him for a year, and then convey him to a wood, where they slew him, sacrificed his body with their customary ritual, partook of his flesh, and, while immolating the Greek, swore an oath of hostility to the Greeks. The remains of their victim were then thrown into a pit.

[96]The man (Apion continues) stated that he had now but a few days left to live and implored the king, out of respect for the gods of Greece, to defeat this Jewish plot upon his lifeblood and to deliver him from his miserable predicament.

NOTES

1. See the discussion in John J. Collins, *The Apocalyptic Vision of the Book of Daniel,* Harvard Semitic Monographs 16 (Missoula: Scholars Press, 1977).

2. See Philip Davies, "Hasidim in the Maccabean Period," *JJS* 28 (1977) 127–40.

3. For this reason too, Philo of Alexandria (ca. 25 B.C.E.–50 C.E.) showed great interest in the Essenes and in another similar Jewish sect, the Therapeutae who lived in Egypt (see above, pp. 41–44).

4. War 2:119–61 and again in Ant. 18:18–22; Philo, Every Good Man Is Free 75–91.

5. Other fragments of his writings on the Jews have survived in Josephus, *Against Apion* 1:183ff. See further Menaham Stern, *Greek and Latin Authors on Jews and Judaism*, 20–25.

BIBLIOGRAPHY

PRIMARY SOURCES

The Bible and Apocrypha are quoted from the RSV; the Samaritan Chronicle from J. **MacDonald**, *The Samaritan Chronicle II* (Berlin: De Gruyter, 1969) 110–13; Josephus and Philo from LCL, with occasional adaptations (see notes); Apocryphal Psalm from James A. **Sanders**, *The Dead Sea Psalms Scroll* (Ithaca, N.Y.: Cornell University Press, 1967) 105–7; Commentary on Nahum from Theodor H. **Gaster**, *The Dead Sea Scriptures*, 3d ed. (Garden City, N.Y.: Anchor, 1967); The Rule of the Community and the Damascus Document from Geza **Vermes**, *The Dead Sea Scrolls in English*, 2d ed. (Harmondsworth: Penguin, 1975); The Fathers According to Rabbi Nathan from Judah **Goldin**, *The Fathers According to Rabbi Nathan*, Yale Judaica Series 10 (New Haven: Yale University Press, 1955); the extracts from Hecataeus and Apollonius Molon from Menaham **Stern**, *Greek and Latin Authors on Jews and Judaism* (Jerusalem: Israel Academy, 1974), vol. 1.

SECONDARY SOURCES

GENERAL

Michael E. **Stone**, "Judaism at the Time of Christ," *Scientific American 228* (January 1973) 80–87. Paul D. **Hanson**, *The Dawn of Apocalyptic* (Philadelphia: Fortress, 1975) 1–13, 209–27. Morton **Smith**, "The Dead Sea Sect in Relation to Ancient Judaism," *New Testament Studies 7*, no. 4 (1961) 347–60.

SECTS

SAMARITANS

The article by Ayala **Löwenstamm** in *Encyclopedia Judaica* (New York: Macmillan, 1971) 14:725–28 is an excellent survey of Samaritan history, religion, literature, and chronology. Frank M. **Cross**, "Papyri of the Fourth Century B.C. from Dâliyeh," *New Directions in Biblical Archaeology*, ed. D. Noel Freedman and Jonas C. Greenfield (Garden City, N.Y.: Doubleday, 1969) 41–62. Idem, "Aspects of Samaritan and Jewish History in Late Persian and Hellenistic Times," *HTR* 59 (1966) 201–11. Idem, "A Reconstruction of the Judean Restoration," *JBL* 94 (1975) 4–18.

HASIDEANS

Shmuel **Safrai**, "Teaching of Pietists in Mishnaic Literature," *JJS* 16 (1965) 15–33. Adolph **Büchler**, *Types of Jewish-Palestinian Piety from 70 B.C.E. to 70 C.E.*, Jews' College Publications 8 (London: Jews' College, 1922).

PHARISEES AND SADDUCEES

"Pharisees" in *IDBSup* has extensive bibliography. Ralph **Marcus**, "The Pharisees in the Light of Modern Scholarship," *Journal of Religion* 32 (1952) 153–65 (with bibliography). Louis **Finkelstein,** *The Pharisees* (Philadelphia: Jewish Publication Society, 1962). Jacob **Neusner,** *From Politics to Piety* (Englewood Cliffs, N.J.: Prentice-Hall, 1972).

ESSENES

Josef T. **Milik,** *Ten Years of Discovery in the Wilderness of Judaea* (Naperville, Ill.: Allenson, 1959). Frank M. **Cross,** *The Ancient Library of Qumran,* 2d ed. (Garden City, N.Y.: Doubleday, 1961). A. **Adam,** *Antike Berichte über die Essener* (Berlin: De Gruyter, 1972) contains a collection of all ancient sources on the Essenes. John **Strugnell,** "Flavius Josephus and the Essenes: *Antiquities* 18:18–22," *JBL* 77 (1958) 106–15. Morton **Smith,** "The Description of the Essenes in Josephus and the Philosophumena," *Hebrew Union College Annual* 29 (1958) 273–313.

ZEALOTS

IDBSup, s.v., and *Encyclopedia Judaica* 16:947–50 both have good bibliographies.

PAGANS

John G. **Gager,** *Moses in Greco-Roman Paganism,* Society of Biblical Literature Monograph Series 16 (Nashville: Abingdon, 1972).

2
Temple
and Cult

Temples and sanctuaries were a common feature of the religions of the ancient Mediterranean world. As early as the time of their wilderness wanderings, we are told, the people who would become Israel erected a building where they and their leaders could meet God and worship him.[1]

For many centuries after the conquest of Canaan, various sites in Israel were considered to be sacred and hence to provide the opportunity for encounter with God. David made a strong move toward centralization when he established the tabernacle in Jerusalem, and Solomon's construction of a magnificent temple on Mount Zion reinforced the religious significance of Jerusalem. This attempt at centralization, however, was never completely successful. For one thing, the division of the kingdom in 922 B.C.E. led to the erection of two shrines in the north at the ancient sacred sites of Bethel and Dan. An Israelite temple at Arad in the south flourished for a couple of centuries. Moreover, the reforms of Hezekiah (ca. 700 B.C.E.) and Josiah (622 B.C.E.) and the preaching of Jeremiah and other prophets indicate that worship at a multiplicity of sacred sites and high places in the land had not been completely suppressed.

This plurality notwithstanding, in the southern kingdom of Judah, Jerusalem reigned supreme as the sacred place par excellence, as the writer of Deuteronomy never tired of saying. The temple, Mount Zion, and Jerusalem were virtually synonymous with a kind of earthly sacred space where God's glory dwelt, where sacrifice was offered to him, and to which pious Jews made pilgrimage. Thus the destruction of Jerusalem and the temple in 587 B.C.E. inflicted deep trauma upon the Jews. Not only were they uprooted from their land and homes and exiled in Babylon, they were cut off from their cultic center, which now lay useless and ruined.

Essential to the Jews' return to their homeland in the late sixth century B.C.E. was their reconstruction of the temple. After some delay, this rebuilding was accomplished under the direction of Zerubbabel, the Davidide, but it was a far cry from the splendor of its Solomonic predecessor. Nonetheless, for almost five centuries this structure was the cultic center of Judaism, and its high priest served also as the ruler of the people. Late in the first century B.C.E., in an attempt to curry the favor of his subjects, King Herod "the Great" began a massive expansion and rebuilding of the temple and its courts which made the sanctuary one of the architectural wonders of the contemporary world.

The second temple, like the first, stood at the center of Jewish piety. Hymns and prayers once composed for use in the first temple were collected together with others into our Book of Psalms, which served, so to speak, as the hymn book of the second temple.[2] Assaults upon the temple and its purity by King Antiochus IV of Syria (168 B.C.E.), and by the Romans, Pompey (63 B.C.E.) and Varus (4 B.C.E.), were viewed with horror, and its final destruction by Titus in 70 C.E. left a vacuum in Jewish life comparable to that inflicted in 587 B.C.E.

Its centrality notwithstanding, the second temple was not the only sanctuary of Judaism in the Hellenistic and Roman periods, and attitudes toward it varied. Other Jewish temples existed at Elephantine and Leontopolis in Egypt and at Tyros (Araq el-Emir) in Transjordan. The old sacred site of Dan seems to have been held in esteem by some apocalyptic Jewish writers of the Hellenistic period.[3] The Samaritans worshiped at their own temple on Mount Gerizim (see above, pp. 13–16, 18–19). Critiques of temple and priesthood stand in tension with words of high praise.

IN PRAISE OF THE TEMPLE

In three passages with clear emotional overtones, we hear the Jews expressing their longing for, devotion to, and joy in this precious and central part of their lives.

A Song of Pilgrimage

Psalm 84:1–10

In this song of preexilic origin, the author anticipates a pilgrimage to Jerusalem, where the temple brings one into the presence of God and even offers shelter for the birds of the air.

1 How lovely is your dwelling place,
    O Lord of hosts!
[2]My soul longs, yea, faints
    for the courts of the Lord;
  my heart and flesh sing for joy
    to the living God.
[3]Even the sparrow finds a home,
    and the swallow a nest for herself,
    where she may lay her young,
  at your altars, O Lord of hosts,
    my king and my God.
[4]Blessed are those who dwell in your house,
    ever singing your praise! *Selah*
[5]Blessed are the men whose strength is in you,
    in whose heart are the highways to Zion.
[6]As they go through the valley of Baca
    they make it a place of springs;
    the early rain also covers it with pools.
[7]They go from strength to strength;
    the God of gods will be seen in Zion.
[8]O Lord God of hosts, hear my prayer;
    give ear, O God of Jacob! *Selah*
[9]Behold our shield, O God;
    look upon the face of your anointed![a]
[10]For a day in your courts is better
    than a thousand elsewhere.
  I would rather be a doorkeeper in the house of my God
    than dwell in the tents of wickedness.

a. A reference to the king.

An Apostrophe to Zion

Apocryphal Psalms, col. 22

This psalm is one of several apocryphal compositions included in a scroll of the Book of Psalms found at Qumran. It is implicitly ascribed to David, but its date is unknown. The psalm is striking because it is addressed to the personified Zion rather than to God.[4] In it the author anticipates a time when Zion will be freed from the domination of her enemies and will be the place of true and perfect righteousness and blessing.

1 I remember you for blessing, O Zion;
>   with all my might have I loved you.
>   May your memory be blessed forever!
2Great is your hope, O Zion:
>   that peace and your longed-for salvation will come.
3Generation after generation will dwell in you,
>   and generations of saints will be your splendor:
4Those who yearn for the day of your salvation,
>   that they may rejoice in the greatness of your glory.
5On (the) abundance of your glory they are nourished,
>   and in your splendid squares will they toddle.
6The merits of your prophets will you remember,
>   and in the deeds of your pious ones will you glory.
7Purge violence from your midst;
>   falsehood and evil will be cut off from you.
8Your sons will rejoice in your midst,
>   and your precious ones will be united with you.
9How they have hoped for your salvation;
>   your pure ones have mourned for you.
10Hope for you does not perish, O Zion,
>   nor is hope in you forgotten.
11Who has ever perished (in) righteousness,
>   or who has ever survived in his iniquity?
12Man is tested according to his way;
>   every man is requited according to his deeds,
13All about are your enemies cut off, O Zion,
>   and all your foes have been scattered.
14Praise from you is pleasing to God, O Zion,
>   ascending through all the world.
15Many times do I remember you for blessing;
>   with all my heart I bless you.
16May you attain everlasting righteousness,
>   and blessings of the honorable may you receive.
17Accept a vision spoken of you,
>   and dreams of prophets sought for you.
18Be exalted, and spread wide, O Zion;
>   praise the Most High, your savior:
>   let my soul be glad in your glory.

A "Pagan" Views the Temple and Its Cult

Aristeas to Philocrates 83–92

Writing some time in the second century B.C.E. in the guise of an
Egyptian official, the Egyptian Jewish author of this passage employs

superlatives to describe the marvels of the Jerusalem temple and the ministrations of its priests.

83 When we arrived in the land of the Jews we saw the city situated in the middle of the whole of Judea on the top of a mountain of considerable altitude. [84]On the summit the temple had been built in all its splendor. It was surrounded by three walls more than seventy cubits high and in length and breadth corresponding to the structure of the edifice. All the buildings were characterized by a magnificence and costliness quite unprecedented. [85]It was obvious that no expense had been spared on the door and the fastenings, which connected it with the doorposts, and the stability of the lintel. [86]The style of the curtain too was thoroughly in proportion to that of the entrance. Its fabric owing to the draft of wind was in perpetual motion, and as this motion was communicated from the bottom and the curtain bulged out to its highest extent, it afforded a pleasant spectacle from which a man could scarcely tear himself away. [87]The construction of the altar was in keeping with the place itself and with the burnt offerings which were consumed by fire upon it, and the approach to it was on a similar scale. There was a gradual slope up to it, conveniently arranged for the purpose of decency, and the ministering priests were robed in linen garments down to their ankles. [88]The temple faces the east and its back is toward the west. The whole of the floor is paved with stones and slopes down to the appointed places, that water may be conveyed to wash away the blood from the sacrifices, for many thousand beasts are sacrificed there on feast days. [89]And there is an inexhaustible supply of water, because an abundant natural spring gushes up from within the temple area. There are, moreover, wonderful and indescribable cisterns underground, as they pointed out to me, at a distance of five furlongs all around the site of the temple, and each of them has countless pipes so that the different streams converge together. [90]And all these were fastened with lead at the bottom and at the sidewalls, and over them a great quantity of plaster had been spread, and every part of the work had been most carefully carried out. There are many openings for water at the base of the altar which are invisible to all except to those who are engaged in the ministration, so that all the blood of the sacrifices which is collected in great quantities is washed away in the twinkling of an eye. . . . [92]The ministration of the priests is in every way unsurpassed both for its physical endurance and for its orderly and silent service, for they all work spontaneously, though it entails much painful exertion, and each one has a special task allotted to him. The service is carried on without interruption—some provide the wood, others the oil, others the fine wheat flour, others the spices; others again bring the pieces of flesh for the burnt offering, exhibiting a wonderful degree of strength.

THE PLACE OF
THE TEMPLE IN JEWISH LIFE

What were the roles played by this institution—so greatly admired and warmly praised?

The Presence of God

Most basically, the temple was the place where one found God, where one came "before" or "into the presence of" God. The idea is expressed in a variety of ways, for example, through the older terms "tent of meeting" (where one met God) and "tabernacle" (where God dwelt), the expression "house of God," and in descriptions of the "glory of the Lord" filling and dwelling in the temple.

1 Kings 8:27–34

In his description of the dedication of Solomon's temple, the seventh-century author of the Deuteronomistic history (Deuteronomy through 2 Kings) relates how the glorious cloud filled the temple, thus manifesting God's presence (1 Kgs 8:10–11). Solomon then blessed the people (8:14–21) and offered a lengthy prayer that is a kind of compendium of the functions of the temple and their relationship to the temple as God's dwelling place.

27 But will God indeed dwell on the earth? Behold, heaven and the highest heaven cannot contain you, how much less this house which I have built! 28Yet have regard to the prayer of your servant and to his supplication, O Lord my God, hearkening to the cry and to the prayer which your servant prays before you this day; 29that your eyes may be open night and day toward this house, the place of which you have said, "My name shall be there," that you may hearken to the prayer which your servant offers toward this place. 30And hearken to the supplication of your servant and of your people Israel, when they pray toward this place; yea, hear in heaven your dwelling place; and when you hear, forgive.

31If a man sins against his neighbor and is made to take an oath, and comes and swears his oath before your altar in this house, 32then hear in heaven, and act, and judge your servants, condemning the guilty by bringing his conduct upon his own head, and vindicating the righteous by rewarding him according to his righteousness.

33 When your people Israel are defeated before the enemy because they have sinned against you, if they turn again to you and acknowledge your name and pray and make supplication to you in this house, 34then

hear in heaven and forgive the sin of your people Israel, and bring them again to the land which you gave to their fathers.

The notion that God's "name" dwells in the temple reflects a tension between the idea that God cannot be confined to any space, let alone a building, and the belief that he is in a special sense present in his temple. Thus repeatedly, as if in a refrain, Solomon makes reference to the temple as the place in which and toward which Israel is to pray and carry out acts of repentance, for there communication with God is established and rapproachement with him is found.

Isaiah 6:1–5

One explanation of the temple as sacred space was that the Jerusalem temple was the counterpart to the heavenly temple. It is expressed in the story of Isaiah's call to be a prophet.

1 In the year that King Uzziah died I saw the Lord sitting upon a throne, high and lifted up; and his train filled the temple. 2Above him stood the seraphim; each had six wings: with two he covered his face, and with two he covered his feet, and with two he flew. 3And one called to another and said:
  "Holy, holy, holy is the Lord of hosts;
    the whole earth is full of his glory."
4And the foundations of the thresholds shook at the voice of him who called, and the house was filled with smoke.[a] 5And I said, "Woe is me! For I am lost; for I am a man of unclean lips, and I dwell in the midst of a people of unclean lips; for my eyes have seen the King, the Lord of hosts!"

a. A reference to the incense in the holy place.

While he is in the Jerusalem temple, Isaiah sees the bottom parts of the garment of the Deity, who is enthroned in his heavenly temple. The earthly temple provides access, however, to the heavenly sanctuary, and Isaiah is able to "see" the Lord of the heavenly hosts and his attendants. Nonetheless, paradoxically, *the whole earth* is full of his glorious presence (cf. 1 Kgs 8:27). The notion that the heavenly and earthly sanctuaries were counterparts of one another appears to be implied in the claim that the plan of the tabernacle was based on a "pattern" which God showed to Moses (Exod 25:9) and in the account of Ezekiel's vision of the new temple (Ezek 40–48). It also appears in later texts that reflect Ezekiel 40–48 (see below, p. 84, nn. e, f, g, j; p. 87, n. 8).

The Place of Cultic Activity

As Solomon's prayer indicates (see above, pp. 56–57), God's presence in the temple is intimately connected with the temple's role as the place in which cultic activity took place. Here sacrifice was offered before God, prayers were directed to him, his praise was sung, and his blessing was spoken over the people.

Wisdom of ben Sira 50:5–21

The cult of the temple was directed and implemented by the priests, "the sons of Aaron," who were assisted by the Levites. Writing between 196 and 175 B.C.E., the Jerusalem sage, Joshua ben Sira, climaxes his catalog of Israelite heroes with a remarkable hymn in praise of the high priest Simon II (219–196 B.C.E.). Noteworthy throughout the passage are ben Sira's awe of and deep emotional attachment to the person and office of this high priest and to the service of worship over which he presides. Of no small importance were the pageantry and spectacle which have always been an important part of most religious traditions.

5 How glorious he was when the people gathered round him
    as he came out of the inner sanctuary![a]
[6]Like the morning star among the clouds,
    like the moon when it is full;
[7]like the sun shining upon the temple of the Most High,
    and like the rainbow gleaming in glorious clouds;
[8]like roses in the days of the first fruits,
    like lilies by a spring of water,
    like a green shoot on Lebanon on a summer day;
[9]like fire and incense in the censer,
    like a vessel of hammered gold
    adorned with all kinds of precious stones;
[10]like an olive tree putting forth its fruit,
    and like a cypress towering in the clouds.

[11]When he put on his glorious robe
    and clothed himself with superb perfection
and went up to the holy altar,
    he made the court of the sanctuary glorious.

¹²And when he received the portions from the hands of the priests,
  as he stood by the hearth of the altar
with a garland of brethren around him,
  he was like a young cedar on Lebanon;
and they surrounded him like the trunks of palm trees,
¹³ all the sons of Aaron[b] in their splendor
with the Lord's offering in their hands,
  before the whole congregation of Israel.
¹⁴Finishing the service at the altars,
  and arranging the offering to the Most High, the Almighty,
¹⁵he reached out his hand to the cup
  and poured a libation of the blood of the grape;[c]
he poured it out at the foot of the altar,
  a pleasing odor to the Most High, the King of all.

¹⁶Then the sons of Aaron shouted,
  they sounded the trumpets of hammered work,
they made a great noise to be heard
  for remembrance before the Most High.
¹⁷Then all the people together made haste
  and fell to the ground upon their faces
to worship their Lord,
  the Almighty, God Most High.
¹⁸And the singers praised him with their voices
  in sweet and full-toned melody.[d]
¹⁹And the people besought the Lord Most High
  in prayer before him who is merciful,
till the order of worship of the Lord was ended;
  so they completed his service.
²⁰Then Simon came down, and lifted up his hands
  over the whole congregation of the sons of Israel,[e]
to pronounce the blessing of the Lord with his lips.
  and to glory in his name;
²¹and they bowed down in worship a second time,
  to receive the blessing from the Most High.

a. Simon has just performed some cultic act in the holy place. There is no clear evidence in the text that he is performing his special office on the Day of Atonement. More likely this is some special occasion on which the high priest chose to preside over the cult. For the presence of the high priest at the daily sacrifice, see M. *Tamid* 7, below, p. 61.

b. A biblical name for the priests denoting their descent from Moses' brother.

c. Libations of wine were a regular part of the daily burnt offering.

d. The Levites sing one of the psalms.

e. A reference to the Aaronic benediction, Num 6:22–26. Cf. M. *Tamid* 7:2, below, p. 61.

Cultic activity in the second temple was diverse in its forms and functions, and the details of its execution differed over the centuries. The sacrificial system was central, of course. The animals slaughtered varied from small birds to whole oxen, depending upon the nature of the sacrifice and one's economic status. Most often, only the fat and inward parts were consumed on the altar, while certain portions of the meat were reserved for the priests, and others were eaten by the person offering the sacrifice. By ancient law the consuming of blood was strictly forbidden.

Sacrifices served a variety of functions: to purify the sanctuary or an individual from ritual impurity; to atone for sin; to fulfill a vow; to offer thanks for some deed of divine deliverance or bounty.

In addition to these sacrifices of ad hoc significance and purpose, there were the daily liturgies of the temple. Twice daily, at daybreak and in the latter part of the afternoon, a whole lamb, together with a portion of grain, was offered. This sacrifice was supported by the half-shekel temple tax collected from all adult male Jews in the holy land and the dispersion.[5] The importance of this sacrifice, the *Tamid*, is reflected in the Book of Daniel, which measures the time of Antiochus's pollution of the temple in terms of the cessation of this sacrifice (Dan 8:11–14; 12:11–12). In the afternoon liturgy a psalm was sung, incense was burned inside the holy place, and the lamps that had been extinguished that morning were lit. The liturgy concluded with the pronouncing of the benediction.

Mishnah *Tamid* 4:1–2 and 7:2

Among the tractates of the Mishnah, *Tamid* is unusual in that it is not prescriptive of practice, but descriptive of the liturgy of the late second temple period. Detailed regulations for the offering of sacrifices are an important part of the Torah (see Lev 1–7). The text that follows is part of the Mishnaic description of the Daily Whole-offering, or *Tamid*.

4 [1]The lamb was not (wholly) bound up but (only) tied, and they to whom it fell to take the members (of the lamb) laid hold on it. And thus was it tied up—with its head to the south and its face to the west. He that slaughtered it stood to the east with his face to the west. (The Daily Whole-offering) of the morning was slaughtered at the northwestern corner at the second ring; that of the afternoon was slaughtered at the northeastern corner at the second ring. He whose lot it was to slaughter

slaughtered it;[a] and he whose lot it was to receive (the blood) received the blood and came to the northeastern corner (of the altar) and sprinkled it to the east and to the north; then he came to the southwestern corner and sprinkled it to the east and to the south. The residue of the blood he poured out at the base (of the altar) on the south side.

²He (that slaughtered it) did not break its hind leg but pierced the knee joint and so hung it up; he flayed it downward as far as the breast; when he reached the breast he cut off the head and gave it to him whose lot it was to take it. He cut off the shanks and gave them to him whose lot it was to take them. He stripped off all the hide, slit the heart, and let out its blood. He cut off the forelegs and gave them to him whose lot it was to take them. He came up to the right hind-leg, cut it off, and gave it with the two stones to him to whose lot they fell. He slit (the carcass) so that all the inward parts lay open before him. He removed the fat and put it above where the head was cut off. He removed the inward parts and gave them to him whose lot it was to swill them. The stomach was swilled as many times as it needed in the swilling chamber, and the inwards were rinsed at least three times on the marble tables between the pillars.

Concerning the blessing we are told:

7 ²They came and stood on the steps of the Porch. They that came first stood to the south of their brothers the priests; and they bore five utensils in their hands, one having the ash bin, another the oil jug, another the fire pan, another the (incense) dish, another the ladle and its cover. They then pronounced the blessing (of the priests) over the people as a single blessing;[b] in the provinces it was pronounced as three blessings, but in the temple as a single blessing. In the temple they pronounced the Name as it was written, but in the provinces by a substituted word. In the provinces the priests raised their hands as high as their shoulders, but in the temple above their heads, excepting the high priest, who raised his hands only as high as the frontlet.[c] Rabbi Judah says: The high priest also raised his hand above the frontlet, for it is written, "And Aaron lifted up his hands toward the people and blessed them" (Lev 9:22).

a. By the time of the late second temple period, lots were cast to determine who would perform the various cultic functions. Cf. Aristeas 92 (above, p. 55) and Luke 1:9.
b. A reference to the Aaronic benediction. See n. *d* on Sir 50:20, above, p. 59.
b. A reference to the Aaronic benediction. See n. *d* on Sir 50:20, above, p. 000.
c. A part of the high-priestly vestment, worn on the forehead.

As we might expect, holy days and festivals were of special significance in the life of the temple. On the Sabbath, the concluding day

of the week, special whole burnt offerings were sacrificed in addition to the *Tamid*. In the morning a new division of presiding priests
replaced those of the previous week.[6] Then twelve new loaves of
shewbread were placed on the table in the holy place, and the ones
from the previous week were divided among the two groups of
priests.

Jerusalem was a place of pilgrimage already in the first temple
period, as is evident from the psalms of pilgrimage in the canonical
Psalter (see above, Ps 84, pp. 52–53). In the second temple period the
festivals of Passover, Pentecost, and Tabernacles brought waves of
pilgrims to Jerusalem, where they participated in the temple services
and rituals. At Passover the lambs were slaughtered in the temple
and were then eaten by groups of Jews within the city precincts.
Pentecost was a festival of wheat-harvesting. Many pilgrims brought
the offerings of first fruits at this time, though they might do so at
other times also. The festival of Tabernacles was a time of great joy
and praise and was marked by elaborate rituals. During these festivals and at other times as well, individual Israelites brought special
sacrifices to the temple. On Yom Kippur, the solemn Day of Atonement, the temple was the focus of national religious attention, for
on this day alone the high priest was permitted to enter the inmost
sanctuary, the holy of holies, where as the climax of a special ritual
he sprinkled blood in atonement for the sins of the nation.

Large-scale pilgrimage to Jerusalem also created problems. Not
the least of these was the difficulty of finding accommodations in the
cramped, crowded city. Other troubles were more severe. On one
occasion the pilgrims pelted the unpopular high priest, Alexander
Janneus, with the citrons they were carrying for ritual purposes on
the feast of Tabernacles. Altercations with the Roman authorities
were not infrequent. The trial and condemnation of Jesus of
Nazareth was probably connected with Pontius Pilate's apprehen-
sion that a popular leader among the Passover pilgrims might well be
a spark that would ignite the powder keg of rebellion against Rome.

Other Aspects of the Temple

The temple served a number of functions not always directly related
to its role as a center of cultic activity. It was the meeting place of the
Sanhedrin, the civil and religious governing body of the Jews. The
study and teaching of the Torah went on in a variety of ways (see Sir

24:10, below, p. 214; cf. also Mark 12:35; 14:49; and Acts 3–4). The temple area also served as a repository for funds (cf. 2 Macc 3:10–11, immediately below) and in times of siege, as a citadel.

The Temple—Indispensable, Threatened, Destroyed

It is evident, then, that the temple played an essential and central role in the religious life of the Jewish people. Its pollution by Antiochus Epiphanes was at the heart of the religious crisis that shook Judaism in the early part of the second century B.C.E., and the writings of this period take due note of the king's idolatrous altar—the sacrilege that left the temple desolate of pious Jews (Dan 11:31; 1 Macc 1:54; 2 Macc 6:5).

2 Maccabees 3:9–39

THE TEMPLE ATTACKED AND DEFENDED

Jason of Cyrene, whose history of the early second century was epitomized in 2 Maccabees, organized this history around the story of the good and evil fortunes of the temple. The opening story of this work recounts how Heliodorus, an official of the Syrian king Seleucus (187–175 B.C.E.), attempted unsuccessfully to plunder the temple treasury. The point of the story is that God protects his temple when his people observe the Torah (3:1). For our present purposes, the story is remarkable also because in it we recognize the same powerful emotional responses that testified in the beginning of this section to the deep impact the temple made on the lives of the Jewish people.[7]

9 When he had arrived at Jerusalem and had been kindly welcomed by the high priest of the city, he told about the disclosure that had been made and stated why he had come, and he inquired whether this really was the situation.[a] [10]The high priest explained that there were some deposits belonging to widows and orphans, [11]and also some money of Hyrcanus, son of Tobias, a man of very prominent position, and that it totaled in all four hundred talents of silver and two hundred of gold. To such an extent the impious Simon had misrepresented the facts. [12]And he said that it was utterly impossible that wrong should be done to those people who had trusted in the holiness of the place and in the sanctity and inviolability of the temple which is honored throughout the whole world. [13]But Heliodorus, because of the king's commands which he had,

said that this money must in any case be confiscated for the king's treasury. [14]So he set a day and went in to direct the inspection of these funds.

There was no little distress throughout the whole city. [15]The priests prostrated themselves before the altar in their priestly garments and called toward heaven upon him who had given the law about deposits, that he should keep them safe for those who had deposited them. [16]To see the appearance of the high priest was to be wounded at heart, for his face and the change in his color disclosed the anguish of his soul. [17]For terror and bodily trembling had come over the man, which plainly showed to those who looked at him the pain lodged in his heart. [18]People also hurried out of their houses in crowds to make a general supplication because the holy place was about to be brought into contempt. [19]Women, girded with sackcloth under their breasts, thronged the streets. Some of the maidens who were kept indoors ran together to the gates, and some to the walls, while others peered out of the windows. [20]And holding up their hands to heaven, they all made entreaty. [21]There was something pitiable in the prostration of the whole populace and the anxiety of the high priest in his great anguish.

[22]While they were calling upon the Almighty Lord that he would keep what had been entrusted safe and secure for those who had entrusted it, [23]Heliodorus went on with what had been decided. [24]But when he arrived at the treasury with his bodyguard, then and there the Sovereign of spirits and of all authority caused so great a manifestation[b] that all who had been so bold as to accompany him were astounded by the power of God and became faint with terror. [25]For there appeared to them a magnificently caparisoned horse, with a rider of frightening mien, and it rushed furiously at Heliodorus and struck at him with its front hoofs. Its rider was seen to have armor and weapons of gold.

[26]Two young men also appeared to him, remarkably strong, gloriously beautiful, and splendidly dressed, who stood on each side of him and scourged him continuously, inflicting many blows on him. [27]When he suddenly fell to the ground and deep darkness came over him, his men took him up and put him on a stretcher [28]and carried him away, this man who had just entered the aforesaid treasury with a great retinue and all his bodyguard but was now unable to help himself; and they recognized clearly the sovereign power of God. [29]While he lay prostrate, speechless because of the divine intervention, and deprived of any hope of recovery, [30]they praised the Lord who had acted marvelously for his own place. And the temple, which a little while before was full of fear and disturbance, was filled with joy and gladness, now that the Almighty Lord had appeared.

[31]Quickly some of Heliodorus's friends asked Onias to call upon the

Most High and to grant life to one who was lying quite at his last breath. [32]And the high priest, fearing that the king might get the notion that some foul play had been perpetrated by the Jews with regard to Heliodorus, offered sacrifice for the man's recovery. [33]While the high priest was making the offering of atonement, the same young men appeared again to Heliodorus, dressed in the same clothing, and they stood and said, "Be very grateful to Onias the high priest, since for his sake the Lord has granted you your life. [34]And see that you, who have been scourged by heaven, report to all men the majestic power of God." Having said this they vanished.

[35]Then Heliodorus offered sacrifice to the Lord and made very great vows to the Savior of his life,[c] and having bidden Onias farewell, he marched off with his forces to the king. [36]And he bore testimony to all men of the deeds of the supreme God, which he had seen with his own eyes.[d] [37]When the king asked Heliodorus what sort of person would be suitable to send on another mission to Jerusalem, he replied, [38]"If you have any enemy or plotter against your government, send him there, for you will get him back thoroughly scourged, if he escapes at all, for there certainly is about the place some power of God. [39]For he who has his dwelling in heaven watches over that place himself and brings it aid, and he strikes and destroys those who come to do it injury."

a. I.e., whether, as rumored, the temple was the repository of sizable funds.
b. A term used by this author for miraculous displays of divine power.
c. It was not unusual for a Gentile to offer sacrifice in Jerusalem.
d. The testimony of a Gentile naturally bore more weight than that of a Jew, an insider.

It is little wonder that Titus's destruction of the temple in 70 C.E. shook Judaism to its roots, and it is the more remarkable that the religion survived this momentous event.

CRITIQUES OF TEMPLE, CULT, AND PRIESTHOOD

Although the Jewish people held the temple in high regard, voices of protest were frequently raised against it and its operation. Often these critiques are directed not against temple and cult as such, but against the abuse of them by people whose acts of social injustice contradicted their participation in the cult (see, e.g., Isa 1:10–17).

Jeremiah 7:1–15

The powerful oppress the poor and helpless and then flee to the temple for security, like robbers to their den. Jeremiah warns them that their appeal, "The temple of the Lord, the temple of the Lord, the temple of the Lord," is in vain. Their belief that the sanctuary is indestructible is wrong, for unless the people repent, God will destroy it, as he did with his ancient shrine in Shiloh.

1 The word that came to Jeremiah from the Lord: [2]"Stand in the gate of the Lord's house, and proclaim there this word, and say, Hear the word of the Lord, all you men of Judah who enter these gates to worship the Lord. [3]Thus says the Lord of hosts, the God of Israel, Amend your ways and your doings, and I will let you dwell in this place. [4]Do not trust in these deceptive words: 'This is the temple of the Lord, the temple of the Lord, the temple of the Lord.'

[5]"For if you truly amend your ways and your doings, if you truly execute justice one with another, [6]if you do not oppress the alien, the fatherless, or the widow, or shed innocent blood in this place, and if you do not go after other gods to your own hurt, [7]then I will let you dwell in this place, in the land that I gave of old to your fathers forever.

[8]"Behold, you trust in deceptive words to no avail. [9]Will you steal, murder, commit adultery, swear falsely, burn incense to Ba'al, and go after other gods that you have not known, [10]and then come and stand before me in this house, which is called by my name, and say, 'We are delivered!'—only to go on doing all these abominations? [11]Has this house, which is called by my name, become a den of robbers in your eyes? Behold, I myself have seen it, says the Lord. [12]Go now to my place that was in Shiloh, where I made my name dwell at first, and see what I did to it for the wickedness of my people Israel. [13]And now, because you have done all these things, says the Lord, and when I spoke to you persistently you did not listen, and when I called you, you did not answer, [14]therefore I will do to the house which is called by my name, and in which you trust, and to the place which I gave to you and to your fathers, as I did to Shiloh. [15]And I will cast you out of my sight, as I cast out all your kinsmen, all the offspring of Ephraim."

To the end, many inhabitants of Jerusalem refused to believe that Nebuchadnezzar could sack the holy city and the sanctuary. The words of Jeremiah's critique were echoed later in Mark's account of Jesus' attack on the temple and its leaders (see below, pp. 78–79).

Malachi 1:6–14

Early in the second temple period the prophet known as Malachi ("my messenger," cf. Mal 3:1) scolded the Jerusalem priests for placing "polluted food on God's altar," that is, for offering sacrificial animals with blemishes, which was forbidden by the Torah.

6 A son honors his father, and a servant his master. If then I am a father, where is my honor? And if I am a master, where is my fear? says the Lord of hosts to you, O priests, who despise my name. You say, "How have we despised your name?" [7]By offering polluted food upon my altar. And you say, "How have we polluted it?" By thinking that the Lord's table may be despised. [8]When you offer blind animals in sacrifice, is that no evil? And when you offer those that are lame or sick, is that no evil? Present that to your governor; will he be pleased with you or show you favor? says the Lord of hosts. [9]And now entreat the favor of God, that he may be gracious to us. With such a gift from your hand, will he show favor to any of you? says the Lord of hosts. [10]Oh, that there were one among you who would shut the doors, that you might not kindle fire upon my altar in vain! I have no pleasure in you, says the Lord of hosts, and I will not accept an offering from your hand. [11]For from the rising of the sun to its setting my name is great among the nations, and in every place incense is offered to my name, and a pure offering; for my name is great among the nations, says the Lord of hosts. [12]But you profane it when you say that the Lord's table is polluted, and the food for it may be despised. [13]"What a weariness this is," you say, and you sniff at me, says the Lord of hosts. You bring what has been taken by violence or is lame or sick, and this you bring as your offering! Shall I accept that from your hand? says the Lord. [14]Cursed be the cheat who has a male in his flock, and vows it, and yet sacrifices to the Lord what is blemished; for I am a great King, says the Lord of hosts, and my name is feared among the nations.

1 Enoch 89:73–74

The so-called Animal Apocalypse is a vision in which a seer writing under the name of Enoch saw the course of history from Adam to the end-time (1 Enoch 85–90). It is an extensive allegory in which all the major figures of history are depicted as animals. Following common biblical usage, the Israelites are sheep.

In the present text, the author alludes to the words of Malachi 1:7–12. For him, however, the second temple was polluted from its inception, and the apostasy of the people (the blindness of the sheep) has continued to the author's own time (ca. 165 B.C.E.).

73 And they began again to build as before, and they raised up that

tower, and it was named "the high tower." And they began again to place a table before the tower; and all the bread on it was polluted and was not pure. [74]And besides all this, the eyes of those sheep were blinded, and they did not see, and their shepherds, likewise.

Toward the end of the apocalypse some of the lambs (the young Israelites) begin to open their eyes and to protest the apostasy of their elders. This is undoubtedly a reference to the rise of one or several of the groups of pious Jews, among whose ranks were the Hasideans and who began to protest the Hellenizing ways of their compatriots (see above, pp. 19–24).

This author's protest against the temple is paralleled in another Enochic apocalypse, the "Apocalypse of Weeks" (1 Enoch 93:1–10 and 91:12–17). Although this author is concerned with the tabernacle and the first temple and an eschatological temple, he never so much as mentions the second temple, but describes the second temple period as a time of thoroughgoing perversion and apostasy.

Testament of Levi 14:5–8

This document, Christian in its present form, stems from a Jewish writing of the Hellenistic period. Here the critique is of the priesthood in Jerusalem.

5 The offerings of the Lord you will rob, and from his portions you will steal, and before you sacrifice to the Lord you will take the choice portions, eating contemptuously with harlots. [6]In greediness you will teach the commandments of the Lord. Married women you will pollute, and the virgins of Jerusalem you will defile, and with harlots and adulteresses you will have intercourse. The daughters of the Gentiles you will take for wives, cleansing them with a cleansing that is contrary to the law. And your union will be (like that of) Sodom and Gomorrah, in wickedness. [7]And you will be puffed up because of the priesthood, raising yourselves up against men. And not only that, but you will be puffed up against the commandments of God; you will mock the sanctuary, [8]despising it with laughter.

The section closes with the threat of judgment. This is followed by another description of the disintegration of the priesthood. When it fails, it will be replaced by the great eschatological priest described in Testament of Levi 18 (see below, pp. 168–70).

Psalms of Solomon 2:1–3 and 8:8–21

The Psalms of Solomon were written in response to the conquest of Judea by Pompey the Great in 63 B.C.E. According to Psalms 2 and 8, Pompey was able to enter the temple and its holy precincts because of the sins of the Jerusalemites, not least the cultic transgressions of those who brought sacrifice and the priests who offered them.

2 [1]When the sinner grew proud, with a battering ram he cast down
  fortified walls,
  and you did not prevent him.
[2]Alien Gentiles ascended your altar;
  they trampled it proudly with their sandals;
[3]because the sons of Jerusalem had defiled the sanctuary of the Lord,
  had polluted the offerings of God through lawless deeds.

8 [8]God revealed their sins before the sun;
  all the earth knew the righteous judgments of God.
[9]In secret places underground, their transgressions (were committed) to
  provoke (God's) wrath.
  Son mingled with his mother, and father with daughter;
[10]everyone committed adultery with his neighbor's wife;
  they concluded covenants with one another concerning these things,
  (sealing them) with an oath.
[11]They plundered the sanctuary of God,
  as if there were no heir to redeem (it).
[12]They trod upon the altar of the Lord, (coming) from all uncleanness;
  and with menstrual blood they defiled the sacrifices, as (if these
  were) polluted flesh.[a]
[13]They left no sin undone, in which they did not surpass the Gentiles.

[14]Therefore God mixed for them a spirit of error;
  he made them to drink a cup of undiluted wine to make them drunk.
[15]He led from the end of the earth one who smites mightily;
  he decreed war against Jerusalem and her land. . . .
[19]He captured her fortresses and the wall of Jerusalem,
  for the Lord led him with safety during their wandering.
[20]He destroyed their princes and everyone wise in counsel;
  he poured out the blood of the inhabitants of Jerusalem like lustral
  water.[b]
[21]He led away their sons and daughters,
  whom they had begotten in pollution.

a. Contact with menstrual blood was defiling according to Jewish law (cf. Lev

15:19–24). That a priest should have such contact was the more serious, because it defiled the sanctuary. The reference here and in the Damascus Document (see text immediately below) may reflect halakhic differences as to when a woman was considered to be clean.

b. Cf. Num 19:9; 31:23. Perhaps the author suggests that the blood of the Jerusalemites acted as a purification for these sins.

This passage stresses the sexual sins of the Jerusalemites, and specifically of the priests (v. 12), as was the case also in Testament of Levi 14 (see above, p. 68).

Damascus Document 4:12—5:9

This writing, known from a medieval manuscript and also found among the Qumran Scrolls, expresses one facet of the Essene critique of temple and priesthood.

4 [12]During all those years Satan shall be unleashed against Israel, as he spoke by the hand of Isaiah, son of Amoz, saying, "Terror and the pit and the snare are upon you, O inhabitant of the land" (Isa 24:17). Interpreted, these are the three nets of Satan with which Levi son of Jacob said that he catches Israel by setting them up as three kinds of righteousness. The first is fornication, the second is riches, and the third is profanation of the temple. Whoever escapes the first is caught in the second, and whoever saves himself from the second is caught in the third.

The builders of the wall who have followed after "Precept"—"Precept" was a spouter [20]of whom it is written, "They shall surely spout" (Mic 2:6)—shall be caught in fornication twice by taking a second wife while the first is alive, whereas the principle of creation is "Male and female created he them" (Gen 1:27).[a] 5 [1]Also, those who entered the ark went in two by two. And concerning the prince it is written, "He shall not multiply wives to himself" (Deut 17:17); but David had not read the sealed book of the law which was in the ark (of the covenant), for it was not opened in Israel from the death of Eleazar and Joshua, and the elders who worshiped Ashtoreth. It was hidden [5]and (was not) revealed until the coming of Zadok. And the deeds of David rose up, except for the murder of Uriah, and God left them to him.

Moreover, they profane the temple because they do not observe the distinction (between clean and unclean) in accordance with the law, but lie with a woman who sees her bloody discharge.[b]

And each man marries the daughter of his brother or sister, whereas

Moses said, "You shall not approach your mother's sister; she is your mother's near kin" (Lev 18:13).

a. Gen 1:27 is also cited by Jesus as a critique of divorce (Mark 10:6 par.).
b. Cf. n. a on Ps. Sol. 8:12, above, p. 69.

The critique is noteworthy because once again the sins imputed to the Jerusalem priests are of sexual nature, and the result of such sins is the pollution of the sanctuary.

While the majority of Jews surely continued to regard the temple as holy and effective as a cultic center, the passages we have considered indicate a long-standing and sometimes strong critique and rejection of the temple, or at least of the priesthood and its conduct of the cult.

THE COMMUNITY AS TEMPLE

Alongside the traditions that celebrate the temple as a central Jewish religious institution and those that criticize it, there is a tradition that speaks of the religious community itself as a temple. Although this imagery need not imply that the Jerusalem temple was viewed as polluted or ineffective, it does appear in the sectarian literature of the Essenes, whose criticism of the Jerusalem temple and priesthood is known from other sources.

The Rule of the Community 8:4–10

When these are in Israel, the council of the community shall be established in truth. It shall be an everlasting plantation, a house of holiness for Israel, an assembly of supreme holiness for Aaron. They shall be witnesses to the truth at the judgment, and shall be the elect of good will who shall atone for the land and pay to the wicked their reward. It shall be that tried wall, that "precious cornerstone," whose foundations shall neither rock nor sway in their place.[a] It shall be a most holy dwelling for Aaron, with everlasting knowledge of the covenant of justice, and shall offer up sweet fragrance. It shall be a house of perfection and truth in Israel, [10]that they may establish a covenant according to the everlasting precepts. And they shall be an agreeable offering, atoning for the land and determining the judgment of wickedness, and there shall be no more iniquity.

a. Isa 28:16.

Here the council of the community is described as if it were a building. It is called house, dwelling, wall, cornerstone, foundations. Moreover, cultic terminology is applied to the community: an agreeable offering, atoning for the land.

Hymn Scroll 6:22–31

The hymns of Qumran make frequent reference to the salvation that comes with entry into the community (see below, pp. 149–50). In this hymn the community is depicted as a fortress which provides one with protection from the chaotic waters of hell that assail one in the outside world.

22 [I am] as a sailor in a ship amid furious seas;
  their waves and all their billows roar against me.
[There is no] calm in the whirlwind that I may restore my soul,
  no path that I may straighten my way on the face of the waters.
The deeps resound to my groaning
  and [my soul has journeyed] to the gates of death.[a]

25But I shall be as one who enters a fortified city,
  as one who seeks refuge behind a high wall until deliverance (comes);
I will [lean on] your truth, O my God,
For you will set the foundation on rock[b]
  and the framework by the measuring cord of justice;
and the tried stones [you will lay] by the plumb line [of truth],
  to [build] a mighty [wall] which shall not sway;
and no man entering there shall stagger.

For no enemy shall ever invade [it,
  since its doors shall be] doors of protection
  through which no man shall pass;
and its bars shall be firm,
  and no man shall break them.[c]
No rabble shall enter in with their weapons of war
  until all the [arrows] of the war of wickedness have come to an end.

And then at the time of judgment the sword of God shall hasten,
  and all the sons of his truth shall awake 30to [overthrow] wickedness;
  all the sons of iniquity shall be no more.
The hero shall bend his bow;
  the fortress shall open on to endless space,
  and the everlasting gates shall send out weapons of war.

a. For this expression, cf. Job 38:17; cf. also Jonah 2:2–6 and Matt 16:18, quoted

below. The imagery of death derived originally from Isa 28; see next note.
  b. Cf. Isa 28:16–17.
  c. For a curious reversal of this imagery, cf. Matt 16:18, below, p. 190.

Although this hymn does not refer explicitly to the community as a temple, its application of Isaiah 28:14ff. to the community indicates a common tradition with the previous passage. Similar imagery recurs in Jesus' commissioning of Peter in Matthew 16 (see below, pp. 80–81). The final paragraph, with its reference to the judgment, is reminiscent of 1QS 8, which speaks of the council of the community as witnesses in the judgment. The members of the community will sally forth from the fortress of their community to participate in God's extermination of evil in the world.

THE ESCHATOLOGICAL TEMPLE

The promise of a new Jerusalem and a new temple is at the heart of the oracles of Second Isaiah and Third Isaiah. These oracles are eloquent in their language and universalistic in their conception. The walls of the new city will be studded with precious stones (Isa 54:11–12). There will be no need for the sun or the moon, for the light of the glorious presence of God will fill the city (60:19–21). The Gentiles will flood to the city with their tribute (60:4–14), and God's new house will be called a house of prayer for all peoples—which include foreigners and outcasts within Israel itself (56:1–8). In the new Jerusalem, in a new heaven and a new earth, the peace and blessings of paradise will reign (Isa 65).

The reality that followed was the temple completed by Zerubbabel (ca. 515 B.C.E.). It was a pale reflection of the glory of the Solomonic structure (cf. Hag 2:3), despite Haggai's promises of a glorious future for it (Hag 2:4–9). These and other prophetic promises were turned to the future, and a glorious eschatological temple became a frequent element in the scenarios of the future found in the Jewish writings of the Hellenistic and Roman periods.

Tobit 13:9–18

The author of Tobit, who may well have lived in the dispersion during the third century B.C.E., wrote in the guise of an eighth-century Israelite exiled in Assyria. His longing for Jerusalem is evident. His vision of the future anticipates the reuniting of the twelve tribes and their loyalty to the one sanctuary, whose glory is described in traditional language which stems back to Second and Third Isaiah.

9 O Jerusalem, the holy city,
    he will afflict you for the deeds of your sons,
    but again he will show mercy to the sons of the righteous.[a]
[10]Give thanks worthily to the Lord,
    and praise the King of the ages,
    that his tent may be raised for you again with joy.[b]
May he cheer those within you who are captives,
    and love those within you who are distressed,
    to all generations forever.
[11]Many nations will come from afar to the name of the Lord God,
    bearing gifts in their hands, gifts for the King of heaven.[c]
Generations of generations will give you joyful praise.
[12]Cursed are all who hate you;
    blessed forever will be all who love you.
[13]Rejoice and be glad for the sons of the righteous;
    for they will be gathered together,
    and will praise the Lord of the righteous.
[14]How blessed are those who love you!
    They will rejoice in your peace.
Blessed are those who grieved over all your afflictions;
    for they will rejoice for you upon seeing all your glory,
    and they will be made glad forever.
[15]Let my soul praise God the great King.
[16]For Jerusalem will be built with sapphires and emeralds,[d]
    her walls with precious stones,
    and her towers and battlements with pure gold.
[17]The streets of Jerusalem will be paved with beryl and ruby and stones
    of Ophir;
[18] all her lanes will cry "Hallelujah!" and will give praise,
    saying, "Blessed is God, who has exalted you forever."

a. The language of afflicting and having mercy is typical of Tobit; see George W. E. Nickelsburg, *Jewish Literature Between the Bible and the Mishnah* (Philadelphia: Fortress, 1981) 32–33.
b. An allusion to the temple, here described as the tabernacle.
c. Cf. Isa 60:5–7. The Gentiles will bring sacrifices to the temple.
d. Cf. Isa 54:11–12 and Rev 21:10–21. The jeweled pavement beneath God's throne is mentioned already in Exod 24:10.

The direct address to Jerusalem is reminiscent of the Apostrophe to Zion (above, pp. 53–54). The author's vision of the Gentiles' coming to Jerusalem differs from that poem's hope for the destruction of Jerusalem's enemies, but it is in the spirit of such passages as Isaiah 60.

Sibylline Oracles 3:702–30

This passage appears to have been composed around the middle of the second century B.C.E. in Egypt. For this Jew of the dispersion, life in Jerusalem around God's temple and in his presence was a constitutive part of the eschatological hope.

702 Then again all the sons of the great God shall live quietly around the temple, rejoicing in those gifts which he shall give, who is the Creator and sovereign righteous Judge. [705]For he by himself shall shield them, standing beside them alone in his might, encircling them, as it were, with a wall of flaming fire. Free from war shall they be in city and country. For they shall not feel the touch of horrid war, for the Eternal shall be himself their champion, and the hand of the Holy One. [710]And then all the isles and the cities shall say, "How the Eternal loves those men! For all things work in sympathy with them and help them, the heaven and God's chariot the sun, and the moon." [715]A sweet strain shall they utter from their mouths in hymns. "Come, let us all fall upon the earth and supplicate the Eternal King, the mighty, everlasting God. Let us make procession to his temple, for he is the sole ruler. And let us all ponder the law of the Most High God, [720]who is the most righteous of all on earth. But we had gone astray from the path of the Eternal, and with foolish heart worshiped the works of men's hands, idols and images of men that are dead."[a]

a. On these last lines, see Nickelsburg, *Jewish Literature*, 189, n. 11.

Like Tobit, the author anticipates the end-time conversion of the Gentiles. His many polemics against idolatry and Gentile immorality and his exhortations that they should repent of these evils suggest that he intended his work to be read by these Gentiles and that he hoped it would aid in their conversion.

THE NEW JERUSALEM
AND TEMPLE AFTER 70 c.e.

The Jews viewed the second temple with some disappointment. Perhaps its splendid rebuilding by Herod the Great brought new pride and satisfaction. In any case such pride and satisfaction would have been short-lived. In 70 c.e. Titus's army sacked the city of

Jerusalem and all but leveled the temple. The old belief in a new Jerusalem and temple reemerged.

2 Baruch 4:2–6

Writing in the decades that followed the events of 70 c.e., this author grieves over the loss of city and temple. In the fictional setting of the book, God speaks to Baruch, the scribe of Jeremiah, who has just learned of the coming destruction.

2 Do you think that this is that city of which I said, "On the palms of my hands I have graven you"?[a] [3]This building which is now built in your midst is not that which is revealed with me, that which was prepared beforehand here from the time when I took counsel to make paradise, and showed it to Adam before he sinned, but when he transgressed the commandment, it was removed from him, as also paradise.[b] [4]And after these things I showed it to my servant Abraham by night among the portions of the victims.[c] [5]And again I showed it to Moses on Mount Sinai, when I showed him the likeness of the tabernacle and all its vessels.[d] [6]And now, behold, it is preserved with me, as also paradise.

    a. Isa 49:16, of Mother Zion, following the wording of the Syriac version.
    b. Cf. Life of Adam and Eve 25–28, where Adam is given a vision of paradise and the divine throne room after he has sinned.
    c. Cf. Gen 15:7–21 and Apoc. Abr. 9–18, where this sacrifice is the occasion for Abraham's ascent to heaven and his vision of the enthroned Deity.
    d. Exod 25:9; cf. 2 Bar 59:4.

The idea that the earthly sanctuary has a heavenly counterpart, implied in other texts (see above, pp. 57–58), is explicit.[8] The author uses the idea here to console his readers.

4 Ezra 9:26—10:59

This apocalypse is roughly contemporary with 2 Baruch. In the present episode, the seer meets a woman who is mourning the loss of her son. Ezra consoles her with the promise of the resurrection (10:15–17). When she refuses to accept his consolation, he minimizes her loss by describing the magnitude of the loss suffered with the destruction of Jerusalem.

10 [21]For you see that our sanctuary has been laid waste
    our altar thrown down,
    our temple destroyed.

^{22}Our harp has been laid low,
   our song has been silenced,
   and our rejoicing has been ended.
The light of our lampstand has been put out,
   the ark of our covenant has been plundered.
Our holy things have been polluted,
   and the name by which we are called has been profaned.

Our free men have suffered abuse,
   our priests have been burned to death,
   our Levites have gone into captivity.
Our virgins have been defiled,
   and our wives have been ravished.
Our righteous men have been carried off,
   our saints have been scattered.
Our little ones have been cast out,
   our young men have been enslaved,
   and our strong men made powerless.

^{23}And what is more than all, the seal of Zion—
   for she has now lost the seal of her glory,
   and has been given over into the hands of those that hate us.

Suddenly the woman is transformed into the vision of "an established city" with huge foundations (10:25–27). The angel explains that the woman was Mother Zion. Ezra is to apply his words of consolation to his own grief over Zion. God has shown Ezra the brilliance of the glory of the new Jerusalem and the loveliness of her beauty (10:50)—a revelation from the heavenly realm—as a token of the eschatological restoration.

PARALLEL DEVELOPMENTS

The New Testament

Our information about Jesus' attitude toward the temple is sparse, uncertain, and heavily overlaid with the theology and concerns of the early church. In the Synoptic Gospels (Matthew, Mark, and Luke), the mature Jesus is depicted in Jerusalem only once, at the time of his crucifixion. The Gospel according to John recounts three previous journeys. In all cases Jerusalem, and especially the temple, is the scene of bitter conflicts between Jesus and the Jewish establishment, in particular the chief priests, the scribes, and the elders.

Whether such conflicts actually took place in Jesus' time in Jerusalem, or to what extent the Gospel accounts have been colored by the experience and theology of the early church, are questions that historians debate. In any case, it is clear that early Christian theology picked up those strands of Jewish temple theology that were critical of the temple, or that spoke of the community as temple or of a heavenly or eschatological temple.

CRITIQUE OF THE TEMPLE

Mark 11:15–18

15 And (Jesus and his disciples) came to Jerusalem. And he entered the temple and began to drive out those who sold and those who bought in the temple, and he overturned the tables of the money-changers and the seats of those who sold pigeons; [16]and he would not allow anyone to carry anything through the temple. [17]And he taught, and said to them, "Is it not written, 'My house shall be called a house of prayer for all the nations'? But you have made it a den of robbers." [18]And the chief priests and the scribes heard it and sought a way to destroy him, for they feared him, because all the multitude was astonished at his teaching.

Thus, according to Mark, the conspiracy to put Jesus to death was triggered by his actions of protest in the temple. The words attributed to Jesus are a conflation of Isaiah 56:7 and Jeremiah 7:11. As opposed to Third Isaiah's expectations for the new temple, Jesus describes its operation with words taken from Jeremiah's condemnation of the first temple and of those who frequented it (see above, pp. 65–66). It is quite possible that Mark—or the tradition he used here—also implied that Jesus intended the same threat of destruction that Jeremiah had uttered. Such a threat is explicit in Mark 13:2 and is referred to in 14:58 and 15:29. Whether Jesus himself ever uttered such a threat cannot be ascertained on the basis of our sources; however, it is likely that Christians before Mark transmitted such a tradition.[9] For Mark, who wrote either immediately before or shortly after 70 C.E., the (coming) destruction of city and temple was the fulfillment of a prophecy by Jesus and a comment and critique on temple and cult."[10]

In his account of the trial of Jesus, Luke omits the accusation that Jesus threatened the temple, but in the story of Stephen (Acts 6:8—7:60), the disciple Stephen is accused of saying that Jesus threatened to abolish the Torah and the temple (6:13–14). This seems to reflect

---

Handwritten marginal notes:

They must certainly have occurred or why else was Jesus Christ crucified. Because the Jews liked him?

These hostilities + conflicts undoubtedly did exist in Jesus' life

No!! Jesus referred to the destruction of himself in 3 days (he was the temple) Thus he was prophesying in Mark 13:2 - Not THREATENING just making a statement + he was commenting on his own death on the cross in Mark 14:58, 15:29

No!! Stephen was wrongly accused

historical reality, namely, that some circles in the early church saw in Jesus the end of the old temple order and the beginning of a new order.

THE COMMUNITY AS TEMPLE

The Qumran Rule of the Community speaks of the community as a temple (see above, pp. 71–72). Similar imagery occurs in a number of New Testament contexts.

Ephesians 2:19–22

Concerning the Gentiles who have now been brought into the community of faith, this author says:

19 So then you are no longer strangers and sojourners, but you are fellow citizens with the saints and members of the household of God, [20]built upon the foundation of the apostles and prophets, Christ Jesus himself being the cornerstone [21]in whom the whole structure is joined together and grows into a holy temple in the Lord, [22]in whom you also are built into it for a dwelling place of God in the Spirit.

1 Peter 2:4–10

4 Come to him, to that living stone, rejected by men but in God's sight chosen and precious; [5]and like living stones be yourselves built into a spiritual house, to be a holy priesthood, to offer spiritual sacrifices acceptable to God through Jesus Christ. [6]For it stands in Scripture:
   "Behold, I am laying in Zion a stone,
      a cornerstone chosen and precious,
    and he who believes in him
      will not be put to shame."[a]
[7]To you therefore who believe, he is precious, but for those who do not believe,
   "The very stone which the builders rejected
      has become the head of the corner,"[b]
[8]and
   "A stone that will make men stumble,
      a rock that will make them fall";[c]
for they stumble because they disobey the word, as they were destined to do.
[9]But you are a chosen race, a royal priesthood, a holy nation, God's own people, that you may declare the wonderful deeds of him who called you out of darkness into his marvelous light. [10]Once you were no people but

now you are God's people; once you had not received mercy but now you have received mercy.

a. Isa 28:16; cf. 1QS 8:7; and 1QH 6:25–27, quoted above, p. 72.
b. Ps 118:22.
c. Isa 8:14–15.

For this author the church is the eschatological people of God, his spiritual "house" or "household."[11] To make his point, he incorporates language about building and priesthood that is reminiscent of a similar combination in The Rule of the Community 8 (see above, pp. 71–72).

Matthew 16:13–19

The connection of the name of Peter with the idea of the church as building is of course not unique to the previous passage.

13 Now when Jesus came into the district of Caesarea Philippi, he asked his disciples, "Who do men say that the Son of Man is?" [14]And they said, "Some say John the Baptist, others say Elijah, and others Jeremiah or one of the prophets." [15]He said to them, "But who do you say that I am?" [16]Simon Peter replied, "You are the Christ, the Son of the living God." [17]And Jesus answered him,
[14]"Blessed are you, Simon bar Jona! = son of Jonah
    For flesh and blood has not revealed this to you,
    but my Father who is in heaven.
[18]And I tell you, you are Peter,
    and on this rock[a] I will build my church,
    and the gates of Hades shall not prevail against it.[b]
[19]I will give you the keys of the kingdom of heaven,
    and whatever you bind on earth shall be bound in heaven,
    and whatever you loose on earth shall be loosed in heaven."

a. Gk *petra*, on which Simon's new name, *petros*, is a wordplay.
b. Cf. Isa 28:15, 18–19, where those who have made a covenant with Sheol and death will be swept away.

In view of his foundational confession that Jesus is the Messiah, Simon is commissioned to be "Peter," the rock on which the building of the church is set. The imagery of this passage, including its probable allusion to Isaiah 28:14–18, is reminiscent of the Qumran hymn cited above (pp. 72–73).

The passages we have quoted in this section are all drawn from writings composed after 70 C.E. While they need not have been reactions to the destruction of the temple, they reflect one strain of Christian theology that enabled the Jewish sect known as the church to have a viable existence apart from the Jerusalem temple. Obvious but still noteworthy is the explicit identification of this temple not simply with the God of Israel, but with Jesus, his Anointed One and the Lord of the church.

THE HEAVENLY TEMPLE

Hebrews 9:1–24

The Epistle to the Hebrews stresses Jesus' role as the mediator of a new covenant. In chapters 7–10 the author contrasts the old sanctuary (the tabernacle) and the Aaronid priesthood with the heavenly temple and Jesus the great and final high priest.

1 Now even the first covenant had regulations for worship and an earthly sanctuary.[a] [2]For a tent was prepared, the outer one, in which were the lampstand and the table and the bread of the Presence; it is called the Holy Place. [3]Behind the second curtain stood a tent called the Holy of Holies, [4]having the golden altar of incense and the ark of the covenant covered on all sides with gold, which contained a golden urn holding the manna, and Aaron's rod that budded, and the tables of the covenant; [5]above it were the cherubim of glory overshadowing the mercy seat. Of these things we cannot now speak in detail.

[6]These preparations having thus been made, the priests go continually into the outer tent, performing their ritual duties; [7]but into the second only the high priest goes, and he but once a year, and not without taking blood which he offers for himself and for the errors of the people.[b] [8]By this the Holy Spirit indicates that the way into the sanctuary is not yet opened as long as the outer tent is still standing [9](which is symbolic for the present age). According to this arrangement, gifts and sacrifices are offered which cannot perfect the conscience of the worshiper, [10]but deal only with food and drink and various ablutions, regulations for the body imposed until the time of reformation.

[11]But when Christ appeared as a high priest of the good things that have come, then through the greater and more perfect tent (not made with hands, that is, not of this creation), [12]he entered once for all into the Holy Place, taking not the blood of goats and calves but his own blood, thus securing an eternal redemption. [13]For if the sprinkling of defiled persons with the blood of goats and bulls and with the ashes of a heifer sanctifies for the purification of the flesh, [14]how much more shall the

blood of Christ, who through the eternal Spirit offered himself without blemish to God, purify your conscience from dead works to serve the living God.

[15]Therefore he is the mediator of a new covenant, so that those who are called may receive the promised eternal inheritance, since a death has occurred which redeems them from the transgressions under the first covenant. [16]For where a will is involved, the death of the one who made it must be established. [17]For a will takes effect only at death, since it is not in force as long as the one who made it is alive. [18]Hence even the first covenant was not ratified without blood. [19]For when every commandment of the law had been declared by Moses to all the people, he took the blood of calves and goats, with water and scarlet wool and hyssop, and sprinkled both the book itself and all the people, [20]saying, "This is the blood of the covenant which God commanded you."[c] [21]And in the same way he sprinkled with the blood both the tent and all the vessels used in worship. [22]Indeed, under the law almost everything is purified with blood, and without the shedding of blood there is no forgiveness of sins.

[23]Thus it was necessary for the copies of the heavenly things to be purified with these rites, but the heavenly things themselves with better sacrifices than these.[d] [24]For Christ has entered, not into a sanctuary made with hands, a copy of the true one, but into heaven itself, now to appear in the presence of God on our behalf.

a. In contrast to the heavenly sanctuary to be mentioned later.
b. A reference to the rituals of the Day of Atonement.
c. Exod 24:6–8, which describes Moses' ratification of the Sinaitic covenant.
d. Cf. Exod 25:9, here explicitly interpreted to refer to a heavenly sanctuary; cf. also 2 Bar 4:2–6, above, p. 76.

Through his death and exaltation, Jesus has made perfect atonement for sin and has been installed as high priest in the heavenly sanctuary (see also below, pp. 190–93). For this author the idea of the heavenly temple as an archetype of the earthly is part of a broader, platonically oriented world-view.

THE ESCHATOLOGICAL JERUSALEM

Revelation 21—22:5

The revelation to John on the island of Patmos concludes with a vision of the new Jerusalem. In its form, concepts, and language it is heavily influenced by Second and Third Isaiah and Ezekiel 40–48.

21 [1]Then I saw a new heaven and a new earth;[a] for the first heaven and the first earth had passed away, and the sea was no more.[b] [2]And I saw the holy city, new Jerusalem, coming down out of heaven from God, prepared as a bride adorned for her husband;[c] [3]and I heard a great voice from the throne saying, "Behold, the dwelling of God is with men. He will dwell with them, and they shall be his people, and God himself will be with them; [4]he will wipe away every tear from their eyes, and death shall be no more, neither shall there be mourning nor crying nor pain anymore, for the former things have passed away."

[5]For he who sat upon the throne said, "Behold, I make all things new." Also he said, "Write this, for these words are trustworthy and true." [6]And he said to me, "It is done! I am the Alpha and the Omega, the beginning and the end. To the thirsty I will give water without price from the fountain of the water of life. [7]He who conquers shall have this heritage, and I will be his God and he shall be my son. [8]But as for the cowardly, the faithless, the polluted, as for murderers, fornicators, sorcerers, idolators, and all liars, their lot shall be in the lake that burns with fire and brimstone, which is the second death."[d]

[9]Then came one of the seven angels who had the seven bowls full of the seven last plagues, and spoke to me, saying, "Come, I will show you the Bride, the wife of the Lamb." [10]And in the Spirit he carried me away to a great, high mountain, and showed me the holy city Jerusalem coming down out of heaven from God,[e] [11]having the glory of God, its radiance like a most rare jewel, like a jasper, clear as crystal. [12]It had a great, high wall with twelve gates, and at the gates twelve angels, and on the gates the names of the twelve tribes of the sons of Israel were inscribed; [13]on the east three gates, on the north three gates, on the south three gates, and on the west three gates. [14]And the wall of the city had twelve foundations, and on them the twelve names of the twelve apostles of the Lamb.

[15]And he who talked to me had a measuring rod of gold to measure the city and its gates and walls.[f] [16]The city lies foursquare, its length the same as its breadth; and he measured the city with his rod, twelve thousand stadia; its length and breadth and height are equal. [17]He also measured its wall, a hundred and forty-four cubits by a man's measure, that is, an angel's. [18]The wall was built of jasper, while the city was pure gold, clear as glass. [19]The foundations of the wall of the city were adorned with every jewel; the first was jasper, the second sapphire, the third agate, the fourth emerald, [20]the fifth onyx, the sixth carnelian, the seventh chrysolite, the eighth beryl, the ninth topaz, the tenth chrysoprase, the eleventh jacinth, the twelfth amethyst. [21]And the twelve gates were twelve pearls, each of the gates made of a single pearl, and the street of the city was pure gold, transparent as glass.

[22]And I saw no temple in the city,[g] for its temple is the Lord God the

Almighty and the Lamb. [23]And the city has no need of sun or moon to shine upon it, for the glory of God is its light, and its lamp is the Lamb.[h] [24]By its light shall the nations walk; and the kings of the earth shall bring their glory into it, [25]and its gates shall never be shut by day—and there shall be no night there; [26]they shall bring into it the glory and the honor of the nations. [27]But nothing unclean shall enter it, nor anyone who practices abomination or falsehood, but only those who are written in the Lamb's book of life.[i]

22 [1]Then he showed me the river of the water of life, bright as crystal, flowing from the throne of God and of the Lamb [2]through the middle of the street of the city; also, on either side of the river, the tree of life with its twelve kinds of fruit, yielding its fruit each month; and the leaves of the tree were for the healing of the nations.[j] [3]There shall no more be anything accursed, but the throne of God and of the Lamb shall be in it, and his servants shall worship him; [4]they shall see his face, and his name shall be on their foreheads. [5]And night shall be no more; they need no light of lamp or sun, for the Lord God will be their light, and they shall reign for ever and ever.

a. Isa 65:17.

b. The sea, the symbol of chaos, has been removed.

c. Here the heavenly Jerusalem descends to become the eschatological Jerusalem. Cf. Isa 65:17–18, where the new Jerusalem is part of the new earth. See also Jub. 1:29. On the bridal imagery in connection with Jerusalem, cf. Isa 54.

d. On the exclusion of certain persons here and in v. 27, cf. Ezekiel's vision of Jerusalem (44:9).

e. Ezek 40:2; cf. Ezek 8:3. On the description that follows, cf. Isa 54:11–12 and Tob 13:16–17 (see above, p. 74).

f. Cf. Ezek 40:3; Zech 2:2.

g. A striking idea. The presence of God himself eliminates the necessity of a temple. Cf. the next verse, where a similar idea has a biblical basis. In Ezek 40–48, the new temple is coterminous with the city.

h. Cf. Isa 60:19–20.

i. See n. *d*, above.

j. Cf. Ezek 47:1–12. V. 12 is here altered to refer to the healing of the Gentiles.

John writes toward the end of the first century and is a contemporary of the authors of 2 Baruch and 4 Ezra. His reuse of the vision in Daniel 7 to refer to the Roman Empire and its demise parallels the traditions in these Jewish apocalypses. However, his description of the new Jerusalem is not primarily a response to the destruction of 70 but the climax of God's promise to vindicate the faithful, who have suffered persecution at the hands of the Roman emperor Diocletian.

Rabbinic Literature

We can scarcely overestimate the effect which Titus's destruction of the temple in 70 C.E. had upon Jews and Judaism. The pseudepigraphic 2 Baruch and 4 Ezra are the best-known literary works responding specifically to this traumatic event. We have quoted relevant texts from both works (see pp. 75–77). Although these authors have their own emphases, they reflect a common viewpoint. They lament over the loss of Zion and are perplexed about why God allowed it to happen. They anticipate an eschatological temple and the return of God's glory, but for the present time they counsel obedience to the Torah as the primary obligation of God's people. These same themes, with different nuances, characterize the writings of the rabbis and the piety and practice of Judaism as the rabbis reshaped and re-formed it.

In the decades that followed the year 70, Rabbi Johanan ben Zakkai gathered scholars and students in the city of Jamnia (or Yavneh) on the Mediterranean coast, where they set about the work of reconstruction. Many laws that had had their seat in the cult were reshaped and reformulated so that their intent and function could be carried out in the absence of the temple and its cult.

The Fathers According to
Rabbi Nathan, A 4

The following anecdote about Rabbi Johanan ben Zakkai expresses the tension between grief over the loss of the temple and the belief that this loss was not insuperable. That acts of charity can have an atoning function is a well-known motif in the literature of second temple Judaism (cf. Tob 4:7–11, below, p. 91; Sir 35:1–3; 1QS 8:1–10; see above, pp. 71–72). The present story is noteworthy because it attributes to the architect of post-70 Judaism the assertion that such deeds could provide the atonement that was no longer possible through the temple cult.[12]

Once as Rabban Johanan ben Zakkai was coming forth from Jerusalem, Rabbi Joshua followed after him and beheld the temple in ruins.

"Woe unto us," Rabbi Joshua cried, "that this, the place where the iniquities of Israel were atoned for, is laid waste!"

"My son," Rabban Johanan said to him, "be not grieved; we have another atonement as effective as this. And what is it? It is acts of lovingkindness, as it is said, 'For I desire mercy and not sacrifice' " (Hos 6:6).

Matthew 9:13 "But go and learn what this means: I desire mercy, not sacrifice ...

This viewpoint notwithstanding, the collectors of the Mishnah, the Tosefta, and the Talmudim devoted a whole division in each of these works to *kodashim,* or "hallowed things," in which they preserved laws about the temple, its measurements, and the operation of its cult (see, e.g., above, pp. 60–61). They transmitted this material not simply as a remembrance of the past, but also in the hope of a future restoration of the temple and its cult.

The *Amida* for the Ninth of Av

Over the centuries, Jewish liturgy and liturgical practice have continued to express both grief over the loss of the temple and hope for a restoration. Each year Jews observe four fast days in connection with the destruction of the temple. Chief among these is the Ninth of Av, the date on which, according to tradition, both the first and the second temples were destroyed. On this day the biblical Book of Lamentations is read in the synagogue, and special *qinot,* or "laments," are recited. In the main prayer, or *Amida,* a special petition strikes a balance between grief and comfort.

Comfort, O Lord our God, the mourners of Zion and the mourners of Jerusalem and the city that mourns—laid waste and despoiled and desolate.[a] . . . Legions[b] have devoured her, and idolators have inherited her; and they have put your people Israel to the sword, and they have willfully murdered the pious ones[c] of the Most High. Therefore, let Zion weep bitterly and let Jerusalem utter her voice. . . . For you, O Lord, have consumed her with fire, and with fire you will rebuild her. As it is said, "'And I shall be to her,' says the Lord, 'a wall of fire round about, and I shall be a glory in her midst'"(Zech. 2:5). Blessed are you, O Lord, who comforts Zion and rebuilds Jerusalem.

    a. The Hebrew for "desolate" is the same word used in Dan 11:31 and elsewhere of Antiochus's sacrilege—the abomination that makes (the temple) desolate.
    b. In transliterating the Latin word *legion,* the prayer retains vivid memory of the Roman destruction of 70 C.E.
    c. The Hebrew *ḥasidim* has a long history; see above, pp. 19–24, and cf. also the Apostrophe to Zion 3b ("saints") and 6b ("your pious ones"), above, pp. 53–54.

The Weekday *Shemoneh Esreh,* Petition 17

The liturgical focus on Zion and its restoration is not limited to fasts commemorating the destruction of the temple. This hope has been expressed also in the daily prayer ("Eighteen Benedictions") since the decades following the year 70.

O Lord our God, accept your people Israel and their prayer. Restore the service of the innermost room of your house, and accept with love and favor the offerings of Israel and their prayer. And let the service of Israel your people be acceptable forever. And let our eyes behold your return to Zion in mercy. Blessed are you, O Lord, who restores his presence to Zion.

God's acceptance now of the worship of Israel is a token and promise of the time when he will again be present on Zion to accept the worship and offerings of his people.

NOTES

1. The many historical problems relating to the "tent of meeting" or "tabernacle" cannot be discussed here, but the early existence of some such institution seems most likely. — IS REALITY- DID EXIST!!

2. For this scroll, see James A. Sanders, *The Dead Sea Psalms Scroll.*

3. See George W. E. Nickelsburg, "Enoch, Levi, and Peter: Recipients of Revelation in Upper Galilee," *JBL* 100 (1981) 575–90.

4. The personification of Zion as a woman, often a mother with children, is frequent in Isa 40–66 and texts dependent on these chapters.

5. On the collection of the tax, see the Mishnah tractate *Shekalim.*

6. The priests were divided into twenty-four divisions, each of which served for one week.

7. An emphasis on the emotions is part of the historical style of the whole of 2 Maccabees (called pathetic history, from the Greek *pathos*). Another version of this story occurs in 3 Macc 1–2, where the culprit is Ptolemy IV.

8. Ezek 40–48 was a source from which developed traditions that described a tour of the new Jerusalem led by an angelic guide; cf. the Description of the New Jerusalem, trans. G. Vermes, *Scrolls,* 262–64; and Rev 21, quoted below. On the broader traditions about the heavenly model of Jerusalem, see Michael E. Stone, "Lists of Revealed Things in the Apocalyptic Literature," in Frank M. Cross et al., eds., *Magnalia Dei* (Garden City, N.Y.: Doubleday, 1976) 415.

9. See George W. E. Nickelsburg, "The Genre and Function of the Markan Passion Narrative," *HTR* 73 (1980) 176–84.

10. Cf. Matt 22:7, where the destruction of Jerusalem is seen as punishment for the Jews' rejection of Jesus as the Messiah.

11. See John H. Elliott, *A Home for the Homeless* (Philadelphia: Fortress, 1981) 168–70.

12. A similar dynamic may be at work in 1QS 8:1–10, cited above, p. 71. At

a time when they consider the temple to be defiled and its cult ineffective, the Qumranites speak of their status as temple and of the atoning function of their deeds.

BIBLIOGRAPHY

PRIMARY SOURCES

The Bible and the Apocrypha (including 4 Ezra) are quoted from the RSV, with some revision and adaptation; Aristeas to Philocrates, 2 Baruch, 1 Enoch, the Psalms of Solomon, the Sibylline Oracles, and the Testament of Levi from *APOT*, vol. 2, with some revision; the Apostrophe to Zion from James A. **Sanders,** *The Dead Sea Psalms Scroll* (Ithaca, N.Y.: Cornell University Press, 1967) 125–27, with some adaptation; the Mishnah *Tamid* from Herbert **Danby,** *The Mishnah* (London: Oxford University Press, 1933) 585–86; the Qumran Scrolls from Geza **Vermes,** *The Dead Sea Scrolls in English,* 2d ed. (Harmondsworth: Penguin, 1975), with some adaptation and the prosodic structure altered in the Hymn Scroll; The Fathers According to Rabbi Nathan from Judah **Goldin,** *The Fathers According to Rabbi Nathan,* Yale Judaica Series 10 (New Haven: Yale University Press, 1955).

SECONDARY SOURCES

DESCRIPTION OF TEMPLE, PRIESTHOOD, AND CULT

Shmuel **Safrai,** "The Temple," in *The Jewish People in the First Century,* Compendia Rerum Iudaicarum ad Novum Testament 1/2 (Assen: Van Gorcum, 1976) 2:865–907. Theodor H. **Gaster,** "Sacrifices and Offerings, OT," in *IDB* 4:147–59. William F. **Stinespring,** "Temple, Jerusalem," in *IDB* 4:534–60. Jacob **Milgrom,** "Sacrifices and Offerings, OT," in *IDB Sup* 763–71.

ARCHAEOLOGY OF THE SECOND TEMPLE

Meir **Ben-Dov,** "Temple of Herod," in *IDB Sup* 870–72. Yigael **Yadin,** ed., *Jerusalem Revealed* (Jerusalem: Israel Exploration Society, 1975) 1–91, a collection of illustrated articles.

THE COMMUNITY AS TEMPLE

Bertil **Gärtner,** *The Temple and the Community in Qumran and the New Testament,* Society of New Testament Studies Monographs #1 (Cambridge: At the University Press, 1965).

3
Ideals
of Piety

Piety and righteousness lie at the heart of much religious literature; ethics and morals, proper conduct toward God and neighbor, and reward and punishment are part of this. In Judaism, ideals of piety are not only set forth in moral tracts, they also infuse prayers and psalms, determine the description of saints and heroes, and are expressed in exhortations and life-styles. Here we seek insight into these ideals by examining, as far as possible, one particular type of text, the summons to the righteous life. Other types of literature could have been quoted, but we have selected these exhortations and other similar passages because of their brevity and their succinct presentation of a broad range of virtues.

The faith of Judaism has been characterized from most ancient times by the covenant or legal agreement which lies at its heart. This was embodied in the Torah, which is a code of law, and much more besides. In the development of Jewish ideals of piety, the Torah plays a central role. Every code of law engenders a tradition of interpretation as it responds to the challenges of social, economic, political, and intellectual change and development. The Torah was no different. By the last centuries before the Common Era a number of different traditions of interpretation of the Torah were cultivated by various groups and sects, such as the Sadducees and Essenes. But it was the Pharisees' exposition of the Torah that was to have the most enduring and significant implications.

The interpretation of the Torah was one of the chief characteristics of the Pharisees (see above, pp. 25–30). Too often their attitude toward the Torah is characterized as a dry legalism, as a petty accounting of virtuous deeds, or as reflecting a mentality orientated toward "works" rather than "grace." In fact, Pharisaic Judaism (like most other forms of Judaism) regarded the Torah as the unique expression of God's will, and the ideal of a life in accordance with that will became central. This did not mean that there were *x* number of specific injunctions and that people had to see how many of them they could fulfill in a kind of race against the clock or a battle against their own natures. The Torah was loved. Its study was a primary religious duty; indeed, it was one of the supreme religious values. Life in accordance with the Torah was considered the highest virtue. To observe the commandments of God was not a burden but a joy— God's gift of them expressed his love.

In his polemic against anti-Semitic detractors of Judaism, Josephus offers the following explanation of the role of the Torah in Judaism:

> 173 Starting from the very beginning with the food of which we partake from infancy and the private life of the home, he (i.e., Moses) left nothing, however insignificant, to the discretion and caprice of the individual. 174What meats a man should abstain from and what he may enjoy; with what persons he should associate; what period should be devoted respectively to strenuous labor and to rest—for all this our leader made the law the standard and rule, that we might live under it as under a father and master and be guilty of no sin through willfulness or ignorance. 175For ignorance he left no pretext. He appointed the law to be the most excellent and necessary form of instruction, ordaining not that it should be heard once for all or twice or on several occasions but that every week men should desert their other occupations and assemble to listen to the law and to obtain a thorough and accurate knowledge of it, a practice which all other legislators seem to have neglected. (Josephus, Against Apion 2:173–75)

This admirably illustrates how the Torah was taken as the will of God; similar comments are also made by Philo, Hypothetica 6:8–9.

Rabbinic Judaism developed out of Pharisaism, and all later forms of Judaism spring from the rabbinic stock. The rabbis, like the Pharisaic sages before them, undertook to interpret the Torah in light of and in response to the developing and changing needs of the people and the age. Jewish law was Israel's greatest expression of the ideals of justice and righteousness, and it developed even more under the rabbis' guidance. It is in the light of these observations that we should understand injunctions to walk in the way of the Lord or to keep his commandments.

In the period of the second temple there were many forms of Judaism (see Chapter 1). There was also a great diversity of ideals, of types of religious life, to which people aspired. This diversity of form and emphasis is to be viewed against the desire to live according to God's will as it was revealed to the Jewish people.

THE EXHORTATION TO PIETY

Tobit 4:5–21

In this document, probably written in the third century B.C.E., the protagonist, Tobit, a righteous man stricken by blindness, addresses his son Tobias, whom he is about to send on a perilous mission.

REMEMBER THE LORD AND
HIS COMMANDMENTS

5 Remember the Lord our God all your days, my son,
  and refuse to sin or to transgress his commandments.
Live uprightly all the days of your life,
  and do not walk in the ways of wrongdoing.[a]
[6]For if you do what is true,
  your ways will prosper through your deeds.[b]

BE CHARITABLE

[7]Give alms from your possessions to all who live uprightly,
  and do not let your eye begrudge the gift when you make it.
Do not turn your face away from any poor man,
  and the face of God will not be turned away from you.
[8]If you have many possessions, make your gift from them in proportion;
  if few, do not be afraid to give according to the little you have.[c]
[9]So you will be laying up a good treasure for yourself
  against the day of necessity.
[10]For charity delivers from death
  and keeps you from entering the darkness;[d]
[11]And for all who practice it, charity is an excellent offering in the presence of the Most High.[e]

BEWARE OF IMMORALITY

[12]Beware, my son, of all immorality. First of all take a wife from among the descendants of your fathers and do not marry a foreign woman who is not of your father's tribe, for we are the sons of the prophets.[f] Remember, my son, that Noah,[g] Abraham, Isaac, and Jacob, our fathers of old, all took wives from among their brethren. They were blessed in their children, and their posterity will inherit the land.[h] [13]So now, my son, love your brethren, and in your heart do not disdain your brethren and the sons and daughters of your people by refusing to take a

wife for yourself from among them. For in pride there is ruin and great confusion; and in shiftlessness there is loss and great want, because shiftlessness is the mother of famine.

DO NOT HOLD OVER WAGES

[14]Do not hold over until the next day the wages of any man who works for you, but pay him at once; and if you serve God you will receive payment.[i]

ETHICAL INJUNCTIONS

Watch yourself, my son, in everything you do,
>   and be disciplined in all your conduct.[j]
[15]   And what you hate, do not to any man.[k]
Do not drink wine to excess
>   or let drunkenness go with you on your way.
[16]Give of your bread to the hungry,
>   and of your clothing to the naked.
Give all your surplus to charity,
>   and do not let your eye begrudge the gift when you make it.
[17]Place your bread on the grave of the righteous,
>   but give none to sinners.[l]
[18]Seek advice from every wise man,
>   and do not despise any useful counsel.
[19]Bless the Lord God on every occasion;
>   ask him that your ways may be made straight
>   and that all your paths and plans may prosper.
For none of the nations has understanding;
>   but the Lord himself gives all good things,
>   and according to his will he humbles whomever he wishes. . . .

CONCLUSION

[21]Do not be afraid, my son, because we have become poor. You have great wealth if you fear God and refrain from every sin and do what is pleasing in his sight.

a. For the imagery of the two ways, see above, pp. 36–37. There are many biblical parallels to these exhortations.

b. See, more explicitly, vv. 9–10, below.

c. Emphasis on the support of the needy through charity is deeply rooted in the biblical sources. It is a continuing theme of Jewish ethics and exhortations.

d. Compare the Day of Atonement liturgy "Repentance, praise, and charity avert the evil decree."

e. Charity as an offering: this implies the spiritualization of sacrifice. Cf. also Apocryphal Psalms (Ps 154) 18:10–11, "And a man who glorifies the Most High, he accepts as one who brings a meal offering, as one who offers he-goats and bullocks, as one who fattens the altar with many burnt offerings, as a sweet-smelling fragrance from the hand of the righteous." This old idea underwent different developments in Judaism and Christianity. See below, p. 109.

f. The expression "sons of the prophets" is difficult. Perhaps the endogamy emphasized here is a function of the exilic situation.

g. Noah's wife is not identified in the Bible. According to Jub. 4:33, Noah married " 'Emzara, daughter of Rake'el, the daughter of his father's brother." Therefore he married endogamously, according to Jubilees. Perhaps Tobit knew the same tradition, or a similar one.

h. This is a citation of Ps 37:11; cf. Matt 5:5—there of the meek.

i. In the Bible, cf. Lev 19:13; Deut 24:15. Virtues bring their reward (also vv. 7, 10, 12), vices their punishment (v. 13).

j. The list that commences in this verse is distinct from the preceding. No sanctions are given. See the comments at the end of this section.

k. With v. 15a, compare Hillel, quoted in Babylonian Talmud *Shabbat* 31a.

l. This strange commandment is perhaps to be related to some sort of funerary rite. An alternative explanation is that the verse means "In spite of all said above, it is better to place your bread on the grave of the righteous than to give it to a sinner."

In this list the injunctions are primarily ethical and noncultic in character. They are clearly related to commandments and Torah (vv. 5, 21), and even the commandment to endogamy (of seemingly particularist, cultic type) is given this ethical dimension. Here a rather practical view, concentrating on a man's relationship with his fellow, reflects a distinct type of righteousness that is encouraged by Tobit. There are no ascetic overtones in it, no concentration on virtues determined by role, and none of the preoccupation with sex and drinking found, for example, in the Testaments of the Twelve Patriarchs (see below, p. 101.)

In the first part of this exhortation, Tobit sets forth a motive for righteous action—the reward of pious deeds and the punishment of wicked ones (vv. 5–14a), but from v. 14b on, no sanctions are stated. In Jewish writings the motive for action is not always the sanction that follows on it; ambiguity sometimes surrounds this point, while at other times people are urged to be "as servants who serve their master without any expectation of reward" (Ethics of the Fathers 1:3). Yet the men who propounded even this last viewpoint believed in reward and punishment. They deliberately chose not to use the sort of statement Tobit has made here.

THE WISE MAN

Wisdom of ben Sira 39:1–11

In the previous chapter, ben Sira has enumerated various craftsmen—farmers, smiths, potters: "All these rely upon their hands. . . .

Without them, a city cannot be established, and men can neither sojourn nor live there" (38:31–32). Yet, Joshua ben Sira observes, "the wisdom of the scribe depends on the opportunity of leisure . . ." (38:24). This passage, then, draws not on the ethical tradition rooted in the Pentateuchal legislation which had influenced Tobit, but on the teaching and ideals of the wisdom tradition as cultivated by Joshua ben Sira, who taught in Jerusalem at the start of the second century B.C.E.

This is a good example of an ideal of life which is determined by social role. The wise man is an ideal that a teacher of wisdom can propound and to which a student of wisdom can aspire. It is comparable, therefore, to the priestly ideals propounded in the Testament of Levi (below, pp. 100–101) or the Testament of Isaac (below, pp. 108–10). That the ideal is a religious one is clear from the subject of study—the Torah—and from the shift from technical and intellectual accomplishments to religious devotion that may be observed in vv. 5–8. See also notes *b–e* on the text.

STUDY OF TORAH

1 On the other hand, he who devotes himself
    to the study of the law of the Most High[a]
will seek out the wisdom of all the ancients
    and will be concerned with prophecies;
[2]he will preserve the discourse of notable men
    and penetrate the subtleties of parables;
[3]he will seek out the hidden meanings of proverbs
    and be at home with the obscurities of parables.

THE ROLE OF THE WISE MAN

[4]He will serve among great men
    and appear before rulers;
he will travel through the lands of foreign nations,
    for he tests the good and the evil among men.[b]
[5]He will set his heart to rise early
    to seek the Lord who made him,
    and will make supplication before the Most High;
he will open his mouth in prayer
    and make supplication for his sins.[c]

THE TEACHING OF THE WISE MAN

[6]If the great Lord is willing,
    he will be filled with the spirit of understanding;[d]

he will pour forth words of wisdom
   and give thanks to the Lord in prayer.
[7]He will direct his counsel and knowledge aright,
   and meditate on his secrets.[e]
[8]He will reveal instruction in his teaching,
   and will glory in the law of the Lord's covenant.

THE RENOWN OF THE WISE MAN

[9]Many will praise his understanding,
   and it will never be blotted out;
his memory will not disappear,
   and his name will live through all generations.
[10]Nations will declare his wisdom,
   and the congregation will proclaim his praise;
[11]if he lives long, he will leave a name greater than a thousand,
   and if he goes to rest, it is enough for him.

   a. Typical of ben Sira's combination of Torah with wisdom is the idea that devotion to the study of Torah brings about study of ancient wisdom. This in turn is related to understanding proverbs and parables.

   b. These are among the traditional roles of the scribal class. Note how quickly, however, ben Sira shifts from them to specifically religious virtues.

   c. The role of prayer is notable; cf. also v. 6b. Here not just learning and acumen are demanded, but also devotion to God.

   d. Wisdom is given by God; it includes insight and teaching. Cf. Isa 11:2, which is permeated with wisdom terminology.

   e. Like a number of passages in the Wisdom of ben Sira, this may refer to secret, mystical knowledge; cf., e.g., 3:20ff.

Joshua ben Sira's words describe the ideal teacher of wisdom, whose understanding is granted by God. The wise man must, through his prayer and devotion to God, show submission to him. Elsewhere in the book, in the "Praise of the Fathers of Old" (chaps. 44–49), ben Sira selects figures from the biblical past and emphasizes their exemplary characteristics. Chapter 50 is an extraordinary description of the high priest Simon, whom ben Sira obviously revered (see above, pp. 58–59). The "Praise of the Fathers of Old" and the "Praise of Simon" both highlight characteristics which ben Sira valued. Yet they differ from the exhortations to virtue, since they are often deeply influenced by particular biblical circumstances of the figures described.[1] This obviates their becoming patterns or paradigms for all men to follow.

RIGHTEOUS ISRAEL

4 Ezra 14:28–35

The setting of this passage is Ezra's address to Israel before his death which concludes this book. It was actually written about 100 C.E. in the aftermath of the Roman destruction of the temple.

28 Hear these words, O Israel. [29]At first our fathers dwelt as aliens in Egypt, and they were delivered from there, [30]and received the law of life which they did not keep; which you also have transgressed after them. [31]Then land was given to you for a possession in the land of Zion; but you and your fathers committed iniquity and did not keep the ways which the Most High commanded you. [32]And because he is a righteous judge, in due time he took from you what he had given. [33]And now you are here and your brethren are farther in the interior.[a] [34]If you then will rule over your minds and discipline your hearts, you shall be kept alive, and after death you shall obtain mercy. [35]For after death the judgment will come, when we shall live again; and then the names of the righteous will become manifest and the deeds of the ungodly will be disclosed.[b]

a. The speech is set in the time of the Babylonian Exile. The reference is to the ten tribes of the northern kingdom, which had been exiled a century or more before; cf. 4 Ezra 13:39–40.

b. Note the author's firm belief in the resurrection and eternal life. On this see below, pp. 142–44.

This passage emphasizes the observance of God's commandments. The tone and form of the address are modeled on Moses' speeches as reported by the Book of Deuteronomy; both Ezra and Moses are lawgivers. Men are exhorted not just to a formal or external observance of the commandments, but also to "rule over your minds and discipline your hearts." The sanction invoked is the ultimate one—life or death, to be decreed on the day of judgment. This is reminiscent of Deuteronomy (30:15), but by it 4 Ezra clearly means eternal life and eternal death.

ABRAHAM'S CHILDREN

Jubilees 20:1–10

This address, given by Abraham to his children five years before his death, was probably composed in the first part of the second century B.C.E. in circles not unlike those from which the Dead Sea sect sprang.[2]

THE WAY OF THE LORD

1 And in the forty-second jubilee, in the first year of the seventh week,[a] Abraham called Ishmael and his twelve sons,[b] and Isaac and his two sons, and the six sons of Keturah, and their sons. [2]And he commanded them that they should observe the way of the Lord; that they should work righteousness, and love each his neighbor, and act on this matter among all men; that they should each so walk with regard to them as to do judgment and righteousness on the earth.

CIRCUMCISION AND SEXUAL RECTITUDE

[3]That they should each circumcise their sons according to the covenant which he had made with them, and not deviate to the right hand or the left of all the paths which the Lord had commanded us; and that we should keep ourselves from all fornication and uncleanness and renounce from among us all fornication and uncleanness. [4]And if any woman or maid commit fornication among you, burn her with fire,[c] and let them not commit fornication with her after their eyes and their heart; and let them not take to themselves wives from the daughters of Canaan, for the seed of Canaan will be rooted out of the land.[d]

JUDGMENTS IN HISTORY

[5]And he told them of the judgment of the giants, and the judgment of the Sodomites, how they had been judged on account of their wickedness and had died on account of their fornication and uncleanness, and mutual corruption through fornication. [6]And guard yourselves from all fornication and uncleanness, and from pollution of sin, lest you make our name a curse, and your whole life a hissing,[e] and all your sons be destroyed by the sword, and you become accursed like Sodom, and all your remnant as the sons of Gomorrah.

IDOLATRY, LOVE OF GOD

[7]I implore you, my sons, love the God of heaven and cleave to all his commandments. And walk not after their idols and after their uncleannesses, [8]and make not for yourselves molten or graven gods; for they are vanity, and there is no spirit in them; for they are work of (men's) hands, and all who trust in them trust in nothing. [9]Serve them not, nor worship them.[f] but serve the most high God, and worship him continually and hope for his countenance always, and work uprightness and righteousness before him,

GOD'S BLESSINGS

that he may have pleasure in you and grant you his mercy, and send rain upon you morning and evening, and bless all your works which you have wrought upon the earth, and bless your bread and your water, and bless the fruit of your womb and the fruit of your land and the herds of your cattle and the flocks of your sheep.g [10]And you will be for a blessing on the earth, and all nations of the earth will desire you and bless your sons in my name, that they may be blessed as I am.

    a. This is the way the Book of Jubilees calculates the chronology of the world, counting in fifty-year (jubilee) periods from creation.
    b. Gen 25:13–15.
    c. Contrast Lev 20:10; Deut 22:23–24; Ezek 16:40; cf. Gen 38:24.
    d. See Gen 9:25; this verse is a kind of summary of the injunctions set forth in the following lines.
    e. Isa 65:15; Jer 29:18.
    f. Exod 20:5.
    g. Deut 7:13.

Abraham sets forth rigorous ethical injunctions—love God, love your neighbor, and observe God's commandments. The latter relate particularly to circumcision, fornication, endogamy, and idolatry. Such commands are clearly appropriate to Abraham's generation. Yet to judge from Jubilees' usual willingness to read back details of the Mosaic legislation into the patriarchal or even the antediluvian periods, Abraham could easily have included ritual or other similar instructions without apparent anachronism. Instead he gives his sons a succinct summary of the basic way of the righteous man. Contrast it with Noah's exhortation in Jubilees 7:26–39, which is centered around other issues that arise from Noah's "historical" context.[3] Circumcision, fornication, idolatry, and endogamy may have been particularly close to Jubilees' concerns, since the book was written during the early period of Hellenization. At that time, those particular offenses were rampant.

SINS TO AVOID

1 Enoch 99:11–16

The Epistle of Enoch (1 Enoch 92–105) is a sustained exhortation to avoid certain evils and seek certain virtues. These chapters call down divine judgment on the wicked and promise eschatological reward to the righteous. The section we reproduce is a list of sins, a reverse key to righteousness.

11 Woe to you who spread evil for your neighbors;
    for in Sheol you shall be slain.

¹²Woe to you who lay the foundations of sin and deceit
    and are rebellious upon the earth,
    for because of it they will come to an end.
¹³Woe to those who build their houses not with their own labors,ᵃ
    and they make the whole house of the stones and bricks of sin.
  Woe to you; you will have no peace.
¹⁴Woe to those who reject the foundation and eternal inheritance of
        their fathers;ᵇ
    and a spirit of error pursues you;
    you will have no rest.
¹⁵Woe to you who practice lawlessness and aid iniquity,
    murdering their neighbor until the day of the great judgment.
¹⁶For he will destroy your glory and lay affliction on your hearts,
    and arouse his wrath against you,
    and destroy all of you with the sword;
  And all the righteous will remember your unrighteous deeds.

    a. Jer 22:13; see also 1 Enoch 94:7.
    b. This apparently refers to the Torah and stands in opposition to "foundations of
sin and deceit" (v. 12).

This passage sets forth a series of moral imperatives formulated as
woe-sayings. These are easily compared with the Beatitudes that
occur in the Sermon on the Mount (Matt 5, Luke 6) and in Slavonic
Enoch (see below, pp. 105–6). Again righteous conduct, but this time
social justice and the rejection of religious error, stands at the heart
of the preaching. This emphasis gives the document a cast quite
different from that of texts like Jubilees 20:1–10.

[handwritten margin note: These have NOTHING in common w/the Beatitudes. These have negative statements about wrongdoers. The Beatitudes are positive statements about rewards people who do well will receive.]

MORAL VIRTUES

The Testaments of the Twelve Patriarchs is one of the most important
repositories of Jewish moral exhortations. It is formulated as the last
wills and testaments of the twelve sons of Jacob. Each son devotes
his last words to one particular moral quality or failing. Thus Reuben
preaches chastity and against fornication, Simeon against envy, Judah against drunkenness and fornication, and Dan against anger.
Because of this structure, the overall picture of the pious man can be
drawn best by presenting a number of passages.

The problems of composition and dating of the Testaments of the
Twelve Patriarchs are notorious: some parts are drawn from Jewish
originals,⁴ while other passages in the book are Christian. There is

much debate as to whether these passages were the work of the author-editor or are later interpolations.

Testament of Levi 13:1–6

ON LEARNING AND WISDOM

1 And now, my children, I command you:
  Fear the Lord your God with your whole heart,
    and walk in simplicity according to all his law.[a]
²And also teach your children letters,
    that they may have understanding all their life,
    reading unceasingly the law of God.[b]
³For every one that knows the law of the Lord shall be honored,
    and shall not be a stranger wherever he goes.
⁴Yea, he shall gain many more friends than his parents,
    and many men shall desire to serve him,
    and to hear the law from his mouth.[c]
⁵Do righteousness, therefore, my children upon the earth,[d]
    that you may have (it) as a treasure in heaven.
⁶And sow good things in your souls,
    that you may find them in your life.

a. The virtue of simplicity of heart occurs elsewhere in the Testaments; cf. T. Iss. 3–5. Note particularly T. Iss. 4:1–3, cited below, p. 101.

b. See also observations in the preceding comment. See also Mal 2:7; Sir 45:17; T. Reub. 4:1; cf. Jub. 4:17 of Enoch.

c. Vv. 3–4 set forth the results and the rewards gained from the study of the Torah; cf. Sir 24:32–34.

d. The last two verses of the quotation are a more general exhortation to righteousness.

Levi was seen as the ancestor of the priestly families, one of whose functions was to "teach Jacob your ordinances and Israel your Torah" (Deut 33:10). This idea is already present in the Aramaic Testament of Levi (paras. 83–95), one of the sources used by the Testaments of the Twelve Patriarchs. Compare also the functions of the priest as seen by an early pagan author, quoted above on p. 45.

This passage, therefore, like that dealing with the wise man (see above, pp. 94–95), presents a type of pious, God-fearing behavior which is appropriate to a particular role in society, that played by the Jewish priests. Its particular emphasis is determined by certain functions of the priest, not primarily in the sacrificial cult. Once wisdom becomes identified with the Torah, the wise man's study and instruction become very like those of the priest. They are both devoted to the Torah.

Testament of Judah 14:1–4

ON DRUNKENNESS AND FORNICATION

1 And now, my children, I say to you, be not drunk with wine; for wine turns the mind away from the truth and inspires the passion of lust and leads the eyes into error. ²For the spirit of fornication has wine as a minister to give pleasure to the mind; for these two also take away the mind of man. ³For if a man drinks wine to drunkenness, it disturbs the mind with filthy thoughts leading to fornication and heats the body to carnal union; and if the occasion of the lust is present, he does the sin and is not ashamed. ⁴Such is the inebriated man, my children, for he who is drunken reverences no man.

Judah preaches particularly against these two sins because of his own sin with Tamar (Gen 38), as this deed is described in Testament of Judah. The same two sins are of concern elsewhere in the Testament and perhaps reflect upon the contemporary scene; see Testament of Issachar 4:4. Compare Testament of Judah 14:5 and also Bilhah's drunkenness according to Testament of Reuben (but not Genesis).

Testament of Issachar 4:1—5:3

ON SIMPLICITY OF MIND

4 ¹And now, hearken to me, my children,
　　And walk in singleness of your heart,
　　for I have seen in it all that is well-pleasing to the Lord.
²The single-(minded) man covets not gold,
　　he overreaches not his neighbor,
　he longs not after manifold dainties,
　　he delights not in varied apparel.

THE CHARACTER OF THE SIMPLE MAN

³He does not desire to live a long life,ᵃ
　　but only waits for the will of God.
⁴And the spirits of deceit have no power against him,
　　for he looks not on the beauty of women,
　　lest he should pollute his mind with corruption.
⁵There is no envy in his thoughts,

no malicious person makes his soul pine away,
   nor worry with insatiable desire in his mind.
[6]For he walks in singleness of soul,
   and beholds all things in uprightness of heart,
shunning eyes (made) evil through the error of the world,
   lest he should see the perversion of any of the commandments of the
   Lord.

ABIDING BY THE LAW GIVES SIMPLENESS

5 [1]Keep, therefore, my children, the law of God,
   and get singleness,
and walk in guilelessness,
   not playing the busybody with the business of your neighbor.

LOVE THE LORD

[2]But love the Lord and your neighbor,
   have compassion on the poor and weak.
[3]Bow down your back unto husbandry,
   and toil in labors in all manners of husbandry,
   offering gifts to the Lord with thanksgiving.[b]

   a. This may be a reaction to such biblical injunctions as the Fourth Commandment,
which have the length of days as a reward.
   b. In T. Iss. 7:1–6 we are told that Issachar has performed these virtues and is
sinless; cf. Gen 49:15.

Issachar is the simple laborer, whose love of God and of manual toil
have kept him free of sins. There is an almost "primitivistic" strain to
this nostalgic exhortation, which hearkens back to a simple life of
toil and virtue. Perhaps the exhortation comes from a society in
which these virtues are not common but in which luxury and sophis-
tication are prevailing values.

Testament of Dan 5:1–3

ON LYING AND ANGER

1 Observe, therefore, my children, the commandments of the Lord,
   and keep his law;
depart from anger,
   and hate lying,
that the Lord may dwell among you,
   and Beliar[a] may flee from you.
[2]Speak truth each one with his neighbor,[b]
   so you shall not fall into anger and confusion;

but you shall be in peace, having the God of peace,[c]
   so shall no war prevail over you.
[3]Love the Lord through all your life,
   and one another with a true heart.[d]

a. Beliar is another name for the Satan found chiefly among the Dead Sea sectaries. It is a by-form of the Hebrew Belial.
   b. Zech 8:16.
   c. For this expression see also Rom 15:33; 1 Thess 5:23; Phil 4:9.
   d. Lying and anger are the particular subjects of T. Dan.

Testament of Benjamin 3:1–5

JOSEPH AS THE IDEAL RIGHTEOUS MAN:
LOVE OF NEIGHBOR

1 You also, therefore my children, love the Lord God of heaven and earth and keep his commandments, following the example of the good and holy man Joseph.[a] [2]And let your mind be unto good, even as you know me, for he that has his mind right sees all things rightly. [3]Fear the Lord and love your neighbor; and even though the spirits of Beliar claim you to afflict you with every evil, yet shall they not have dominion over you even as they had not over Joseph my brother.[b] [4]How many men wished to slay him, and God shielded him! For he that fears God and loves his neighbor cannot be smitten by the spirit of Beliar, being shielded by the fear of God. [5]Nor can he be ruled over by the device of men or beasts, for he is helped by the Lord through the love which he has toward his neighbor.

a. Joseph serves often in the Testaments of the Twelve Patriarchs as the paradigm of the righteous man. In later Christian texts he becomes a type of Christ.
   b. The world view of the Testaments of the Twelve Patriarchs, like that of other writings of the time, is permeated by a belief in angels and evil spirits. Much of the evil that man does is ascribed to the influence of demonic spirits, but these can be repelled if a man observes the commandments of God.

This selection of texts from the Testaments of the Twelve Patriarchs illustrates some of the particular emphases of the book. There is great concern with sexual chastity, but matters like lying, drunkenness, and craving after luxuries are also objects of exhortations. The love of God is emphasized; so are the love of brother or neighbor, the observance of the divine commandments, and simplicity of heart. The range of virtues and vices seems to imply a rather pious, moralistic context of composition, reacting against "dangers" of urban living as it developed in the Hellenistic and Roman periods.

THE CHARACTER OF
THE JEWISH PEOPLE

When we turn to the Sibylline Oracles we enter a different world. These books were composed in the Hellenistic Diaspora as propaganda for Judaism, set in the mouth of the famous Greek oracles, the Sibyls. They are written in carefully constructed Greek poetry. The section reproduced here is drawn from the oldest of the Jewish Sibylline Oracles. It describes the virtues of the Jewish people as a whole, and not the ideal for the individual to aspire to. It is not an exhortation, but instead states a range of virtues succinctly.

Sibylline Oracles 3:218–47

THE WISDOM OF THE JEWS IN REJECTING
CHALDEAN SCIENCES

218 There is a city, Camarina, down in the land of Ur of the Chaldees from which comes a race of most righteous men,[a] 220who ever give themselves up to sound counsel and fair deeds. For they search not out the circling course of the sun or the moon, nor monstrosities beneath the earth, nor the depth of Ocean's shimmering sea, nor portent of sneezes,[b] and birds of augurers,[c] 225nor wizards, nor magicians, nor enchanters, nor the deceits of ventriloquists' foolish words, nor do they study the predictions of Chaldean astrology, nor do they astronomize: for all these things are in their nature prone to deceive, such things as witless men are searching out day by day, 230exercising their souls for a work of no profit. Yes, and they have taught deceits to ill-starred men, from which come many evils to mortals on the earth, so that they are led astray from good paths and righteous acts.

RIGHTEOUSNESS OF THE JEWS

But these diligently practice justice and virtue 235and not covetousness, which is the source of myriad ills to mortal men, of war and desperate famine.

SOCIAL JUSTICE, CHARITY, AND VIRTUE

But they have just measures in country and city, nor do they carry out night robberies against one another, nor do they drive off herds of oxen and sheep and goats, 240nor does a neighbor remove his neighbor's landmarks, nor does a man of much wealth vex his lesser brother, nor does anyone afflict widows, but rather assists them, ever ready to supply them with corn and wine and oil. And always the wealthy man among the people sends a portion of his harvest to those who have nothing,

[245]but are in want, fulfilling the command of the Mighty God,[d] the ever-abiding strain: for Heaven[e] wrought the earth for all alike.

a. Abraham came from Ur of the Chaldees. In the Hellenistic period the Chaldeans were famous as teachers of the occult sciences, augury, astrology, and the like. The author makes the point that the Jews, even though they came from Chaldea, rejected this type of Chaldean learning. Instead, they practice righteousness in their society at the command of God.

b. In the Greek world, sneezes were regarded as omens or portents, and the type of involuntary movement of the head was an indication of the future.

c. Augurers foretold the future by studying the flight of birds.

d. The reference is to the biblical injunctions about parts of the harvest that were set aside for the poor.

e. A common substitute for the name of God which was regarded with particular sacrosanctity in the second temple period.

Certain of the points made here derive from the author's opposition to his Hellenistic context. Thus, for example, he violently rejects the "Chaldean sciences"—astrology, portents and omens, and the like, which were rampant in the Hellenistic world. Instead he stresses the virtues of social justice practiced by the Jewish nation. The picture given by this presentation is very like that given by the author of the Epistle of Enoch (see 1 Enoch 99:11–16, above, pp. 98–99). For the Jewish Sibyl, however, it is an indictment of contemporary Greek society. These virtues, the Sibyl claims, are practiced by the Jews *as a nation*.

SOCIAL JUSTICE

2 Enoch B 42:6–14

THE BEATITUDES OF ENOCH

Above we observed the place of woe-sayings in the Epistle of Enoch (1 Enoch 99:11–16, etc.). In the Slavonic Book of Enoch, or 2 Enoch, there is a set of beatitudes of special interest to us. They reflect the same concern for social justice observed in the Sibylline Oracles and the Epistle of Enoch. They conclude with praise of a number of moral virtues.

6 Blessed is he who fears God and serves him. And you, my children, learn to bring gifts to the Lord, that you may enjoy life.
[7]Blessed is he who judges a judgment justly to the widow and orphan, [8]and helps everyone that is wronged, [9]clothing the naked with garments and giving bread to the hungry.

[10]Blessed is he who turns back from the changeable path and walks along the straight path.

[11]Blessed is he who sows the seeds of righteousness, for he shall reap sevenfold.

[12]Blessed is he in whom is truth, that he may speak truth to his neighbor.

[13]Blessed is he in whose mouth is mercy and gentleness.

[14]Blessed is he who understands the Lord's works and glorifies the Lord God.

WHY OBSERVE THE LAW?

4 Maccabees 5:16–27

In 4 Maccabees the stories of the martyrs under Antiochus Epiphanes illustrate the thesis that reason—which is the observance of the Torah—can overcome the passions. The passage we quote is from the speech which Eleazar—"a priest by birth, trained in knowledge of the law, a man advanced in years"—addresses to the king, who demands that he eat swine's flesh.

16 We, O Antiochus, who have been persuaded to govern our lives by the divine law, think that there is no compulsion more powerful than our obedience to the law. [17]Therefore we consider that we should not transgress it in any respect. [18]Even if, as you suppose, our law were not truly divine and we had wrongly held it to be divine, not even so would it be right for us to invalidate our reputation for piety. [19]Therefore do not suppose that it would be a petty sin if we were to eat defiling food; [20]to transgress the law in matters either small or great is of equal seriousness, [21]for in either case the law is equally despised. [22]You scoff at our philosophy as though living by it were irrational, [23]but it teaches us self-control, so that we master all pleasures and desires, and it also trains us in courage, so that we endure any suffering willingly; [24]it instructs us in justice, so that in all our dealings we act impartially, and it teaches us piety, so that with proper reverence we worship the only real God.

[25]Therefore we do not eat defiling food, for since we believe that the law was established by God, we know that in the nature of things the Creator of the world in giving us the law has shown sympathy toward us. [26]He has permitted us to eat what will be most suitable for our lives, but he has forbidden us to eat meats that would be contrary to this. [27]It would be tyrannical for you to compel us not only to transgress the law, but also to eat in such a way that you may deride us for eating defiling foods, which are most hateful to us.

This passage admirably illustrates the attitude of Hellenistic Judaism to the law. All virtues come from the observance of the law, and those virtues can be discussed in a style and language appropriate to Greek philosophic discourse. The observance of the Torah is thus the true philosophical life.

Philo, On Dreams 1.124–25

124 None such is a disciple of the holy Word (i.e., Logos), but only those who are really men, enamored of moderation, propriety, and self-respect: men who have laid down as the foundation, so to speak, of their whole life self-control, abstemiousness, endurance, which are safe road-steads of the soul, in which it can lie firmly moored and out of danger; men superior to the temptations of money, pleasure, popularity, regardless of meat and drink and of the actual necessities of life, so long as lack of food does not begin to threaten their health; men perfectly ready for the sake of acquiring virtue to submit to hunger and thirst and heat and cold and all else that is hard to put up with; men keen to get things most easily procured, who are never ashamed of an inexpensive cloak, but on the contrary regard those which cost much as a matter for reproach and a great waste of their living. 125To these men a soft bit of ground is a costly couch; bushes, grass, shrubs, a heap of leaves, their bedding; their pillow some stone or mound rising a little above the general level. Such a mode of life as this the luxurious call hard-faring, but those who live for what is good and noble describe it as most pleasant, for it is suited to those who are not merely called but really are men.

The view proposed is related to the Cynic school of Greek philosophy, but in other places Philo is equally dependent on Platonic and Stoic concepts.

THE WAY OF
THE SPIRIT OF TRUTH

The Rule of the Community 4:2–6

Quite different are the atmosphere and assumptions of the rule book of the Dead Sea sectaries, which was probably written in the early first century b.c.e. The passage quoted is not an exhortation proper, but part of a statement of sectarian theology.

And these are the ways of these (spirits) in the world.[a]
It is [of the Spirit of Truth] to enlighten the heart of man,
   and to level before him the ways of true righteousness,
   and to set fear in his heart of the judgment of God.

And (to it belong) the spirit of humility and forbearance,
  of abundant mercy and eternal goodness,
  of understanding and intelligence,
  and almighty wisdom with faith in all the works of God
  and trust in his abundant grace,
  and the spirit of knowledge in every design,
  and zeal for just ordinances,
  and holy resolution [5]with firm inclination,
  and abundant affection toward all the sons of truth,
  and glorious purification from hatred of all the idols of defilement,
  and modesty with universal prudence,
  and discretion concerning the truth of the Mysteries of Knowledge.[b]
Such are the counsels of the Spirit to the sons of truth in the world.

a. The Dead Sea sect believed that two opposing powers had control of the destiny of men. These were often called the Spirit of Truth and the Spirit of Falsehood. Men are in the lot or portion of one or the other.

b. This term perhaps refers to the special sectarian interpretation of the world and divine rule in it. Note the extensive reapplication of wisdom language in this section, and see below, Chapter 6.

Notable is the strongly dualist and sectarian character of this teaching. The true way to follow is that of the sect. The pious member loves his fellows, hates those outside, pursues the paths of right thought and action according to sectarian teaching, and does not reveal esoteric secrets. The virtues encouraged are spoken of in abstract terms: "goodness," "understanding," "intelligence," and so forth. This is significant since in the past some have claimed that such abstractions are characteristically Greek; but here they occur in a document composed in Hebrew.

ASCETICISM AND PRIESTLY VIRTUE

Testament of Isaac, p. 64

JACOB'S LAST INSTRUCTIONS

But the priest[a] of God said unto him: Show me the way to a word of
  consolation. He said unto him:
Keep your body holy, because it is the temple of God and the spirit of
  God dwells in it.
  Keep also your little flesh pure and holy.
Keep yourself, mingle not with men, so that no word of wrath may come
  out of your mouth.[b]
  Keep yourself from slander.

Keep yourself from vainglory.

Keep yourself, speak not alone with a woman.

Keep yourself, speak no idle word from your mouth.

Keep your hands, so that they may not be stretched out to that which is not yours.

Offer not up a sacrifice when there is a blemish in you.[c]

a. The term "priest" is ambiguous here, but the book may be drawing on the idea of a priesthood in the patriarchal and antediluvian periods.

b. A fairly strong ascetic tone is evident in this passage.

c. This is probably a deliberate variation on the Pentateuchal injunctions not to offer blemished sacrifices. The passage continues with a number of other instructions that have strongly ethical overtones.

Traditions about antediluvian and patriarchal priesthoods and sacrificial cults are very ancient and occur in unmistakably Jewish writings, such as the Aramaic Testament of Levi, and Slavonic Enoch. The Testaments of Isaac and Jacob are later Christian embellishments of Jewish traditions, and it is interesting that ideas about ancient priesthood were preserved and developed in some Christian circles. There, although they took on certain ethical or spiritualizing features, they remained rooted in the idea of sacrifice. The spiritualization of ritual injunctions was under way in Judaism well before the founding of Christianity; Christianity, however, used this instrument in a radical way in its grappling with the ritual and cultic laws of the Bible.

Testament of Isaac, pp. 66–67

PRIESTLY CONDUCT

It is fitting for everyone among the priests . . . not to be filled with bread, not to be filled with water, not to speak of the happenings of this world nor listen to them that speak (of them); but they should lead all their life instant unto prayer and watching and ascetic practice, until the Lord comes to seek them in peace.

ASCETICISM AND WITHDRAWAL

Every man that is upon the earth, whether monk or priest, it is fitting for them to love the well-chosen withdrawing of themselves after a little time, and that they should renounce the world and its evil cares and remain in the holy angelic service in purity, and become purified before the Lord and his angels, because of their holy sacrifices and their angelic service, which is the type that they shall perform in the heavens. And the angels shall be their companions because of their perfect faith and their purity, and great is their honor before God.

SINS AND SINLESSNESS

Simply, whether he be small or great, it is sinlessness that the Lord seeks from him; but as for the wicked that commit sin, they should repent before God. You shall not sin in any of these sins; you shall not slay with the sword; you shall not slay with the tongue; you shall not commit fornication in your body; you shall not commit fornication in your thoughts; you shall not defile yourself; you shall not envy; you shall not be angry until the sun sets nor remain in pride. You shall not rejoice at the fall of your enemy nor at that of your neighbor; you shall not blaspheme; you shall not teach your mouth to slander; your eye shall not look after a woman with lust.

Testament of Jacob, pp. 87–88

JACOB'S LAST WORDS

Now therefore, my sons, let us not fail in prayer and fasting but let us remain in expectation, for these are the things that drive away the devils. My sons, keep yourselves from fornication and wrath and adultery and every evil thing, but especially violence and blasphemy and theft, for there is no violence that shall inherit the kingdom of the heavens. . . . My sons, glorify the saints, for it is they who pray for you that your descendants may multiply. . . . My sons, be hospitable . . . love the poor . . . clothe the poor man that is naked . . . have a care unto the word of God here and remember the saints. . . .[a]

a. Compare these injunctions with the beatitudes of 2 Enoch B 42:6–14 (above, pp. 105–6).

FURTHER DEVELOPMENTS

The New Testament

There are numerous texts in early Christian writing which set forth the way of life men should struggle to attain. A small selection from the New Testament is offered here, chiefly of texts that show some relationship to the Jewish sources quoted above.

Luke 6:20–23

BEATITUDES FROM
THE SERMON ON THE PLAIN

20 And he lifted up his eyes on his disciples, and said:
"Blessed are you poor,
    for yours is the kingdom of God.
21Blessed are you that hunger now,
    for you shall be satisfied.

Blessed are you that weep now,
>for you shall laugh.

[22]Blessed are you when men hate you,
>and when they exclude you and revile you,
>and cast out your name as evil, on account of the Son of Man!

[23]Rejoice in that day, and leap for joy,
>for behold, your reward is great in heaven;
>for so their fathers did to the prophets."

The beatitudes here are very similar in form to 2 Enoch B 42:6–14 (above, pp. 105–6). They deal with a number of states of life. In 1 Enoch 99:11–16 a series of woe-sayings (reversed beatitudes) occur (see above, pp. 98–99). In Matthew 5:3–12, in another form of this passage (the Sermon on the Mount), the social qualities are transmuted into spiritual ones, the "poor" become the "poor in spirit," and so on.

In the Sermon on the Plain in Luke, woe-sayings also occur. They are clearly reversals of the Beatitudes. Their inclusion may be the work of Luke; however, they are consonant with the Jewish apocalyptic tradition, as is evident from 1 Enoch.

Luke 6:24–26

24 But woe to you that are rich,
>for you have received your consolation.

[25]Woe to you that are full now,
>for you shall hunger.
Woe to you that laugh now,
>for you shall mourn and weep.

[26]Woe to you, when all men speak well of you,
>for so their fathers did to the false prophets.

Galatians 5:16–24

Much of the writing in the Pauline Epistles could be described as hortatory. A list of sins to avoid and virtues to pursue is given in the Epistle to the Galatians, and this list of sins has many parallels in Jewish and Christian writing.

16 But I say, walk by the Spirit, and do not gratify the desires of the flesh. [17]For the desires of the flesh are against the Spirit, and the desires of the Spirit are against the flesh; for these are opposed to each other, to prevent you from doing what you would. [18]But if you are led by the Spirit you are not under the law. [19]Now the works of the flesh are plain:

immorality, impurity, licentiousness, [20]idolatry, sorcery, enmity, strife, jealousy, anger, selfishness, dissension, party spirit, [21]envy, drunkenness, carousing, and the like. I warn you, as I warned you before, that those who do such things shall not inherit the kingdom of God.[22] But the fruit of the Spirit is love, joy, peace, patience, kindness, goodness, faithfulness, [23]gentleness, self-control; against such there is no law. [24]And those who belong to Christ Jesus have crucified the flesh with its passions and desires.

It is notable that the sins and virtues relate to social relations and community life. On this passage see also below, p. 52.

James 1:19–27

Another sustained exhortation to the life of piety is preserved in the Epistle of James. A short excerpt suffices to give some insight into its atmosphere.

19 Know this, my beloved brethren. Let every man be quick to hear, slow to speak, slow to anger, [20]for the anger of man does not work the righteousness of God. [21]Therefore put away all filthiness and rank growth of wickedness and receive with meekness the implanted word, which is able to save your souls.
    [22]But be doers of the word and not hearers only, deceiving yourselves. [23]For if anyone is a hearer of the word and not a doer, he is like a man who observes his natural face in a mirror; [24]for he observes himself and goes away and at once forgets what he was like. [25]But he who looks into the perfect law, the law of liberty, and perseveres, being no hearer that forgets but a doer that acts, he shall be blessed in his doing.
    [26]If anyone thinks he is religious and does not bridle his tongue, but deceives his heart, this man's religion is vain. [27]Religion that is pure and undefiled before God and the Father is this: to visit orphans and widows in their affliction and to keep oneself unstained from the world.

As can be observed in v. 25 and elsewhere, this epistle sets "the perfect law" in opposition to the Jewish law. This comes out more powerfully in 2:8–13. Yet the point stated in 2:10 does not reflect any Jewish attitude to the Torah that can be documented, but is probably a polemical overstatement.

Rabbinic Literature

The body of rabbinic literature is extensive, and a considerable amount of it deals with the question of how one should live. The following are merely samples; see also the Bibliography for further information. The texts given here were selected for their context, which is similar to that of many of the texts we quoted from the earlier literature.

The Fathers According to
Rabbi Nathan, A 19

When Rabbi Eliezer (ben Hyrcanus) fell ill, his disciples came in to visit him. They sat before him and said to him, "Our Master, teach us one thing." He said to them, "I will teach you. Go forth and be careful of each other's honor; when you pray, know before whom you are standing in prayer, for through that you will win the life of the world to come."

Babylonian Talmud *Berakot* 61b

"And you shall love the Lord your God. . . ." Rabbi Aqiba says, "with all your soul," that is, even if it takes your soul (life). Our sages taught: Once the wicked government decreed that Israel should not study the Torah. Pappos ben Yehuda came and found Rabbi Aqiba assembling groups in public and studying the Torah. He said to him, "Aqiba, are you not afraid of the government?" He replied, "Let me tell you a parable. It resembles a fox who was walking along the river bank and saw fish moving in schools from one place to another. He said to them, 'What do you flee?' They replied, 'From the nets that men are using against us.' He said to them, 'Do you wish to come up on to the ground and you and I will dwell together as my ancestors dwelt with your ancestors?' They replied, 'You are he whom men say to be wisest of the beasts; you are not wise, but foolish. If we are afraid in the place in which we can live, how much more would we fear in a place in which we die?' So it is with us. Now while we are sitting and studying the Torah, of which it is written 'It is your life and the length of your days' (Deut. 30:20) (we are afraid); how much more when we do not study it."

The text goes on to tell the story of Aqiba's martyrdom at the hands of the Romans and thus his fulfillment thereby of his own interpretation, "even if it takes your life." Although its literary form is very different from that of the other texts we quoted, this passage shares with them the presentation of the quintessence of its view of the life of true piety in a limited compass.

Ethics of the Fathers 2:5–8

Other types of rabbinic ideals permeate the sayings of Hillel, one of the most radical Jewish thinkers of antiquity.

5 Hillel said,[a] "Do not separate from the community, do not trust yourself until the day of your death, and do not judge your fellow until you reach his situation; and say not of anything that it is unbearable, for in the end it will be heard; and do not say, 'When I have time I will study,' lest you have no time."

[6]He said, "The boor fears not sin, nor is the ʿam haʾareṣ (ignoramus) pious, nor is the shy man learned, nor can the short-tempered man teach, nor does he who is chiefly engaged in business become wise. In a place where there are no men, strive to be a man."

[7]He also saw a skull floating on the surface of the water. He said to it, "Because you drowned someone, you were drowned, and the fate of those who drowned you is to be drowned."

[8]He said, "The more flesh, the more worms;[b] the more possessions, the more worries; the more women, the more sorcery; the more maidservants, the more unchastity; the more menservants, the more robbery; the more Torah, the more life; the more learning, the more wisdom; the more counsel, the more understanding; the more charity, the more peace. If a man has acquired a good name, he has acquired it for himself; if he has acquired knowledge of the Torah, he has acquired life in the world to come."

a. It is possible that this is Hillel the Elder (last century B.C.E.), although many scholars have held the contrary view.
b. Or translate throughout, "He who increases . . . increases. . . ."

NOTES

1. Chapter 9 of the Wisdom of Solomon gives what purports to be the self-understanding of a true monarch. It shares with the Wisdom of ben Sira the idea of the God-givenness of wisdom and the responsibility of the wise king to observe God's commandments.

2. It should be observed that the Pentateuch ascribes no farewell speech to Abraham prior to his death.

3. For an exhortation similar to that of Abraham, see Jub. 21:5–6, 22–24.

4. Some sections seem to have been written in Semitic languages; others seem to reflect Jewish Greek sources.

BIBLIOGRAPHY

PRIMARY SOURCES

The Bible and Apocrypha are quoted from the RSV; the Pseudepigrapha from *APOT*, vol. 2; Philo from LCL; The Rule of the Community from A. **Dupont-Sommer,** *The Essene Writings from Qumran* (Cleveland: Meridian, 1962); and the Testaments of Isaac and Jacob, adapted from S. **Gaselee** in G. H. Box, *The Testament of Abraham* (London: SPCK, 1927).

SECONDARY SOURCES

There is no extensive discussion of the type of texts collected here. However, very similar problems are treated from a rather different focus in John J. **Collins** and George W. E. **Nickelsburg,** *Ideal Figures in Ancient Judaism,* SBLSCS 12 (Chico, Calif.: Scholars Press, 1980).

TYPOLOGICAL ANALYSIS OF TYPES
OF JEWISH PIETY

Gershom **Scholem,** "Three Types of Jewish Piety," *Eranos Jahrbuch* 38 (1969) 331–48.

POPULAR PALESTINIAN PIETY

Saul **Lieberman,** *Greek in Jewish Palestine* (New York: Jewish Theological Seminary, 1942) 68–90, uses tombstones as a source for study of ideals of piety.

PHILO

Hans **Lewy,** *Philo* (Oxford: Phaidon, 1946) 18–20, and also many of the texts excerpted there.

RABBINIC VIEWS

Adolph **Büchler,** *Types of Jewish-Palestinian Piety from 70 B.C.E. to 70 C.E.,* Jews' College Publications 8 (London: Jews' College, 1922). Solomon **Schechter,** *Some Aspects of Rabbinic Theology* (London: A. & C. Black, 1909) 199–218. Ephraim E. **Urbach,** *The Sages: Their Concepts and Beliefs* (Jerusalem: Magnes, 1975) 1:420–523.

4
Deliverance, Judgment, and Vindication

Israel's understanding of itself as a nation chosen by God and bound to him by a covenant is the fundamental presupposition of Judaism from biblical times on. This covenantal relationship began, we are told, with God's choice and call of Abraham to be the patriarch of a people who would inherit the land. The covenant was executed and formalized at Sinai. By delivering Israel from their Egyptian oppressors, God claimed them as his own people, and their possession of the land followed. The Israelites, in turn, were to be faithful to their God, obeying the Torah, the divine laws that Moses received on Mount Sinai. God would respond appropriately in judgment; he would reward and bless them when they obeyed and would punish and bring a curse on them when they disobeyed. Yet even though disobedience brought punishment, it did not annul the covenant. Repentance and the divinely instituted sacrificial system would turn God's wrath to mercy, bringing forgiveness and atonement. The divine Judge would vindicate his people; he would put them in the right. The enemy whom God used to punish his people would himself be punished for arrogantly rejecting the sovereignty of God. The basic pattern of this covenantal theology is sketched in the Song of Moses in Deuteronomy 32 and is spelled out in more detail in Deuteronomy 28–30.

Within this general framework, the biblical prophets and sages interpret the history of Israel and events in the lives of individuals. Covenantal language is not always explicit, but Israel's status as God's people and his dealings with them in response to their fidelity or rebellion are always presumed. Thus the authors of the Deuteronomistic history (Deuteronomy through 2 Kings) structure their narrative of Israel's history largely in terms of obedience and disobedience, reward and punishment for righteousness and sin.

While the narrative literature and the prophetic writings of the

Bible speak mainly in terms of God's dealings with the nation, the focus of the wisdom literature is largely on the individual. Many of the individual sayings in the Book of Proverbs posit a cause-and-effect relationship between one's deeds and one's lot in life. Thus, for example,

> No ill befalls the righteous,
> > but the wicked are filled with trouble (Prov 12:21).

The psalmist puts the matter more specifically:

> Blessed is everyone who fears the Lord,
> > who walks in his ways!
> You shall eat the labor of your hands;
> > you shall be happy, and it shall be well with you.
> Your wife will be like a fruitful vine
> > within your house;
> Your children will be like olive shoots
> > around your table.
> Lo, thus shall the man be blessed
> > who fears the Lord (Ps 128:1–4).

Alongside these passages, however, is a recognition and admission that the righteous one may also have to suffer. The obvious example is the Book of Job, which voices a vigorous protest against a simplistic Deuteronomistic view of life. More typical are those psalms in which the righteous one who is suffering illness or persecution at the hands of his enemies pleads with God to vindicate him and reward his piety (e.g., Ps 22, 35, 69).

The prophetic corpus is, in large part, crisis literature, in which God's spokesmen indict Israel for its breaches of covenant. In some cases (e.g., Joel) the prophets interpret current disasters as acts of divine punishment. More often, however, they speak in terms of the future. Because of their sins, the people stand on the brink of calamity: war, defeat, subjugation, exile. Amos speaks of the terrible "Day of the Lord." Hosea sees Israel returning to Egypt because of its adulterous abandonment of its marital covenant with its God. Jeremiah and Ezekiel announce exile to Babylon. Sometimes there is a powerful appeal to repent (Jer 3–4). In other cases the predictions are categorical and disaster seems inevitable.

Alongside these oracles of doom are predictions of a better time, when Israel will be restored to favor with God. According to Isaiah, a remnant will survive God's judgment. Jeremiah envisions a new covenant between God and his people. According to Ezekiel, the nation will be raised from its death in Babylon. For both him and Jeremiah, the people will return to their land and live in a covenantal relationship with their God under a restored Davidic monarchy. These and other royal oracles form the background of Jewish hopes for the Messiah, which we shall consider in the next chapter.

The oracles of the anonymous prophet called Second Isaiah (Isa 40–55) exude high optimism. Writing toward the end of the Exile, he sees Cyrus's victory over Babylon as divine judgment on the enemy (chaps. 45–47). The Israelites, for their part, have paid "double" for the sins that have led to their exile, and God has now pardoned their iniquities (40:1–2). The people stand on the brink of a new era of hope and promise. God is about to do a new thing that will make his mighty deeds of old shrink by comparison (43:18–19). He will lead his people back to Zion in a new Exodus, and in the process he will remold the shape of creation itself (40:3–5; 41:18–19; 51:3; 55:12–13). The glory of God will dwell in Jerusalem, the dispersed children of Mother Zion will return, and all nations will acknowledge the God of Israel. He who created Israel will now redeem the Israelites (43:1).

Integral to the message of Second Isaiah is the complex and mysterious figure of the servant of the Lord, described in 42:1–4; 49:1–7; 50:4–9; and 52:13—53:12. He is at once Israel and a figure or group within or apart from Israel. He receives a call like a prophet (chap. 49), and he speaks on God's behalf (50:4–5). Most notably, the servant suffers. He is persecuted by enemies (50:6). The last servant poem begins as an audience of kings and nations looks on in astonishment at the exalted servant (52:13–15). They confess how they had previously despised him in his lowliness, taking his suffering as evidence of divine punishment. But now they realize and admit that he has suffered on their behalf (53:1–3; cf. 50:7–9). The servant's suffering was God's means of working His purposes, and his exaltation is God's vindication of him, His open demonstration and acclamation of his innocence. This particular passage and its pattern of suffering and exaltation/vindication are fundamental and central to beliefs in resurrection and eternal life in the writings of the later Jewish community.

Sharply contrasted to the optimistic oracles of Second Isaiah are the prophecies of the so-called Third Isaiah (Isa 56–66), which stem from the early decades after the Exile. The people have returned to their homeland, but the glowing promises of Second Isaiah have not been fulfilled. The temple in which God's presence would dwell still lies in ruins. The people—at least those of whom the prophet spoke —are divided. Israel is no longer viewed as God's servant over against the nations. Rather, within Israel there are "the servants" of the Lord, the prophet's own group, and others whom he views as wicked and apostate. But God will soon resolve the situation when he appears with fire (as he did on Mount Sinai) to render judgment.

> For behold, the Lord will come in fire,
>   and his chariots like the stormwind,
> to render his anger in fury,
>   and his rebuke with flames of fire.
> For by fire will the Lord execute judgment,
>   and by his sword upon all flesh;
>   and those slain by the Lord shall be many (66:15–16).

The wicked will be recompensed for their deeds, and their corpses will be pitched into the Valley of Hinnom outside Jerusalem. There they will be viewed with abhorrence by all flesh, who will come to Jerusalem to worship (66:23–24).

For his servants, however, God will create new heavens and a new earth, and in it a new Jerusalem that will be a return to paradise. Here God's chosen servants will enjoy the blessings and rewards which God promised them but which they presently do not experience in their troubled and fragmented world.

> For behold, I create new heavens
>   and a new earth;
> and the former things shall not be remembered
>   or come to mind.
> But be glad and rejoice forever
>   in that which I create;
> for behold, I create Jerusalem a rejoicing,
>   and her people a joy.
> I will rejoice in Jerusalem
>   and be glad in my people;
> no more shall be heard in it the sound of weeping
>   and the cry of distress.
> No more shall there be in it
>   an infant that lives but a few days
>   or an old man who does not fill out his days,
> for the child shall die a hundred years old,
>   and the sinner a hundred years old shall be accursed.

> They shall build houses and inhabit them;
>> they shall plant vineyards and eat their fruit.
> They shall not build and another inhabit;
>> they shall not plant and another eat;
> for like the days of a tree shall the days of my people be,
>> and my chosen shall long enjoy the work of their hands.
> They shall not labor in vain
>> or bear children for calamity,
> for they shall be the offspring of the blessed of the Lord,
>> and their children with them.
> Before they call I will answer,
>> while they are yet speaking I will hear.
> The wolf and the lamb shall feed together,
>> the lion shall eat straw like the ox;
>> the dust shall be the serpent's food.
> They shall not hurt or destroy
>> in all my holy mountain,
>>>> says the Lord (Isa 65:17–25).

In the oracles of Second and Third Isaiah we see some of the major components of later Jewish apocalypticism: a time of deep distress; persons who construe themselves as the righteous expecting an imminent adjudication of present injustices; a scenario for this judgment and the new era that will follow it, described as a repetition of God's deeds of old and a universal return to God's intention at creation. Because Second and Third Isaiah and their successors saw the judgment as ending one era and ushering in a new, qualitatively different, and final era, we may speak of their "eschatology" (Greek for "teaching about the end").

From the biblical texts two aspects of judgment emerge which are relevant for the literature of the postbiblical period. On the one hand, God deals justly within the context of the covenant, rewarding the faithful and punishing the wicked. On the other hand, sometimes experience seems to belie his justice, for indeed the faithful suffer and the wicked prosper. Nonetheless, God's justice is inevitable. In keeping with his promises, he will vindicate the faithful and deliver and redeem them from dire circumstances, just as he will punish the wicked, who seem to have eluded his judgment. In some of the texts that we shall discuss, an event in the life of the nation or of an individual is seen as an act of divine judgment. Increasingly, however, the critical and distressing events of the Hellenistic and early Roman periods test and try belief in God's judgment and create literature whose central thrust is the expectation and assertion that God is about to set right terrible wrongs by means of a final judgment that will usher in a new age. Moreover, judgment cannot be frustrated by death. Whether by means of an end-time resurrection or during one's noncorporeal existence after physical death, God will vindicate and reward the faithful and punish the wicked.

AN EARLY JUDGMENT ORACLE

1 Enoch 1–5

First Enoch is a collection of writings purporting to transmit revelations of the heavenly realm and of future events, especially the coming judgment. Chapters 1–5 announce the judgment and its results and thus constitute a fitting introduction to the collection. They date from 200 B.C.E. or earlier.

GOD'S APPEARANCE AND THE REACTIONS
OF THE COSMOS

1 [3]The Great Holy One[a] will come forth from his dwelling
[4]   and the Eternal God will tread from thence upon Mount Sinai.[b]
And he will appear with his army,
   yea, he will appear with his mighty host
      from the heaven of heavens.

[5]And all the watchers will fear and quake,
   and those who are hiding in all the ends of the earth will sing;[c]
   and trembling and great fear will seize them (the watchers) unto the
      ends of the earth.
[6]And the high mountains will be shaken
   and fall and break apart,
and the high hills will be made low
   and melt like wax before the fire;[d]
[7]And the earth will be wholly rent asunder,
   and everything on the earth will perish,
   and there will be judgment on all.

[8]And with the righteous he will make peace,[e]
   and over the chosen there will be protection,
   and upon them will be mercy.
And they will all be God's,
   and he will grant them his good pleasure.
And he will bless (them) all,
   and he will help (them) all.

And light will shine upon them,
  and he will make peace with them.

[9]Behold, he comes with the myriads of his holy ones,[f]
  to execute judgment on all,
  and to destroy all the wicked,
  and to convict all flesh
    for all the deeds of their wickedness which they have done,
    and the proud and hard words which godless sinners spoke against
    him.

THE INDICTMENT[g]

2 [1]Contemplate all the works, and observe the works of heaven, how
  they do not alter their paths; and the luminaries of heaven, that
  they all rise and set, each one ordered in its appointed time; and
  they appear on their feasts and do not transgress their own appointed order.

[2]Observe the earth, and contemplate the works that come to pass on it
  from the beginning until the consummation, that nothing on earth
  changes, but all the works of God are manifest to you.

[3]Observe the signs of summer and winter. Contemplate the signs of
  winter, that all the earth is filled with water, and clouds and dew
  and rain rest upon it.

3 [1]Contemplate and observe how all the trees appear withered and
  (how) all their leaves are stripped, except fourteen trees which are
  not stripped, which remain with the old until the new comes after
  two or three years.

4 [1]Observe the signs of summer, whereby the sun burns and scorches,
  and you seek shelter and shade from its presence, and the earth
  burns with scorching heat, and you are unable to tread on the dust
  or the rock because of the burning.

5 [1]Contemplate all the trees; their leaves blossom green on them, and
  they cover the trees. And all their fruit is for glorious honor.

Contemplate all these works, and understand that he who lives for all
  the ages made all these works. [2]And his works come to pass from
  year to year, and they all carry out their works for him, and their
  works do not alter, but they all carry his word. . . .

[4]But you have changed your deeds and have not acted according to his
  commandments;
  but you have turned aside, you have spoken proud and hard words
  with your unclean mouth against his majesty.[h]
Hard of heart! There will be no peace for you!

THE VERDICT[i]

A Curse on the Wicked

5 [5]Then you will curse your days, and the years of your life will perish;
and the years of your destruction will increase in an eternal curse.[j]
And there will be no mercy or peace for you!

[6]Then your names will become an eternal curse for all the righteous;
and by you all who curse will curse;
and all the sinners and ungodly will swear by you.[k]

Two Alternating Blessings and Curses[l]

And all the chosen[m] will rejoice;
and for them there will be forgiveness of sins and all mercy and peace
and clemency.
And for them there will be salvation, a good light;
and they will inherit the earth.[n]
But for all you sinners there will be no salvation,
but upon all of you a curse will abide.

[7]And for the chosen there will be light and joy and peace;
and they will inherit the earth.
But for you wicked there will be a curse.

*The Wisdom, Sinlessness, and Blessings
of the Chosen*

[8]Then wisdom will be given to all the chosen
and they will all live;
And they will sin no more
through wickedness or pride.[o]
And in the enlightened man there will be light,
and in the wise man, understanding.
And they will transgress no more,
nor will they sin all the days of their life.
[9]And they will not die in the heat of (God's) wrath;
but the number of the days of their life they will complete;[p]
And their life will grow in peace;
and the years of their joy will increase in rejoicing and eternal peace,
in all the days of their life.

a. This title distinguishes God from the many "holy ones," the angels (cf. v. 9).
Together with the title "the Eternal God" and the references to his appearance from
heaven, it stresses his transcendence.

b. As the avenger of the covenant, God returns to Mount Sinai, where the covenant
was enacted. The language of this verse and vv. 1 and 9 reflects Deut 33:1–2.

c. The meaning of this line is obscure. The parallelism of the verse suggests that it refers to a lament sung by the fallen watchers, the angels whose sin is the subject of 1 Enoch 6–19.

d. For the sources of the theophanic imagery here, cf. esp. Mic 1:3–4; Hab 3:3–6.

e. This promise of a blessing on the righteous is a paraphrase of the Aaronic benediction (Num 6:24–26). It is balanced by the curses in chap. 5.

f. After the blessing in v. 8, the author returns to the topic of v. 7 and elaborates upon it. The present line reflects the wording of Deut 33:2 and Isa 66:15–16 or Jer 25:30–31. This verse is quoted in Jude 14–15, where it is described as a prophecy of Enoch.

g. The translation of this section reflects text-critical judgments made on the basis of the Ethiopic and Greek texts and the Aramaic fragments. The contrast between the constancy of nature, which fulfills God's commands (2:1—5:3), and the inconstancy of the author's audience, which has disobeyed his commandments (5:4), reflects a wisdom tradition found also in Sir 16:26–28; T. Napht. 3:1–3; and Ps. Sol. 18:10–12.

h. As the verbs "change" and "turn aside" indicate, the wicked addressed are apostate Jews. The reference to their words and deeds parallels the double reference in 1:9. On the speaking of proud and hard words, cf. Dan 7:8, 20, which refers to Antiochus Epiphanes. The wording of the present verse and the contrast between nature and humanity is taken up again in 1 Enoch 101.

i. The oracle closes with a description of the contrasting curses and blessings that will come to the sinners and the righteous as a result of the judgment.

j. The wording of this curse anticipates v. 9 and its description of the long life of the chosen. The combination of "curse" and "no mercy and peace" suggests a contrast with the blessing in 1:8.

k. The wording of this verse constitutes a reversal of the blessing in Isa 65:15–16.

l. Vv. 6 and 7 parallel one another in structure (a blessing followed by a curse) and wording.

m. The text is corrupt here. It calls for a word denoting the righteous, and "the chosen" is used by analogy with the parallel v. 7.

n. Cf. Ps 37:9, 11, 22, 29, 34, and the beatitude in Matt 5:5.

o. Reference to the former "wickedness" and "pride" is reminiscent of the twin sins mentioned in 1:9 and 5:4 (see above, n. h) and suggests that the author expects that the ranks of the chosen will include those of his audience (addressed in 2:1—5:4) who repent and follow the wisdom of his teaching.

p. For the wording of this verse, cf. Isa 65:20–22 and contrast v. 5, above.

God is here depicted as the universal judge, rendering to "all flesh" the due rewards and punishments of their deeds. The oracle is heavily influenced by biblical language, especially theophanies (descriptions or announcements of God's appearance) and the promises and predictions in Isaiah 65–66.

The first major part of the oracle (1:3–9) is set in a poetic form reminiscent of prophetic oracles. The second section (2:1—5:4), which is written mainly in prose, draws on wisdom traditions. It is an indictment of the wicked (5:4), whose inconstancy and deviation from God's law is contrasted with nature's constancy and obedience. The third, poetic section, which is especially beholden to Isaiah 65, anticipates God's curse on the wicked but offers the promise of a long and blessed life to those wise enough to hearken to the author's message. Although this passage does not mention a resurrection of the dead, such an event is anticipated in chapter 22, which was part of the book for which chapters 1–5 were composed as an introduction.

GOD'S VINDICATION OF HIS PERSECUTED PEOPLE

Descriptions of the Judgment

The persecution of the Jews in 168–165 B.C.E. by Antiochus IV Epiphanes of Syria ranks as one of the critical and tragic moments of Jewish history. Antiochus defiled the temple and threatened with death anyone who observed the Torah and refused to perform public acts of apostasy and desecration. Many apostasized in order to save their lives. Others died rather than forsake the covenant. The situation created not only a human crisis but also a profound theological problem. This was not simply the perennial problem of the righteous suffering and the wicked flourishing. Instead, the pious suffered precisely *because of* their faithfulness to the Torah, while the apostasy of the wicked led to their safety and deliverance.

Daniel 12:1–3

Chapters 7–12 of the Book of Daniel were written as a response to Antiochus's persecution. They were combined with a cycle of earlier stories to form a tractate that exhorted the Jews to stand fast in the face of the persecution.[1] The four visions that constitute Daniel 7–12 predict that God's final judgment will occur during the time of Antiochus and in response to his misdeeds.

The concluding vision (chaps. 10–12) is a detailed account of events in Israelite history from Alexander the Great to Antiochus Epiphanes. The vision culminates with the death of this king, an act of God's judgment that is simultaneous with the great judgment (11:45—12:1). For this author the wars of history have their counterpart in the heavenly realm, where the guardian angels of the nations and their hosts do battle. The defeat of a kingdom implies the fall of its angelic chieftain (10:13, 21). At the time of the great judgment, Michael the angelic patron of Israel will strike down the angelic chieftain behind the throne of Antioch, and thus Antiochus Epiphanes and his kingdom will come to an end (12:1). This judgment will also separate the apostate Jews from the pious, who will be vindicated for their faithfulness and saved. Moreover, justice will be meted out to those who died in the persecution and to the apostates who have died since; they will be raised to the reward of a long life or suffer perpetual contempt (12:2). Special honor will be granted to the leaders who exhorted the people to faithfulness. The wise, who brought many to righteousness, will be exalted to heaven, where they will shine in glory (12:3).

12 [1]And at that time Michael will arise,
   the great prince who stands up for the sons of your people.[a]
And there will be a time of trouble such as has not been from the time that the nation came into being until that time.[b]
And at that time your people will be delivered,
   everyone who is found written in the book.[c]
[2]And many of those who sleep in the land of dust will awake,[d]
   some to eternal life[e] and some to eternal contempt.[f]
[3]And the wise will shine as the firmament,
   and those who bring many to righteousness, as the stars forever and ever.[g]

   a. Michael is here depicted both as Israel's warrior chieftain and as its advocate in court.
   b. Cf. Jer 30:7.
   c. The register of the citizens of the new Jerusalem; cf. Isa 4:2–6; Mal 3:16–18; Rev 20:15.
   d. Cf. Isa 26:19. The "land of dust" is Sheol, the underworld.
   e. I.e., the long life promised in Isa 65:20–22. Cf. 1 Enoch 5:9 (above, p. 124), where, however, no resurrection is mentioned.
   f. The language is drawn from Isa 66:24.
   g. The author draws on a tradition that is based on Isa 52–53 (see below, p. 132). Like the servant of the Lord, and like the sage Daniel (Dan 6), the wise will be exalted and vindicated.

The resurrection here described is limited to only some of the dead—evidently the righteous and the wicked at the time of Antiochus. It is uncertain, however, whether the author anticipates a resurrection *of the body.*

Testament of Moses 9–10

The Testament of Moses (usually known as the Assumption of Moses) was also composed during Antiochus's persecution.[2] It is a paraphrase of the last chapters of Deuteronomy, in which the historical scheme of those chapters is interpreted as a prediction of the events of the author's own time.[3] The author believes that Antiochus's persecution is divine punishment for the sin of Hellenization. At the same time, he contemplates an act that will trigger God's vengeance and usher in the judgment. The mysterious figure of Taxo, typical of certain pious Jews in Antiochus's time (cf. 1 Macc 2:29–38), believes that a few innocent deaths will force God to avenge his people. Their enemies will be destroyed, and Israel will be exalted to heaven. As 10:2 notes, Taxo's ploy will work. Chapter 10 is a remarkable pastiche of phraseology drawn chiefly from Deuteronomy 33, interwoven with important elements also found in the judgment scene in Daniel 12:1–3 (see above, pp. 126–27).

9 [1]Then in that day there will be a man of the tribe of Levi, whose name will be Taxo,[a] who having seven sons shall speak to them exhorting (them): [2]"Observe, my sons, behold a second ruthless (and) unclean visitation has come upon the people,[b] and a punishment merciless and far exceeding the first. [3]For what nation or what region or what people of those who are impious toward the Lord, who have done many abominations, have suffered as great calamities as have befallen us? [4]Now, therefore, my sons, hear me: for observe and know that neither did the fathers nor their forefathers tempt God, so as to transgress his commands. [5]And you know that this is our strength, and thus we will do.[c] [6]Let us fast for three days, and on the fourth let us go into a cave which is in the field, and let us die rather than transgress the commands of the Lord of lords, the God of our fathers.[d] [7]For if we do this and die, our blood shall be avenged before the Lord.[e]

10 [1]And then his kingdom will appear throughout all his creation;[f]
and then Satan will be no more,[g]
and sorrow will depart with him.
[2]Then the hands of the angel will be filled,
who has been appointed chief;[h]
and he will immediately avenge them of their enemies.[i]
[3]For the Heavenly One will arise from his royal throne;
and he will go forth from his holy habitation[j]
with indignation and wrath on account of his sons.

[4]And the earth will tremble: to its confines shall it be shaken;
and the high mountains will be made low,
and the hills will be shaken and fall.[k]
[5]And the horns of the sun will be broken and he will be turned into darkness;
and the moon will not give her light, and be turned wholly into blood;[l]
and the circle of the stars will be disturbed.

[6]And the sea will retire into the abyss,
  and the fountains of water will fail,
  and the rivers will dry up.

[7]For the Most High will arise, the Eternal God alone;[m]
  and he will appear to punish the Gentiles,
  and he will destroy all their idols.

[8]Then you, O Israel, will be happy,[n]
  and you will mount upon their necks,[o]
  and they will be ended.
[9]And God will exalt you;
  and he will cause you to approach the heaven of the stars,
  in the place of their habitation.
[10]And you will look from on high and will see your enemies on earth;
  and you will recognize them and rejoice,
  and you will give thanks and confess your Creator."

a. On the possible meaning of this obscure name, see George W. E. Nickelsburg, *Resurrection, Immortality, and Eternal Life in Intertestamental Judaism*, 98.

b. The first "visitation" or judgment was Nebuchadnezzar's sack of Jerusalem, described in chap. 3.

c. Cf. Dan 11:32.

d. Cf. 1 Macc 2:20; 2 Macc 7:2. For other stories about retreat to the wilderness and death in caves, cf. 1 Macc 2:29–38; 2 Macc 5:27; 6:11.

e. Cf. Deut 32:43.

f. Reference to God's "kingdom," i.e., his kingly reign, is relatively rare in our literature. Cf. Ps. Sol. 17:3, below, p. 162.

g. Reference to the devil here and the great angel in v. 2 suggests the heavenly antagonism between Michael and the guardian angel of Syria, presumed in Dan 12:1 (see above, p. 126).

h. Filling the hands was part of the ritual of priestly ordination; cf., e.g., Exod 28:41; Lev 21:10; and see Nickelsburg, *Resurrection*, 29, n. 94. This suggests that here or in the tradition behind this text the great angel was construed as a heavenly priest.

i. The angel's function duplicates that of God in the next verse.

j. Cf. Deut 33:2.

k. In biblical literature, theophanies (appearances of God) are customarily attended by cosmic reactions (cf., e.g., Exod 19:16–19; Ps 97:1–5; Hab 3:3–15). Cf. also 1 Enoch 1:6–7 (above, p. 122); here in vv. 5–6 these reactions move beyond those recorded in 1 Enoch to include the sea and the heavens.

l. Cf. Joel 2:10, 30–31, and its description of the "Day of the Lord."

m. For this name of God, cf. 1 Enoch 1:4 (above, p. 122) and Deut 33:27. On the destruction of the idols, cf. Mic 1:7 and 1 Enoch 91:9.

n. Cf. Deut 33:29.

o. The text here is problematic. It reads, "You will mount upon the necks and wings of the eagle." Originally the text probably read approximately as above, a reference to Israel's treading on the necks of their enemies; cf. Deut 33:29 LXX, which reads "necks" for "high places" of the Hebrew. Later, when the book was reedited in Herodian times (see n. 2), reference to the eagles was added, alluding to an incident in the time of Herod, when certain Jews of the persuasion of Taxo and his sons pulled down a Roman eagle which Herod had erected over the temple gate. See Adela Yarbro Collins, "Composition and Redaction of the Testament of Moses 10," *HTR* 69 (1976) 184–86.

According to Daniel 12:2–3, the faithful Jews will be raised to life and the righteous teachers will be exalted to special glory. Here all of righteous Israel will ascend to heaven—the realm of immortality—while earth becomes the place of punishment for their enemies, principally the Gentiles. No reference is made to a resurrection, but a place among the exalted Israel is hardly excluded for the likes of Taxo and his sons.

Jubilees 23:23–31

Jubilees is yet another book attached to the name of Moses and written in the second century B.C.E. It is an extensive reworking of Genesis and part of Exodus. When the author speaks of Abraham's 175 years (Jub. 23:8; cf. Gen 25:7), he launches into a description of future times, when sin and distress will greatly shorten life. Although his language is stereotyped, he appears to refer to the sin of Hellenization and its punishment in the form of foreign oppression (23:12–23). Repentance in the form of studying and obeying the Torah will bring about a gradual return of God's blessing (rather than the cataclysmic change described in Dan 12 and T. Mos. 10). The fabulously long life-spans that characterized antediluvian humanity will return (contrast vv. 27–28 with v. 25, and cf. 23:9), and the reward for righteousness will transcend death (v. 31).

23 And they will use violence against Israel and transgression against Jacob,
    and much blood will be shed on the earth,
    and there will be none to gather and none to bury.
²⁴In those days they will cry aloud,
    and call and pray that they may be saved from the hand of the sinners, the Gentiles;
    but none will be saved.
²⁵And the heads of the children will be white with gray hair,
    and a child of three weeks will appear old like a man of one hundred years,
    and their stature will be destroyed by tribulation and oppression.
²⁶And in those days the children will begin to study the laws
    and to seek the commandments
    and to return to the path of righteousness.

[27]And the days will begin to grow many and increase among those children of men.

till their days approach one thousand years,

and to a greater number of years than (before) was the number of the days.[a]

[28]And there will be no old man,

nor one who has not lived out his full life span,

for all will be (as) children and youths.

[29]And all their days they will complete and live in peace and in joy,

and there will be no Satan nor any evil destroyer,[b]

for all their days will be days of blessing and healing.

[30]And at that time the Lord will heal his servants,

and they will rise up and see great peace

and drive out their adversaries.

And the righteous will see and be thankful[c]

and rejoice with joy forever and ever,

and will see all their judgments and all their curses on their enemies.

[31]And their bones will rest in the earth,

and their spirit will have much joy,

and they will know that it is the Lord who executes judgment,

and shows mercy to hundreds and thousands and to all that love him.

a. Cf. Isa 65:20–22 and the allusion to it in 1 Enoch 5:9 (see above, p. 124).
b. Cf. T. Mos. 10:1.
c. Cf. ibid., and on this verse and the next cf. Isa 66:14.

For this author also, vindication and reward transcend death. But different from Daniel 12, there is no resurrection. While the bones of the righteous rest (from their pain) in the earth, their spirits rejoice—presumably in God's presence, immediately after death.

(For other texts describing the judgment, see below, pp. 142–47.)

Stories about the Vindication of the Persecuted Righteous

The theme of God's vindication of the persecuted righteous is embodied in the form of stories with a relatively stereotyped plot. The most familiar examples are the stories about the three men in the fiery furnace (Dan 3) and Daniel in the lions' den (Dan 6). The heroes are functionaries in the Mesopotamian court. Their rivals at court conspire to destroy them, accusing them of practicing their religion in defiance of the laws of the land. The heroes' choice to be faithful to the Torah leads to their condemnation by the king and the sentence of death. Thus their imminent death becomes an ordeal or test that will demonstrate the rightness or the futility of their decision. Through their startling and unexpected deliverance, their pious behavior is vindicated and rewarded. The monarch acclaims their behavior and, more important, the sovereignty of their God, whose law supersedes the law of the land; and their enemies are punished or threatened with punishment.

Wisdom of Solomon 2–5

Chapters 1–6 of the Wisdom of Solomon are an admonition to "the rulers of the earth," advising them to rule wisely and righteously because God judges justly. Central to the author's exposition is the case of a righteous man, whose enemies condemn him to death, believing that there is no reckoning after death. To their surprise, after their death they are confronted by the righteous man, exalted in the heavenly courtroom. As their judge, he condemns them to that punishment whose existence they had denied.

A remarkable difference between these chapters and other narratives about the righteous man is the manner of the hero's rescue and exaltation; here he dies and is exalted in the heavenly court. In describing this heavenly exaltation, the author draws on the language and format of the last servant poem in Second Isaiah (Isa 52:13—53:12).[4]

In Wisdom of Solomon 2–5 the story of the righteous man is recounted in a pair of speeches by his enemies. In the first speech the wicked muse on the impossibility of immortality and retribution after death (2:1–5).[5] They intend to enjoy life here and now, even if it means oppressing others (2:6–11).

THE WICKED CONSPIRE AGAINST
THE RIGHTEOUS MAN

2 [12]"Let us lie in wait for the righteous man,
  because he is inconvenient to us and opposes our actions;[a]
 he reproaches us for sins against the law
  and accuses us of sins against our training.
[13]He professes to have knowledge of God[b]
  and calls himself a child[c] of the Lord.
[14]He became to us a reproof of our thoughts;
[15] the very sight of him is a burden to us,[d]
 because his manner of life is unlike that of others,
  and his ways are strange.[e]

[16]We are considered by him as something base,
and he avoids our ways as unclean;
he calls the last end of the righteous happy,
and boasts that God is his father."

THE WICKED WILL TEST THE
RIGHTEOUS MAN'S CLAIM TO BE GOD'S SON

[17]"Let us see if his words are true,
and let us test what will happen at the end of his life;
[18]For if the righteous man is God's son, He will help him,
and he will deliver him from the hand of his adversaries.[f]
[19]Let us test him with insult and torture,
that we may find out how gentle he is
and make trial of his forbearance.
[20]Let us condemn him to a shameful death,
for, according to what he says, he will be protected."

THE AUTHOR'S REFUTATION OF THE
BLIND FOLLY OF THE WICKED

[21]Thus they reasoned, but they were led astray,
for their wickedness blinded them;
[22]and they did not know the secret purposes[g] of God,
nor hope for the wages of holiness
nor discern the prize for blameless souls;[h]
[23]for God created man for incorruption,
and made him in the image of his own eternity;
[24]but through the devil's envy[i] death entered the world,
and those who belong to his party experience it.
3 [1]But the souls of the righteous are in the hand of God,
and no torment will ever touch them.
[2]In the eyes of the foolish they seemed to have died,
and their departure was thought to be an affliction,
[3] and their going from us to be their destruction;[j]
but they are at peace.
[4]For though in the sight of men they were punished,
their hope is full of immortality.
[5]Having been disciplined a little, they will receive great good,
because God tested them and found them worthy of himself;
[6]like gold in the furnace he tried them,
and like a sacrificial burnt offering he accepted them.[k]
[7]In the time of their visitation they will shine forth,[l]
and will run like sparks through the stubble.[m]
[8]They will govern nations and rule over peoples,[n]
and the Lord will reign over them forever.[o]

9Those who trust in him will understand truth,
and the faithful will abide with him in love;
because grace and mercy are upon his chosen ones,
and he watches over his holy ones.

[Now follows a section that exemplifies God's rewards and punishments of the righteous and the sinners (3:10—4:9). Enoch is cited as an example of the righteous one who dies prematurely (4:10–15).[p] The author anticipates the end of his story, when the righteous man will condemn his enemies (4:16–19). Then he describes the dreadful scene.]

THE WICKED ACCLAIM THE EXALTED RIGHTEOUS MAN AS GOD'S SON

4 20They will come with dread when their sins are reckoned up,
and their lawless deeds will convict them to their face.
5 1Then the righteous man will stand with great confidence
in the presence of those who have afflicted him
and those who make light of his labors.[q]
2When they see him they will be shaken with dreadful fear,
and they will be amazed at his unexpected salvation.
3They will speak to one another in repentance,
and in anguish of spirit they will groan and say,[r]
4"This is the man whom we once held in derision[s]
and made a byword of reproach—we fools!
We thought that his life was madness
and that his end was without honor.
5Why has he been numbered among the sons of God?[t]
And why is his lot among the holy ones?"

THE WICKED CONFESS THEIR SIN[u]

6"So it was we who strayed from the way of truth,
and the light of righteousness did not shine on us,
and the sun did not rise upon us.
7We took our fill of the paths of lawlessness and destruction,
and we journeyed through trackless deserts,
but the way of the Lord we have not known.
8What has our arrogance profited us?
And what good has our boasted wealth brought us?"

a. A quotation of Isa 3:10 LXX.
b. Like the wise sages in the stories in Dan 1–6.
c. Gk *pais;* it may translate "servant."
d. Cf. Isa 53:2.
e. Perhaps an allusion to religious customs that are the basis for the righteous man's accusations against the wicked; cf. v. 16.
f. Cf. Ps 22:8 and Matt 27:43, which conflates Ps 22:8 and this passage.

g. Gk *mystēria*.

h. Viz., immortality. The wicked deny its possibility.

i. Perhaps an allusion to traditions that attributed the fall of Satan to his envy of Adam; cf., e.g., Life of Adam and Eve 12–17, and see the discussion by David Winston, *The Wisdom of Solomon*, Anchor Bible 43 (Garden City, N.Y.: Doubleday, 1979) 121–22.

j. For the background of this idea of misperception, which runs throughout this passage, cf. Isa 52:13—53:9 and 57:1.

k. Nowhere in his use of Isa 52–53 does this author speak of a vicarious suffering or death; here the language of sacrifice (cf. Isa 53:10) has a totally different function.

l. Cf. Dan 12:3.

m. Cf. Obad 18 and 1 Enoch 48:9.

n. Cf. Dan 7:27.

o. For the parallelism between this and the previous line, cf. Ps. Sol. 17:34 (see below, p. 164): the Messiah is king, but God is his king.

p. The passage is a paraphrase of Isa 57:1.

q. This whole section and the one that follows it employ the structure of the last servant poem of Second Isaiah: exaltation; reaction; confession. See n. 4.

r. Hereafter begins the second speech of the wicked, in which, point by point, they rescind the claims made in their first speech.

s. Cf. Isa 53:2–4.

t. The sons of God and the holy ones are the angelic court. His presence among them vindicates his claim to be son of God.

u. This confession of sin is based on Isa 53:6; cf. also Sib. Or. 3:721 (above, p. 75).

The speech ends as the wicked anticipate their annihilation (5:9–14). Different from their opinion in their first speech, it is not an extinction that comes naturally with death, but a punishment that comes to them, ironically, because they have believed in such an extinction and have acted accordingly.

For "Solomon," "death" and "immortality" do not come at the end of one's life. Death is that state in which the wicked live here and now—the end of which is extinction. Eternal life is already the possession of the righteous, whose immortal soul will survive what *appears to be* their death (3:1–2). For them there is no need for a resurrection.

2 Maccabees 7

Second Maccabees structures Maccabean history according to the scheme of Deuteronomy 28ff. (see above, p. 127). The persecution by Antiochus IV was divine punishment for the sin of Hellenization. The death of the righteous was a turning point that catalyzed God's judgment, bringing victory to the forces of Judas Maccabeus and punishment to Antiochus.[6]

The story of the martyrdom of seven brothers and their mother encapsules the theological tension between interpreting the persecution as a just punishment for the sins of the nation and as unjust punishment of the righteous, who die rather than apostasize. The story is structured around speeches by each of the brothers and their mother which carry these themes.

1 It happened also that seven brothers and their mother were arrested and were being compelled by the king,[a] under torture with whips and cords, to partake of unlawful swine's flesh.

THE FIRST BROTHER
WE OBEY IN ANTICIPATION OF GOD'S MERCY

[2]One of them, acting as their spokesman, said, "What do you intend to ask and learn from us? For we are ready to die rather than transgress the laws of our fathers."[b]

[3]The king fell into a rage, and gave orders that pans and caldrons be heated. [4]These were heated immediately, and he commanded that the tongue of their spokesman be cut out and that they scalp him and cut off his hands and feet, while the rest of the brothers and the mother looked on. [5]When he was utterly helpless, the king ordered them to take him to the fire, still breathing, and to fry him in a pan. The smoke from the pan spread widely, but the brothers and their mother encouraged one another to die nobly, saying, [6]"The Lord God is watching over us and in truth has compassion on us, as Moses declared in his song which bore witness against the people to their faces, when he said, 'And he will have compassion on his servants.' "[c]

THE SECOND, THIRD, AND FOURTH BROTHERS
OUR DEATH FOR THE TORAH WILL BE VINDICATED IN THE RESURRECTION

[7]After the first brother had died in this way, they brought forward the second for their sport. They tore off the skin of his head with the hair and asked him, "Will you eat rather than have your body punished limb by limb?" [8]He replied in the language of his fathers and said to them, "No." Therefore he in turn underwent tortures as the first brother had done. [9]And when he was at his last breath, he said, "You accursed wretch, you dismiss us from this present life, but the King of the universe will raise us up to an everlasting renewal of life because we have died for his laws."[d]

[10]After him the third was the victim of their sport. When it was demanded, he quickly put out his tongue and courageously stretched

forth his hands [11]and said nobly, "I got these from Heaven, and because of his laws I disdain them, and from him I hope to get them back again."[e] [12]As a result the king himself and those with him were astonished[f] at the young man's spirit, for he regarded his sufferings as nothing.

[13]When he too had died, they maltreated and tortured the fourth in the same way. [14]And when he was near death, he said, "One cannot but choose to die at the hands of men and to cherish the hope that God gives of being raised again by him. But for you there will be no resurrection to life!"

THE FIFTH AND SIXTH BROTHERS

WE ARE PUNISHED FOR OUR SINS, BUT GOD WILL PUNISH ANTIOCHUS

[15]Next they brought forward the fifth and maltreated him. [16]But he looked at the king and said, "Because you have authority among men, mortal though you are, you do what you please. But do not think that God has forsaken our people. [17]Keep on, and see how his mighty power will torture you and your descendants!"[g]

[18]After him they brought forward the sixth. And when he was about to die he said, "Do not deceive yourself in vain. For we are suffering these things on our own account, because of our sins against our own God. Therefore astounding things have happened. [19]But do not think that you will go unpunished for having tried to fight against God!"[h]

THE MOTHER TO HER LAST SON

OBEY, FOR THE CREATOR WILL GIVE YOU NEW LIFE IN THE RESURRECTION

[20]The mother was especially admirable and worthy of honorable memory. Though she saw her seven sons perish within a single day, she bore it with good courage because of her hope in the Lord. [21]She encouraged each of them in the language of their fathers. Filled with a noble spirit, she fired her woman's reasoning with a man's courage and said to them,[i] [22]"I do not know how you came into being in my womb. It was not I who gave you life and breath, nor I who set in order the elements within each of you. [23]Therefore the Creator of the world, who shaped the beginning of man and devised the origin of all things, will in his mercy give life and breath back to you again, since you now forget yourselves for the sake of his laws."

[24]Antiochus felt that he was being treated with contempt, and he was suspicious of her reproachful tone. The youngest brother being still alive, Antiochus not only appealed to him in words but promised with oaths that he would make him rich and enviable if he would turn from

the ways of his fathers and that he would take him for his friend and entrust him with public affairs. [25]Since the young man would not listen to him at all, the king called the mother to him and urged her to advise the youth to save himself. [26]After much urging on his part, she undertook to persuade her son. [27]But, leaning close to him, she spoke in their native tongue as follows, deriding the cruel tyrant: "My son, have pity on me. I carried you nine months in my womb and nursed you for three years, and have reared you and brought you up to this point in your life, and have taken care of you. [28]I beseech you, my child, to look at the heaven and the earth and see everything that is in them, and recognize that God did not make them out of things that existed. Thus also mankind comes into being. [29]Do not fear this butcher, but prove worthy of your brothers. Accept death, so that in God's mercy I may get you back again with your brothers."[j]

THE SEVENTH BROTHER
WE APPEAL FOR DIVINE JUDGMENT

[30]While she was still speaking, the young man said, "What are you waiting for? I will not obey the king's command, but I obey the command of the law that was given to our fathers through Moses. [31]But you who have contrived all sorts of evil against the Hebrews will certainly not escape the hands of God.[k] [32]For we are suffering because of our own sins. [33]And if our living Lord is angry for a little while, to rebuke and discipline us, he will again be reconciled with his own servants.[l] [34]But you, unholy wretch, you most defiled of all men, do not be elated in vain and puffed up by uncertain hopes when you raise your hand against the children[m] of heaven. [35]You have not yet escaped the judgment of the almighty, all-seeing God.[n] [36]For our brothers after enduring a brief suffering have drunk[o] of everflowing life under God's covenant; but you, by the judgment of God, will receive just punishment for your arrogance. [37]I, like my brothers, give up body and life for the laws of our fathers, appealing to God to show mercy soon to our nation and by afflictions and plagues to make you confess that he alone is God,[p] [38]and through me and my brothers to bring to an end the wrath of the Almighty which has justly fallen on our whole nation."

[39]The king fell into a rage and handled him worse than the others, being exasperated at his scorn. [40]So he died in his integrity, putting his whole trust in the Lord.

[41]Last of all, the mother died, after her sons.

a. I.e., Antiochus Epiphanes.
b. Cf. the statements of Taxo and Mattathias in T. Mos. 9:6 and 1 Macc 2:20.

    c. A quotation of Deut 32:43, which describes the coming of salvation, the end of the historical scheme.

    d. Because they have disobeyed the law, Antiochus condemns the brothers. The *great* King, however, will reverse this decision in his court, thus vindicating the brothers' obedience of his Law.

    e. Cf. also vv. 23, 27.

    f. Cf. Isa 52:14. The same motif appears in the New Testament passion narratives. See below, pp. 150–51.

    g. See below, n. *p.*

    h. Cf. Acts 5:39 and Gamaliel's warning that persecution of the disciples might constitute fighting against God.

    i. The imagery here may have been influenced by 1 Sam 2:5–8. A later Jewish writer, Yosippon, gives the mother the name of Hannah and has her quote the Song of Hannah.

    j. Cf. the language of Mother Zion and her sons in Isa 49:14–23; 54:1ff.; 60:4–9; and the parallel interpretation of that imagery in Bar 4:19–23.

    k. Cf. Deut 32:39.

    l. The interpretation of suffering as temporary discipline is a popular one in Judaism and in the New Testament. Cf., e.g., Ps. Sol. 3:4, below, p. 141.

    m. Or "servants"; cf. Wis 2:13 for the same ambiguity in an interpretation of Isa 52–53.

    n. God's ability to see all is often mentioned in contexts that speak of him as judge.

    o. Emending *peptōkasi* ("have fallen") to *pepōkasi* ("have drunk").

    p. Cf. chap. 9, which describes this punishment and confession by Antiochus.

Resurrection of the body is a corollary of this author's view that divine judgment involves appropriate compensation (cf., e.g., 2 Macc 4:26, 38, 42; 5:9–10). Thus, in order to vindicate his servants, God will restore to them the lives and limbs that they lost in his service (vv. 9, 10, 23, 24). In his theology of resurrection, this author reinterprets three images that Second Isaiah used to describe Israel's salvation, the return from exile.[7] The brothers are the suffering but vindicated servants of the Lord. In the resurrection the Creator redeems them. Their mother is depicted as Mother Zion who looks forward to receiving back her dispersed children.

GOD'S JUDGMENT AS
REWARD AND PUNISHMENT

We began this chapter by noting the covenantal context within which God rewarded faithfulness and punished disobedience. However, most of our earliest texts, spawned in response to Antiochus's persecution, had to deal with the evident contradiction of the innocent suffering and death of the righteous. Thus God's judgment functioned to vindicate or punish hitherto unrequited pious behavior or apostasy. Of necessity, such judgment took place after death.

Nevertheless, the theme of covenantal rewards and punishments, apart from the problem of persecution, is a constitutive part of the literature of this period.

Tobit 4:5–11

The Book of Tobit was composed some time before Antiochus's persecution. In the present text, Tobit gives his son, Tobias, a bit of paternal advice, exhorting him to pious conduct, with the assurance that piety has its rewards. Particularly noteworthy is the virtue of generosity and the practice of almsgiving, which carry with them the assurance of God's generosity in judgment. Such reward is dispensed in this life, as Tobit himself experiences after some suffering.

5 Remember the Lord our God all your days, my son,
　　and refuse to sin or to transgress his commandments.
　Live uprightly all the days of your life,
　　and do not walk in the ways of wrongdoing.
　[6]For if you do what is true,
　　your ways will prosper through your deeds.
　[7]Give alms from your possessions to all who live uprightly,
　　and do not let your eye begrudge the gift when you make it.
　Do not turn your face away from any poor man,
　　and the face of God will not be turned away from you.
　[8]If you have many possessions, make your gift from them in proportion;
　　if few, do not be afraid to give according to the little you have.
　[9]So you will be laying up a good treasure for yourself
　　against the day of necessity.[a]
　[10]For charity delivers from death
　　and keeps you from entering the darkness.
　[11]And for all who practice it charity is an excellent offering in the
　　presence of the Most High.

　a. Cf., e.g., Matt 6:19–20; Jas 5:3.

(For a more extensive quotation of the above passage, see above, pp. 91–93.)

Psalms of Solomon 3:3–12

This collection of prayers and hymns from the first century B̶C̶ B.C.E. dwells largely on two subjects: God's judgment of his people's sins through Pompey's conquest of Palestine (see also Ps. Sol. 17, below, pp. 162–66); and the life of piety and its rewards. For the author(s) of the psalms, God enacts his judgment in this life as well as in the hereafter.

A PORTRAYAL OF THE RIGHTEOUS

3 The righteous remember the Lord at all times,
    when they confess and declare the Lord's judgments to be just.
[4]The righteous does not despise the chastisement of the Lord;[a]
    his good pleasure is always before the Lord.
[5]The righteous stumbles and considers the Lord to be just;[b]
    he falls and he looks to see what God will do to him;
    he watches whence his salvation will come.
[6]The faithfulness of the righteous (comes) from God their savior;
    sin upon sin do not lodge in the house of the righteous.[c]
[7]The righteous continually searches his house,
    to remove the iniquity of his transgression.
[8]He makes atonement for (sins of) ignorance through fasting and the
    humiliation of his soul;
    and the Lord cleanses every pious[d] man and his house.

THE SINNERS AND THEIR PUNISHMENT

[9]The sinner stumbles and curses his life.
    the day of his birth and his mother's birthpangs.
[10]He adds sin upon sin in his life;
    he falls—for evil is his fall—and he does not rise again.[e]
[11]The destruction of the sinner is forever;
    and he will not be remembered when the righteous is visited.
[12]This is the lot of the sinners forever.

THE REWARD OF THE RIGHTEOUS

But those who fear the Lord will rise to eternal life;
    and their life will be in the light of the Lord and will never fail.[f]

a. The precise translation is uncertain.
b. Contrast v. 9.
c. Contrast v. 10.
d. The Greek word here (*hosios*) very likely translates the Hebrew, *ḥasid*, although the reference is not certainly to the party of that name (see above, pp. 19–24).
e. A wordplay implying sin as "fall" and reward as resurrection, i.e., "rising up."
f. Cf. Isa 60:19–20.

This psalm is interesting for its portrayals of the lives that lead to reward or punishment. The righteous person is not sinless but is concerned about his conduct and seeks to make atonement for his sins. Intention is important. The righteous person "fears" God and "loves" him and seeks to be faithful to the obligations of the covenant. God deals with such a one gently, "chastening" him so as to call his attention to his sins; and in the end he has mercy, removing the chastisement and not dealing with him in strict justice. The sinner, on the other hand, heaps up sins, with no concern for God's demands or their consequences. Him God will judge in strict justice. He will fall and stay down, while the righteous will rise to eternal life. Thus, resurrection is not recompense for a life unjustly taken, as in the previous texts. It is God's final and full reward for the pious. Whether that reward involves a resurrection *of the body* is not stated.

4 Ezra 7:28–42

Writing around 100 A.D. C.E., the pseudonymous author of 4 Ezra puzzles over the disparity between God's covenantal promises and Zion's devastation at the hands of the Romans in 70 A.D. C.E. The author, recognizing the human propensity to sin, wonders who will be saved. That will be determined on the great day of judgment, when *all* of humanity will be raised from the dead and God will divide between the few righteous and the many wicked, judging them on the basis of the Torah.

28 For my son the Messiah shall be revealed with those who are with him, and those who remain shall rejoice four hundred years. 29And after these years my son the Messiah shall die, and all who draw human breath. 30And the world shall be turned back to primeval silence for seven days, as it was at the first beginning; so that no one shall be left. 31And after seven days the world, which is not yet awake, shall be roused, and that which is corruptible shall perish.
32And the earth shall give up those who are asleep in it,
    and the dust those who dwell silently in it;
    and the chambers shall give up the souls which have been committed
        to them.
33And the Most High shall be revealed upon the seat of judgment,
    and compassion shall pass away,
    and patience shall be withdrawn;
34but only judgment shall remain,
    truth shall stand,
    and faithfulness shall grow strong.

[35]And recompense shall follow,
   and the reward shall be manifested;
righteous deeds shall awake,
   and unrighteous deeds shall not sleep.[a]
[36]Then the pit of torment shall appear,
   and opposite it shall be the place of rest;
and the furnace of hell shall be disclosed,
   and opposite it the paradise of delight.[b]

[37]Then the Most High will say to the nations that have been raised from
      the dead,
   "Look now, and understand whom you have denied,
   whom you have not served,
   whose commandments you have despised!
[38]Look on this side and on that;
   here are delight and rest,
   and there are fire and torments!"

Thus he will speak to them on the day of judgment—
[39]a day that has no sun or moon or stars,
[40]or cloud or thunder or lightning,
   or wind or water or air,
   or darkness or evening or morning,
[41]or summer or spring or heat,
   or winter or frost or cold,
   or hail or rain or dew,
[42]or noon or night or dawn,
   or shining or brightness or light,
   but only the splendor of the glory of the Most High, by which all shall
      see what has been determined for them.[c]

a. Here the testimonies of righteous and unrighteous deeds function as defense
and prosecuting attorneys.

b. God's throne appears to be placed between the two gates that lead to paradise
and hell. Cf. T. Abr. 12, below, p. 144.

c. Cf. n. f on Ps. Sol. 3, above, p. 141. Perhaps the cancellation of the times and
seasons is a reversal of Gen 1:14 and alludes to the creation of a new world order.

This passage is noteworthy because it combines two originally separate eschatological scenarios. In the first, to which the author will
return in chapters 11–13, the Davidic Messiah was the principal agent
of judgment. According to the second, God himself is the judge who
dispenses rewards and punishments. In combining these es-
chatologies, the author posits a temporary messianic reign, after

which the Messiah, like the rest of humanity, must die and await the resurrection.

Testament of Abraham 12–14

When Abraham is taken on a low-altitude chariot ride across the face of the earth, he directs Michael, his angelic guide, to strike dead a number of people whom he catches in the act of gross sin. Such summary execution eliminates the possibility that the sinners can repent and be saved, and so God summons Abraham to the heavenly courtroom for a lesson in justice and mercy.

The judgment scene in chapters 12–14 is the most elaborate in our literature and contains a number of unique features. The judge is Adam's son Abel.[8] Perhaps this is reminiscent of the idea of the persecuted righteous one acting as judge (cf. Wis 5). Salvation or damnation depends on the balance between good and evil deeds. Although "weighing" is a frequent metaphor for judging in Jewish literature, this is perhaps the earliest text to incorporate a precise balancing of deeds into the eschatological scenario. The imagery may reflect pagan Egyptian ideas.

THE TWO GATES

12 Behold, two angels of fiery appearance and pitiless mind and severe glance . . . , and they were driving tens of thousands of souls without mercy, striking them with fiery whips. The angel seized hold of one soul. And they drove all the souls into the wide gate to destruction.[a] Then we too followed the angels and we came inside that wide gate.

ABRAHAM'S VISION OF THE
JUDGMENT SCENE

Between the gates there stood a fearsome throne which looked like awesome crystal, flashing lightning like fire. And upon it was seated a wondrous man looking like the sun, like a son of God. Before him there stood a crystalline table, all of gold and byssus. Upon the table lay a book six cubits thick and ten cubits broad. On its right and on its left stood two angels holding parchment and ink and a pen. Before the table sat a luminous angel, holding a scale in his hand. At his left hand there sat a fiery angel altogether merciless and severe, holding a trumpet in his hand, holding within it all-consuming fire for the testing of the sinners.

And the wondrous man who sat upon the throne was himself judging and sentencing the souls. The two angels at the right and at the left were recording. The one on the right was recording the righteous deeds, the one on the left the sins, and the one who was before the table who was holding the scale was weighing the souls, and the fiery angel who was holding in the fire was testing the souls.

ABRAHAM'S QUESTION AND
MICHAEL'S EXPLANATION

Then Abraham asked the Archistrategos Michael, "What are these things that we see?"

And the Archistrategos said, "These things that you see, O holy Abraham, are judgment and recompense."

THE VISION CONTINUED

THE JUDGMENT OF THE ONE SOUL
IS DEFERRED

And behold, the angel who was holding the soul in his hand brought it before the judge, and the judge said to one of the angels who were attending him, "Open this book for me and find me the sins of this soul."

And he opened the book and he found that its sins and righteous deeds were equally balanced, and he delivered it neither to the tormentors nor to those who were saved, but set it in the middle.

ABRAHAM'S QUESTION AND
MICHAEL'S EXPLANATION

THE IDENTIFICATION OF CHARACTERS
AND THEIR FUNCTIONS

13 Then Abraham said, "My lord Archistrategos, who is this most wondrous judge? Who are the recording angels? Who is the sunlike angel who holds the scales? Who is the fiery angel who holds in the fire?"

The Archistrategos said, "Do you see, holy Abraham, the fearsome man who is sitting on the throne? This is the son of Adam, the first created one, who is called Abel. Him Cain the wicked killed,[b] and he sits here to judge all the creation and to examine righteous and sinners. For this reason God said, 'I do not judge you, but each man shall be judged by a man.'

A DIGRESSION ON THE
THREE JUDGMENTS[c]

"For this reason he gave him the judgment, to judge the world until his great and glorious appearance, and then, O righteous Abraham, there will be perfect judgment and recompense, eternal and immutable, which no one can alter. For each man has been born of the first created one, and therefore they first shall be judged by his son. And in the second coming every breath and creation shall be judged by the twelve tribes of Israel. The third, they shall be judged by the Master, God of all, and then the end of that judgment is near and the sentence is fearsome and there is none who releases. And then, through three judgment seats shall be the judgment of the world and the recompense. Therefore, a matter shall not finally be decided according to one or two witnesses, but every matter shall be established according to three witnesses."

MICHAEL'S EXPLANATION CONTINUED

"The two angels, the one on the right and the one on the left, these are those who record the sins and the righteous deeds.[d] The one on the right records the righteous deeds, and the one on the left, the sins. The sunlike angel who holds the scale in his hand is the archangel Dokiel, the just scale-bearer, and he weighs the righteous deeds and the sins by means of the righteousness of God. The fiery and pitiless angel who holds fire in his hand is the archangel Puruel, who has power over fire and tests the deeds of men through fire.[e] If the fire burns the deed of a certain man, at once the angel of judgment takes him and leads him away to the place of the wicked, a most bitter house of correction. But if the fire tests the act of a certain man and does not touch it (or: affect it), this man is found righteous and the angel of righteousness takes him and leads him up to salvation in the lot of the righteous. Thus, O most righteous Abraham, all things in all men are tested by fire and scales."

ABRAHAM'S QUESTION AND
MICHAEL'S EXPLANATION

THE ONE SOUL

14 Abraham said to the Archistrategos, "My lord Archistrategos, how was the soul which the angel held in his hand adjudged to the middle?"

The Archistrategos said, "Hear, O righteous Abraham. Because the judge found that its sins and its righteous deeds were equal, and he neither handed it over to judgment nor to salvation, until the time when the judge of all comes."

Abraham said (to) the Archistrategos, "What additional thing is lacking for the soul to be saved?"

The Archistrategos said, "If it could obtain one righteous deed more than its sins, it will go to salvation."

ABRAHAM AND MICHAEL INTERCEDE
FOR THE SOUL

Abraham said to the Archistrategos, "Come, Archistrategos Michael, let us pray on behalf of this soul and let us see if God will hearken to us."

The Archistrategos said, "I agree." And they implored and prayed for the soul, and God heard them; and arising from the prayer, they did not see the soul standing there.

Abraham said to the angel, "Where is the soul which you held in the middle?"

And the angel said, "It was saved by your righteous prayer, and behold, the luminous angel has taken it and brought it up to the garden (paradise)."

a. The imagery here presumes that judgment takes place at the moment of death. The idea that the mass of humanity is going to perdition also occurs in 4 Ezra. For the two gates, cf. Matt 7:13–14. Cf. also Mark 10:23–25.

b. See Gen 4:1–16.

c. This digression divides Michael's interpretation in two and may be a secondary interpolation into the text.

d. On the two witnesses and their functions, see Nickelsburg, *Resurrection*, 39–40.

e. Cf. 1 Cor 3:13–15, which appears to know the tradition recorded here. Cf. also Didache 16:5.

In the Testament of Abraham the function of the weighing scene is not to expound doctrine about how the judgment takes place. Rather, it presents Abraham with the case of the person with equally balanced deeds. This in turn leads Abraham to intercede for the soul. When he sees that his intercession is efficacious, he intercedes for the people he previously struck dead. Thus righteous Abraham is led from self-righteous condemnation of others to compassionate intercession on their behalf. Ironically, what appears to be a legalistic view of God's judgment and justice is really a warning against self-righteousness and an appeal for compassion.

The Rule of the Community 4:2–14

The idea that there are two ways or roads along which one may travel in one's life is an old and common one in the Mediterranean world. In biblical literature these are the ways of "life" and "death." On the one hand, these ways symbolize modes of living, the one according to the will of God, the other in disobedience to his Torah. On the other hand, they are seen as roads leading to (a long) life and blessing or to (a premature) death and a curse. In the great covenantal section at the end of Deuteronomy, Moses summarizes his recitation of the blessings and curses with these words:

. . . I have set before you *life* and *death*, blessing and curse; therefore choose life, that you and your descendants may live (Deut 30:19; cf. Jer 21:8).

The Qumran Rule of the Community speaks of two types of ways, along which people are led by two spirits. It describes the deeds that pertain to these ways and the "visitations" or rewards and punishments that accrue to the travelers along the respective ways. The rewards are granted both in this life and thereafter; the punishments will be inflicted after death. The Qumranites believed that in a real sense they were already participating in eternal life (see below, pp. 149–50). This idea is compatible with the image of the road, which implies continuity and hence the extension of the categories of life and death back into one's present existence.[9]

THE DEEDS OF THE WAYS OF LIFE

4 [2]These are their ways in the world for the enlightenment of the heart of man, and that all the paths of true righteousness may be made straight before him, and that fear of the laws of God may be instilled in his heart: a spirit of humility, patience, abundant charity, unending goodness, understanding, and intelligence; (a spirit of) mighty wisdom which trusts in all the deeds of God and leans on his great lovingkindness; a spirit of discernment in every purpose, of zeal for just laws, of holy intent with steadfastness of heart, of great charity toward all the sons of truth, of admirable purity which detests all unclean idols, of humble conduct sprung from an understanding of all things, and of faithful concealment of the mysteries of truth. These are the counsels of the spirit to the sons of truth in this world.

THE REWARD OF THESE WAYS

[6]And as for the visitation of all who walk in this spirit, it shall be healing, great peace in a long life, and fruitfulness, together with every everlasting blessing and eternal joy in life without end, a crown of glory and a garment of majesty in unending light.

THE DEEDS OF THE WAYS OF DEATH

[9]But the ways of the spirit of falsehood are these: greed, and slackness in the search for righteousness, wickedness and lies, haughtiness and pride, falseness and deceit, cruelty and abundant evil ill-temper and much folly and brazen insolence, abominable deeds (committed) in a spirit of lust, and ways of lewdness in the service of uncleanness, a blaspheming tongue, blindness of eye and dullness of ear, stiffness of neck and heaviness of heart, so that man walks in all the ways of darkness and guile.

THE PUNISHMENT OF THESE WAYS

[12]And the visitation of all who walk in this spirit shall be a multitude of plagues by the hand of all the destroying angels, everlasting damnation

by the avenging wrath of the fury of God, eternal torment and endless disgrace together with shameful extinction in the fire of the dark regions. The times of all their generations shall be spent in sorrowful mourning and in bitter misery and in calamities of darkness until they are destroyed without remnant or survivor.

THE PRESENCE OF ETERNAL LIFE

Hymn Scroll 11:3–14

Among the hymns of thanksgiving in the Qumran Hymn Scroll are several in which the author praises God for having delivered him from the realm of ignorance, death, and damnation and having brought him into the sphere of knowledge, life, and salvation, that is, the sectarian community. The author of the present hymn employs the language of resurrection to describe how he has been "raised from the dust" and made a member of the community that stands with the angels in God's presence. What traditional Jewish eschatology places in the future—or beyond death—the Qumranites ascribe to their present situation, although they still await the final consummation and perfection of their salvation.[10] The author alternates between wonder that God would deal graciously with the lowly sinner and celebration of this remarkable act of grace.

3 I give thanks to you, my God,
 for you have dealt marvelously with dust;
 you have shown your power mightily, mightily in a creature of clay.
 ⁴And I, what am I,
 that you have [taught] me the secret of your truth
 and given me insight into your marvelous deeds?
 And you have put hymns of thanksgiving in my mouth,
 ⁵ [a song of praise] on my tongue. . . .

⁸All chastisements are in your wrath,
 ⁹ but much forgiveness is in your goodness,
 and your mercies are on all who are acceptable to you.
 For you have taught them the secret of your truth,
 ¹⁰ and you have given them insight into your marvelous mysteries.
 And for the sake of your glory you have cleansed man from sin,
 ¹¹that he might be holy for you from all unclean abomination and
 faithless guilt;
 that he might be joined [with] your true sons,

¹²   and in a lot with your holy ones;
    that (you) may raise up the mortal worm from the dust to the secret [of
        your truth]
    and from a perverse spirit to [your] understanding;
¹³and that he may be stationed in his position before you
    with the everlasting host and the spirits [of holiness];
¹⁴that he may be renewed with all that will be,
    and with those who know in a community of joy.

PARALLELS AND DEVELOPMENTS

The New Testament

JESUS, THE PERSECUTED AND VINDICATED RIGHTEOUS ONE

The two central and controlling facts of life for the earliest Christian community were: (a) the belief that God had delivered Jesus of Nazareth from his death on the cross and exalted him to a high status in heaven; and (b) the belief that the gift of God's Spirit to his church was a guarantee that God had brought near the judgment and the new age through the death and resurrection of Jesus.

If the church believed that Jesus had been raised from the dead, they also felt the need to explain that death. Such explanations are evident already in the church's earliest credal formulations, which are embedded in the letters of the apostle Paul. In some cases the crucifixion is understood as God's means of dealing with sin. "He died for our sins" (see, e.g., Rom 4:25; 1 Cor 15:3). Thus Jesus' death is construed positively. In other cases, however, his death is that evil deed from which God delivered him by means of the resurrection. God "raised him *from the dead*" (Rom 10:9). Here the death and resurrection are interpreted according to the Jewish pattern of the persecution and vindication of the righteous one. Most often the focus is not on the death as persecution but on the resurrection as deliverance and vindication. However, in the Book of Acts, whose author holds considerable brief against "the Jews" for troubling the church, the theme of persecution and vindication is frequent and formulaic (see, e.g., Acts 2:23–24, 36; 3:15; 4:10–11).

Scholars have long noted that language from the last servant poem of Second Isaiah (Isa 52:13—53:12) has influenced New Testament language about Jesus. This fact is to be explained at least partly by the earlier Jewish usage of this biblical passage in material about the persecution and vindication and exaltation of the righteous one (thus, e.g., Wis 2–5). The pattern of suffering and exaltation structures the Christ hymn embedded in Philippians 2:6–11, which reflects the language of the servant poem and probably also its interpretation in Wisdom 2–5 (see below, pp. 187–88).

The theology of persecution and vindication, epitomized in these credal and hymnic formulas, is fleshed out in detail in the passion narratives that form the last chapters of the four Gospels. These narratives are a Christianized version of the old stories of the vindication and exaltation of the persecuted righeous one.[11] Looking at Mark, for example, we find: the conspiracy (11:18; 14:1); the trial and accusations (14:55–64; 15:2–15); the death as an ordeal (15:26–32); the vindication (15:38–39). At stake are several things: Jesus' (alleged) words against the temple; his claim to be Son of God; his alleged status as "Christ," "the king of Israel (or: the Jews)." Remarkably the vindication comes at the moment of his death, when the centurion utters a confession parallel to that of the enemies in Wisdom of Solomon 5:4. In any event, Mark surely sees Jesus' resurrection as the vindication of his claims. Within these Gospel accounts, which are structured like the old Jewish stories, are many allusions to or quotations from the biblical psalms about the vindication and exaltation of the persecuted or suffering righteous one (e.g., Mark 15:24, 34, 36; cf. Ps 22:18, 1; 69:21). In proclaiming Jesus to be Messiah and Lord, the church had to deal with the embarrassing fact of his execution by the Romans (cf. 1 Cor 1:23–24). In order to do so, they borrowed the ready-made categories that the Jewish community had created and re-formed many times to speak to their own circumstances of persecution and oppression.

THE RESURRECTION AND JUDGMENT OF CHRISTIANS

The resurrection of Jesus implies the coming resurrection of the Christians. The connection is explicit, for example, in Romans 8:11 and in great detail in 1 Corinthians 15. In the New Testament apocalypse, the Book of Revelation, the general resurrection is both the vindication of the martyrs and the occasion for the final judgment. Revelation 20–22 is indebted at many points to the language and ideas of such Jewish works as Daniel 7 and 12, but also to earlier biblical works on which these and other Jewish works are based (see the notes on p. 84).

The theme that one is to be judged according to one's deeds is far more frequent in the New Testament than many Christians recognize. The idea is explicit in the parable of the great judgment in Matthew 25:31–46 (see below, pp. 195–96). For the apostle Paul, one is made right with God ("justified") by the grace of God, which is appropriated through faith. Nonetheless, one can annul this relationship by a life of deeds that contradict it. Thus Paul speaks of a judgment according to one's deeds in Romans 2:5–8 and in 2 Corinthians 5:10. In Galatians 5:16—6:8 (see above, pp. 111–12), he employs the language and categories of the two ways (see above, pp. 147–49). Corresponding to the two Spirits of Qumran are Sin, which is resident in the flesh, and the Spirit of God (or Christ), which is resident in the human spirit. The two are locked in a mortal combat (5:17). The deeds (*or* fruits) of the two ways in which one "walks" are enumerated, and the apostle indicates that the life according to the flesh leads to eternal corruption, while the life according to the Spirit will bring eternal life. The same pattern appears to stand behind Paul's language in Romans 5–8.

THE PRESENCE OF ETERNAL LIFE

The Qumranic idea that one participates in eternal life already in the present time is central to the theology of the Gospel according to John. One who believes already *has* eternal life (3:36) and "has passed from death to life" (5:24). The one who does not believe "is already condemned" (3:18). In comparison with this heavy emphasis on the present experience of eternal life (and of Jesus' return already now in the Spirit), Johannine references to a *future* resurrection and judgment are few and far between. Although Paul's thought is dominated with the hope of the imminent return of Christ and the resurrection and judgment, he too can speak of the presence of eternal life, albeit in a muted way (cf. Rom 6:11–14, within the context of the two ways idea; cf. 5:18). Paul's restrained use of this theological conception probably reflects his dealings with people whose experience of the Spirit led them to suppose that the end had already arrived. Thus in 1 Corinthians 15 his repetition of those events that must yet precede the end (vv. 23–28) and his insistence that "flesh and blood" must be transformed before it can inherit the kingdom of heaven (vv. 42–54) are probably directed against people who supposed that they "already reigned" (1 Cor 4:8). Second Thessalonians 2 contains a similar restraining argument against people who claimed that "the day of the Lord has come."

Rabbinic Literature

God's role as judge was central to the theology of the rabbis, as it had been for the theology of their predecessors. In the view of some, judgment awaited God's people *individually* after death. On the other hand, the rabbinic writings are replete with references to the resurrection of the dead and the dispensing of final reward and punishment. Moreover, although the writing of full-blown apocalypses seems to have diminished sharply around the end of the first century C.E., the rabbinic literature offers ample evidence that eschatological scenarios were still a part of the Jewish religious tradition. As we have seen (above, pp. 85–87), the restoration of the temple remained a living hope. Similarly, the expectation of the Messiah(s), especially the Davidic Messiah, was reaffirmed, and some rabbis speculated on the time of his appearance and the length of his reign (see below, pp. 196–99). Along with the resurrection, Jewish prayer continued, and continues, to express belief in the final triumph of God and the annihilation of evil.

Babylonian Talmud *Berakot* 28b

According to this story, when Rabbi Joḥanan ben Zakkai anticipates judgment after death he presumes the idea that there are two ways leading to paradise and Gehinnom (see 4 Ezra 7:36, above, p. 143; T. Abr. 12, above, pp. 144–45). As in the Testament of Abraham, judgment takes place immediately after death.

When Rabban Joḥanan ben Zakkai fell ill, his disciples went in to visit him. When he saw them he began to weep. His disciples said to him, "Lamp of Israel, pillar of the right hand, mighty hammer! Why do you weep?"

He replied, "If I were being taken today before a human king who is here today and tomorrow in the grave, whose anger if he is angry with me does not last forever, who if he imprisons me does not imprison me forever, and who if he puts me to death does not put me to everlasting death, and whom I can appease with words and bribe with money, even so I would weep. Now that I am being taken before the supreme King of kings, the Holy One, blessed be he, who lives and endures forever and ever, whose anger if he is angry with me is an everlasting anger, who if he imprisons me imprisons me forever, who if he puts me to death puts me to death forever, and whom I cannot appease with words or bribe with money—nay more, when there are two ways before me, one leading to paradise and the other to Gehinnom, and I do not know by which I shall be taken, shall I not weep?"

Although Johanan was a great leader and teacher of Israel (as emphasized here by the titles with which he is addressed), whose decisions were viewed as the definition of God's will for his people, this remarkable anecdote portrays him as a mortal before his God, all too aware of his own personal shortcomings—for which God the judge could hold him responsible.[12]

Tosefta *Sanhedrin* 13:3–5[13]

Although it appears to have been axiomatic for the rabbis that "all Israel has a share in the world to come" (M. *Sanhedrin* 10:1), exceptions were enumerated. The present excerpt is part of a lengthy enumeration of both Israelites and Gentiles who would be damned because of gross sin.

Paragraph 3 contrasts the stricter and more liberal viewpoints of the followers of Shammai and Hillel, and as such the passage is an artificial construct. Nonetheless, the reference to three groups and the evident references to a kind of weighing process in the judgment suggest a common imagery reminiscent of the judgment scene in the Testament of Abraham (see above, pp. 144–47).

3 The house of Shammai says,[a] "There are three classes (of people). One is (destined) 'for eternal life' and one 'for shame, for eternal contempt' (Dan 12:2). One for eternal life—these are the perfectly righteous. One for shame, for eternal contempt—these are the perfectly wicked. Those who are equally righteous and wicked descend to Gehinnom[b] and are singed[c] and (later) come up from there and are healed; for it says, 'And I will put this third into the fire and refine them as one refines silver and test them as one tests gold. He will call on my name, and I will be his God' (Zech 13:9).[d] Concerning them Hannah said, 'The Lord kills and brings to life; he brings down to Sheol and raises up'" (1 Sam 2:6).[e]

But the house of Hillel says, "'He who is great in mercy' (Exod 34:6) inclines (the scale) toward mercy."[f] Concerning them, David says, 'I love (the Lord) because he has heard (my voice)' (Ps 116:1). . . .

[4]Those Israelites who have transgressed with their body[g] and those of the nations of the world who have transgressed with their body descend to Gehinnom and are punished there for twelve months, and after the twelve months, their souls perish and their body is burned;[h] Gehinnom spews them out, and they become ashes, and the wind scatters and disperses them under the soles of the feet of the righteous; for it says, "'You will tread down the wicked, for they will be ashes under the soles

of the feet of the righteous on the day when I act,' says the Lord of hosts"
(Mal 4:3 [in the Hebrew 3:21]).[i]

[5]But the heretics[j] and the apostates and the traitors and the Epicureans[k] and those who deny the Torah and those who depart from the
ways of the community and those who deny the resurrection of the dead[l]
and everyone who has sinned or caused the multitude to sin,[m] such as
Jeroboam and Ahab, and those "who have spread their terror in the
land of the living" (Ezek 32:23)[n] and those who have stretched out their
hands against *zebul* (the temple)[o]—against them Gehinnom will be
closed, and they will be punished there for all generations; for it says,
"And they shall go forth and look at the dead bodies of the men that have
rebelled against me; for their worm shall not die, and their fire shall not
be quenched, and they shall be an object of contempt to all flesh" (Isa
66:24).[p]

a. The "houses of Shammai and Hillel" represent differing traditions of interpretation of the Torah associated with the first century B.C.E. rabbis Shammai and Hillel.
Their opposing opinions, often strict as opposed to liberal, are frequently juxtaposed
in rabbinic literature.

b. Gehinnom, "the valley of (the sons of) Hinnom," skirts the west and south sides
of Jerusalem. The point of its junction with the Kidron valley, southeast of Jerusalem,
was the place where sacrifices were offered to the god Molech, and the sight of the
fires there may be related to the tradition that this would be the place of punishment.
The idea is mentioned in Isa 66:24 (see below in this passage) and is expanded in 1
Enoch 27. Eventually Gehinnom, or Gehenna (often translated "hell" in English
Bibles), comes to be thought of as a subterranean place of eternal punishment,
doubtless reflecting the Greek idea of Tartarus.

c. The meaning is uncertain; some scholars translate "squeal."

d. This foreshadows the later medieval idea of purgatory, which was often substan-
tiated by reference to 2 Macc 12:39–45, according to which Judas Maccabeus prays
that certain of his men who had died in sin might be forgiven and be enabled to
participate in the resurrection. Since the present passage quotes the last sentence of
Zech 13:9, the author may believe that intercessory prayer or the prayer of those
being purged helps to effect their ascent from Gehinnom.

e. A quotation from the prayer of Hannah, the mother of Samuel. See above, p. 139,
n. *i.*

f. If this interpretation is correct, we appear to have a parallel in a Coptic Enochic
writing in which an unidentified figure places his staff on one of the pans of the
balance when the weight of evil deeds inclines it toward damnation; see Birger A.
Pearson, "The Pierpont Morgan Fragments of a Coptic Enoch Apocryphon," in *Studies on the Testament of Abraham,* ed. George W. E. Nickelsburg, SBLSCS 6 (Missoula:
Scholars Press, 1976) 275. This theme is often represented in art, in paintings of the last
judgment.

g. Probably a reference to sexual sins. In making reference to certain Israelites and
Gentiles who will be punished, this paragraph implies that not all Gentiles will be
damned.

h. For a different kind of calculation about the time of certain punishments after
death, cf. 4 Ezra 7:78–87.

i. The wording of Malachi is slightly altered to fit its usage in the context here.

j. Heb *minim*—a word whose precise referent is debated.

k. The Epicureans believed that the body was composed of atoms, which were dispersed at the time of death. Suitably those who deny existence after death are denied participation in the resurrection. For a similar idea, cf. Wis 2–5, discussed above, pp. 132–35; and 1 Enoch 102:4—103:8.

l. The principle is the same as that described in the previous note.

m. Cf. the similar expression "those who lead many astray," found in the Qumran literature and the apocalypses in the synoptic Gospels.

n. A reference to tyrants. See Børge Salomonsen, *Die Tosefta: Seder IV: Nezikin, 3: Sanhedrin—Makkot* (Stuttgart: Kohlhammer, 1976) 207, n. 48.

o. The identification of *zebul* as the temple is made explicit at the end of para. 5, not quoted here. In 1 Macc 7:47, 2 Macc 14:33, and 15:32, Nicanor stretches out his hand against the temple. He is killed in battle, and the transgressing limb is amputated and displayed in public.

p. Our earliest reference to the valley of Hinnom as the place of punishment (see above, n. *b*). The Hebrew for "object of contempt" occurs in only one other place in the Bible—Dan 12:2, quoted at the beginning of this passage, which is undoubtedly alluding to Isa 66:24.

Although this passage indulges in some of the speculation about the process and nature of post-mortem judgment that we have seen in earlier texts, in one respect it is distinct. Its assertions are explicitly anchored in Scripture and employ its phraseology. This is typical of rabbinic writing and reflects the developing authority of the ancient writings as Scripture.[14]

The *Amida* for New Year, Petition 3

In keeping with the theme of Rosh Hashana, this petition of the festival prayer anticipates the time when God will make all things new. God's kingly power will be finally and fully evident. As judge he will vindicate his people and annihilate evil. His promised Messiah will appear, and his glorious presence will again dwell in Zion.

Therefore place the fear of you, O Lord our God, upon all your works, and the awe of you upon all that you have created. That all your works may revere you and all your creatures prostrate themselves before you,[a] that they may all be made a single company, to do your will with a perfect heart. Even as we know,[b] O Lord our God, that dominion is in your presence, power is in your hand, and might is in your right hand, and your name is to be revered above all that you have created.

Therefore give glory, O Lord, to your people, praise to them that revere you, hope to them that seek you, and confidence to them that wait for you, joy to your land and rejoicing to your city, burgeoning of strength for David your servant and the preparing of a lamp for the son of Jesse your anointed,[c] speedily in our days.[d]

Then the righteous will see and be glad, and the upright will exult, and the pious will rejoice greatly. Iniquity will close her mouth,[e] and all wickedness will wholly vanish like smoke,[f] when you cause the dominion of insolence to pass away from the earth.

Then, O Lord, you will reign alone over all your works on Mount Zion, the dwelling place of your glory,[g] and in Jerusalem, your holy city, as it is written in your holy words, "The Lord your God will reign forever, O Zion, for all generations. Praise the Lord!"[h]

a. The prayer anticipates the time when all humanity—all that God has created—will worship him. Cf. 1 Enoch 10:21; 91:14; and the biblical antecedents for this idea, e.g., in Isa 60:1–14.

b. The rest of humanity will join with Israel, which already acknowledges the sovereignty of God.

c. A clear allusion to v. 17 of the royal Psalm 132. "Anointed" translates Heb *mashiah,*there the reigning king, here the awaited "Messiah."

d. For a similar idea, cf. Ps. Sol. 17:44, below, p. 165.

e. This complements the previous petition, which speaks of the confidence, lit. the "opening of the mouth" of God's people in the end-time.

f. The annihilation of evil is a common apocalyptic idea. Cf. 1 Enoch 10:16, 20–22; 1QS 4:20–23.

g. An allusion to Mic 4:7. For the motif of the renewal of Zion, see also above, p. 86.

h. Ps 146:10.

This passage is especially worth noting for the universality of its vision. The petition harks back to old Jewish liturgical usage, which is also pithily expressed in the prayer of Jesus in Matthew 6:10.[15] The ultimate and complete triumph of God anticipated in the Rosh Hashana liturgy here is consonant with the viewpoint of the classic apocalyptic literature.

NOTES

1. Two of the earlier stories depicted the deliverance of Daniel and his friends, who chose to go to their deaths rather than disobey their God (chaps. 3 and 6, below, pp. 131–32).

2. On this dating and the later revision of the book during the time of the Herods, see George W. E. Nickelsburg, *Resurrection, Immortality, and Eternal Life in Intertestamental Judaism,* 43–45; and the papers by John J. Collins, George W. E. Nickelsburg, and Jonathan A. Goldstein in *Studies on the Testament of Moses,* ed. G. W. E. Nickelsburg, SBLSCS 4 (Cambridge: Society of Biblical Literature, 1973) 15–52.

3. On this scheme of sin, punishment, repentance, and salvation and its background in Deuteronomy, see George W. E. Nickelsburg, *Jewish Literature Between the Bible and the Mishnah* (Philadelphia: Fortress, 1981) 80–81.

4. Here the author draws on an older tradition that appears to be reflected also in Dan 12:3 and its context. For details, see George W. E. Nickelsburg, *Resurrection*, 62–65.

5. In these and the verses that follow, the wicked express themselves in language used by some Greek philosophers, but the combination of motifs also has parallels in the Book of Ecclesiastes.

6. On the relationship of this story to T. Mos. 9 and to the story of Mattathias's revolt in 1 Macc 2, see Nickelsburg, *Resurrection*, 97–102.

7. For details, see ibid., 102–8.

8. There may be some connection between this judgment scene and that described in the Parables of Enoch (see below, Chapter 5), where a "son of man" (in Hebrew, Adam means "man") sits on a glorious throne judging. On this and the text as a whole, see George W. E. Nickelsburg, "Eschatology in the Testament of Abraham," in *Studies on the Testament of Abraham*, ed. G. W. E. Nickelsburg, SBLSCS 6 (Missoula: Scholars Press, 1976) 23–63.

9. Catechetical traditions based on the imagery of the two ways and connected with the tradition found in The Rule of the Community are found also in early Christian literature. Cf. Didache 1–6, Barnabas 18–20, and the Mandates in the Shepherd of Hermas. On their relationship to The Rule of the Community, see J. P. Audet, "Affinités littéraires et doctrinales du 'Manuel de Discipline,'" *RB* 59 (1952) 219–38; 60 (1953) 41–82.

10. See Nickelsburg, *Resurrection*, 152–56.

11. See George W. E. Nickelsburg, "The Genre and Function of the Markan Passion Narrative," *HTR* 73 (1980) 153–84.

12. See E. P. Sanders, *Paul and Palestinian Judaism*, 223–33.

13. The translation and commentary here are indebted to Børge Salomonsen, *Die Tosefta: Seder IV: Nezikin, 3: Sanhedrin—Makkot* (Stuttgart: Kohlhammer, 1976) 204–9.

14. The same practice is evident at many points in the New Testament, especially in the Gospels and the Epistle to the Hebrews.

15. "Your kingdom come, your will be done, on earth as it is in heaven." For a detailed discussion of this subject see Jakob J. Petuchowski and Michael Brocke, *The Lord's Prayer and Jewish Liturgy* (New York: Seabury, 1978).

BIBLIOGRAPHY

PRIMARY SOURCES

The Bible (except for Dan 12) and the Apocrypha (including 4 Ezra) are quoted from the RSV, with some revision; Jubilees and the Testament of Moses from *APOT*, vol. 2, with some revision and adaptation; the Testament of Abraham from Michael E. **Stone,** *The Testament of Abraham* (Missoula: Society of Biblical Literature, 1972); The Rule of the Community from Geza **Vermes,** *The Dead Sea Scrolls in English*, 2d ed. (Harmondsworth: Penguin, 1975); the Hymn Scroll from George W. E. **Nickelsburg,** *Resurrection, Immortality, and Eternal Life in Intertestamental Judaism*, Harvard Theological Studies 26 (Cambridge: Harvard University Press, 1972) 154–55; the Babylonian Talmud *Berakot* from I. **Epstein,** *The Babylonian Talmud: Seder Zera'im* (London: Soncino, 1948).

SECONDARY SOURCES

George W. E. **Nickelsburg,** *Resurrection, Immortality, and Eternal Life In Intertestamental Judaism,* Harvard Theological Studies 26 (Cambridge: Harvard University Press, 1972), a fuller discussion of the topic and texts treated in this chapter. E. P. **Sanders,** *Paul and Palestinian Judaism* (Philadelphia: Fortress, 1977), an extensive treatment of the relationship to covenant and Torah. Klaus **Koch,** *The Rediscovery of Apocalyptic,* Studies in Biblical Theology, 2:22 (Naperville: Allenson, 1972), highly influential in the recent discussion. John J. **Collins,** "The Apocalyptic Literature," in *Early Judaism and Modern Research,* ed. Robert A. Kraft and George W. E. Nickelsburg (Philadelphia: Fortress; Chico, Calif.: Scholars Press, forthcoming), critical evaluation of the modern discussion of apocalyptic thought and literature, copious bibliography. Michael E. **Stone,** "Apocalyptic Literature," in Compendia Rerum Iudaicarum ad Novum Testamentum 2:2 (forthcoming).

5
The Agents of
Divine Deliverance

The texts in the previous chapter express a wide variety of Jewish expectations about God's future deliverance and judgment. This variety extends to the agents who will effect this deliverance and judgment: God himself (1 Enoch 1 and T. Mos. 10); the archangel Michael or his unnamed counterpart (Dan 12; T. Mos. 10); the glorified Abel and a number of angelic functionaries (T. Abr. 12–13).

In this chapter we present other texts that focus especially on the agents of deliverance and judgment. The variety evident in Chapter 4 can be seen here also. God's agents may be clearly human, wholly transcendent, or somewhere in between. Their specific functions also vary. They may administer justice, dividing between the righteous and the wicked. They may deliver from one's enemies or conquer Satan. They may preside over God's world after deliverance and judgment have taken place.

HUMAN AGENTS

The Davidic Messiah

The monarchy was an institution of central importance in preexilic Judah. The king was ruler and judge of his people and the nation's defender against its enemies. The office of king belonged to the dynasty founded by David. It was an institution based on an everlasting covenant between God and David and his descendants (2 Sam 7:8–16; 23:5; Ps 89:3–4). The king was God's "Anointed One" (Heb *mashiaḥ;* 1 Sam 2:10), his vice-regent, executing and enacting his reign (or "kingdom") not only among his people but also over the nations (Ps 2). As such he shared in certain divine qualities and characteristics. All this was recited, proclaimed, and celebrated in such prophetic oracles as Isaiah 7:10–17; 9:2–7; 11:1–10; and such royal psalms as Psalms 2, 45, 89.

The exile to Babylon broke the continuity of the Davidic line promised in the ancient oracles. Nonetheless, other prophets foretold a restoration of the Davidic dynasty (e.g., Jer 23:5–6; Ezek 34:23–24; 37:24–25). Zechariah and Haggai rested the hopes for such a restoration in Zerubbabel (Zech 4, 6; Hag 1:2–3), but these hopes never came to fruition. Thus, during the years of Persian, Hellenistic, and Roman rule the ancient biblical oracles about the Lord's Anointed One and the promises of the restoration of the dynasty were interpreted to refer to a king yet to come.

Psalms of Solomon 17

Late in the second century B.C.E., members of the Hasmonean house began to take for themselves the title of king. The inner-dynastic battles that followed led, within half a century, to the Roman annexation of Palestine into its empire. The present text invokes divine judgment on both the Hasmoneans and the Romans. Employing the language of the ancient oracles, the psalmist appeals to God to remember his covenant and to send the Davidic deliverer, who will drive the enemy from the land and rule and judge his people in the peace and equity that are embodied in the reign of God.

GOD IS OUR KING

1 Lord, you are our King forever and ever,
for in you, O God, our soul makes its boast.
²And what is the time of a man's life upon the earth?
as is his time, so also is his hope in himself;[a]
3   but we hope in God, our savior.
For the might of our God is forever, in mercy;
and the reign of our God is forever over the nations, in judgment.

THE SONS OF DAVID WERE TO BE
THE AGENTS OF GOD'S REIGN

⁴You, O Lord, chose David to be king over Israel;[b]
and you made an eternal oath with him concerning his descendants,
that his kingdom would not come to an end in your sight.

ISRAEL'S SIN IS PUNISHED THROUGH
THE RISE OF THE HASMONEANS

⁵But because of our sins, sinners rose up against us;
they, to whom you made no promise, assailed us and thrust us out.[c]
They took by force and did not give glory to your honorable name;
6   with splendor they set up a kingdom because of (their) pride;
they laid waste the throne of David through innovative arrogance.

GOD PUNISHES THE HASMONEANS
THROUGH POMPEY

[7]But you, O God, cast them down and removed their descendants from
   the land
   when a man alien to our race rose up against them.[d]
[8]According to their sins you recompensed them, O God,
   so that it befell them according to their deeds.
[9]God showed them no pity;
   he searched out their progeny
   and did not let one of them escape.
[10]Faithful is God in all his judgments.
   which he executes upon the earth.
[11]The lawless one depopulated our land of its inhabitants;
   he destroyed young and old, and their children with them.
[12]In the heat of his anger,[e] he sent them off to the west;
   and the rulers of the land (he made) a reproach, and he did not spare
   (them).
[13]Being an alien, the enemy acted arrogantly;
   and his heart was alien from our God. . . .[f]

A PRAYER TO RESTORE THE
DAVIDIC DYNASTY

[21]Behold, O Lord, and raise up for them their king, the son of David;
   at the time you know,[g] O God, to rule over Israel your servant.
[22]And gird him with strength to crush unrighteous rulers;
   to cleanse Jerusalem from the Gentiles that trample her in
   destruction.
[23] in righteous wisdom to cast out sinners from the inheritance;
   to shatter the arrogance of the sinner as a potter's vessel,[h]
[24] with a rod of iron to crush all their substance;
   to destroy transgressing Gentiles with the word of his mouth,[i]
[25] by his rebuke to cause the nations to flee from his presence,
   and to convict sinners for the thoughts[j] of their heart.

A DESCRIPTION OF THE MESSIAH
AND MESSIANIC TIMES

[26]And he will gather a holy people, whom he will lead in righteousness,
   and he will judge the tribes of the people that has been sanctified by
   the Lord his God.[k]
[27]And he will not permit unrighteousness to lodge any longer in their
   midst;
   and no man who knows wickedness will dwell with them,
   for he will know that they are all sons of their God.
[28]And he will divide them according to their tribes on the land;[l]
   and the sojourner and foreigner will no longer reside with them.

[29]He will judge peoples and nations in his righteous wisdom,

30   and he will make the peoples of the nations serve him under his
       yoke,
     and he will glorify the Lord openly over all the earth.[m]
   And he will purify Jerusalem, making it holy as it was from the
       beginning

31   so that the Gentiles will come from the corners of the earth to see his
       glory,
     bearing as gifts her sons who had fainted;[n]
     and to see the glory of the Lord with which God glorified her.

[32]And he will be a righteous king over them, taught by God;
     and in his days there will be no unrighteousness in their midst,
     for all will be holy and their king, the Anointed of the Lord.[o]

[33]For he will not put his hope in horse and rider and bow;
     nor will he multiply for himself gold or silver for war;[p]
     And for the multitude he will not accumulate hopes for a day of war.

[34]The Lord himself is his King, the hope of him who is mighty through
       his hope in God.
     And he will have mercy on all the Gentiles (who stand) before him
       in fear;

[35]For he will smite the earth with the word of his mouth forever;
     he will bless the people of the Lord with wisdom and gladness.

[36]And he will be pure from sin to rule a great people,
     to convict rulers and to remove sinners by the strength of his word.

[37]And he will not grow weak in his days because of his God;
     for God will make him mighty by (his) holy spirit[q]
     and wise in the counsel of understanding, with strength and
       righteousness.

[38]And the blessing of the Lord will be with him in strength;
     and he will not grow weak.

[39]His hope (will be) in the Lord,
     and who will prevail against him?

[40]He will be strong in his deeds, and mighty in the fear of God,
     shepherding the flock of the Lord in faithfulness and righteousness;[r]
   And he will not permit any among them to grow weak in their pasture;

41   he will lead them all with equity,
     and there will be no arrogance among them, that any of them be
       oppressed.

[42]This (will be) the beauty of the king of Israel, which God knows,
     so that he may raise him up over the house of Israel, to correct it.

[43]His words (will be) purified more than gold of highest quality;
     in the assemblies he will pass judgment on the tribes of a sanctified
       people;

his words (will be) as the words of the holy ones in the midst of the
sanctified peoples.
[44]Blessed are those who live in those days,
to see the good things of Israel which God will bring to pass, when
the tribes are gathered.
[45]May God hasten his mercy on Israel;
may he rescue us from the uncleanness of defiled enemies.
[46]The Lord himself is our king forever and ever.

a. Contrast with the next line. "Natural man," as long as he lives, trusts in himself;
the child of God trusts in God.
b. The oracle is in 2 Sam 7:8–16. For a treatment of it similar to this psalm, cf. Ps
89:3, 19–37.
c. Does this line hint that the author sees himself as a member of the Davidic
house?
d. I.e., Pompey; cf. also v. 5a.
e. The text is corrupt: "In the wrath of his beauty." The next clause is an allusion to
the events of 63 B.C.E. Pompey took many Jewish prisoners to Rome—among them the
Hasmonean prince Aristobulus and his family.
f. Seven verses describing conditions in Jerusalem are here omitted.
g. Some mss. read "you see"; this could be a corruption of "you have chosen."
h. This and the next line paraphrase Ps 2:9. This is perhaps the earliest use of this
psalm to refer to the future king. It is often applied to Jesus in the New Testament. For
this verse, see Rev 2:27; 12:5; 19:15.
i. Cf. Isa 11:4; see also v. 35, below.
j. Lit., "the word of their heart."
k. Cf. Isa 49:5–6.
l. Cf. Ezek 47–48.
m. Possibly an allusion to Isa 11:10.
n. Cf. Isa 60, for the glorifying of Jerusalem and the return of Jerusalem's children.
o. The Greek mss. all read "the Anointed, the Lord." This is almost certainly a
Christian emendation or a Christian translation of a Hebrew original that read as
above. In either case, the Hebrew would have looked the same. "The Anointed, the
Lord" is a most unlikely Jewish formulation. "The Anointed of the Lord" is a typical
title for the Israelite king.
p. In keeping with the command in Deut 17:16–17.
q. Cf. Isa 11:2 for this and the next line.
r. Cf. Ezek 34.

Although the messianic king will be a human being, by virtue of his
role as God's agent on earth, he shares in and embodies divine
qualities: wisdom, strength, righteousness (vv. 23, 27, 37, 40), purity
from sin (v. 36), and speech whose power is reminiscent of the
mighty, creative, and effective power of God's word (vv. 35–36).
As to his functions, when the king has driven the Romans from the
promised inheritance of God's people (vv. 4, 22–25, 45), he will
gather the dispersed (vv. 26, 44) and restore the old tribal boundaries
(v. 28), thus expanding the nation to the boundaries of the Davidic-

Solomonic kingdom. The days of the Messiah are depicted as ideal times. Israel will be cleansed of sin (vv. 27, 32, 40), and as the nations flow to Jerusalem to bring their tribute, God's kingly power will be evident not only in Israel but also over all the earth.

4 Ezra 11–12

Here the hope for the Davidic Messiah is embodied in an apocalyptic vision that reflects a reinterpretation of Daniel 7. The fourth beast of Daniel's vision represented the Macedonian kingdom, which had come to its terrible climax under the rule of Antiochus IV Epiphanes, the arch-persecutor of the Jews and their religion. The present vision focuses on the fourth beast, which is here depicted as an eagle, the Roman Empire's own symbolic representation of itself. The fearful deeds of Antiochus are now overshadowed by the Roman devastation of Jerusalem in 70 C.E.

Employing and elaborating the allegorical technique of Daniel 7, the author enumerates the Roman emperors and pretenders, using as symbols the multiple wings and heads of the eagle. While the precise identification of all the symbolized people is a matter of dispute, the three heads appear to be best identified with the three Flavian emperors: Vespasian (69–79 C.E.), Titus (79–81 C.E.), and Domitian (81–96 C.E.). Thus the author appears to have written in the last years of the first century C.E. and to have placed the demise of the Roman Empire in the imminent future.

Ezra's vision concludes with the following passage:

11 ³⁷And I looked, and behold, a creature like a lion was aroused out of the forest, roaring; and I heard how he uttered a man's voice to the eagle and spoke, saying, ³⁸"Listen and I will speak to you. The Most High says to you, ³⁹'Are you not the one that remains of the four beasts which I had made to reign in my world, so that the end of my times might come through them? ⁴⁰You, the fourth that has come, have conquered all the beasts that have gone before; and you have held sway over the world with much terror, and over all the earth with grievous oppression; and for so long you have dwelt on the earth with deceit. ⁴¹And you have judged the earth, but not with truth; ⁴²for you have afflicted the meek and injured the peaceable; you have hated those who tell the truth, and have loved liars; you have destroyed the dwellings of those who brought forth fruit, and have laid low the walls of those who did you no harm. ⁴³And so your insolence has come up before the Most High, and your pride to the Mighty One. [44]And the Most High has looked upon his times, and behold, they are ended, and his ages are completed![a] [45]Therefore you will surely disappear, you eagle, and your terrifying wings, and your most evil little wings, and your malicious heads, and your most evil talons, and your whole worthless body, [46]so that the whole earth, freed from your violence, may be refreshed and relieved and may hope for the judgment and mercy of him who made it.' "

12 [1]While the lion was saying these words to the eagle, I looked, [2]and behold, the remaining head disappeared. And the two wings that had gone over to it arose and set themselves up to reign, and their reign was brief and full of tumult. [3]And I looked, and behold, they also disappeared, and the whole body of the eagle was burned[b] and the earth was exceedingly terrified.

Awakening from his dream vision, the perplexed Ezra prays for an interpretation (12:7–9). God relates the vision to that of Daniel and explains the meaning of the various wings and heads (12:10–30). The interpretation ends with the following identification of the lion as the Davidic Messiah, the Lion of the tribe of Judah (cf. Gen 49:9–10).

12 [31]And as for the lion whom you saw rousing up out of the forest and roaring and speaking to the eagle and reproving him for his unrighteousness, and as for all his words that you have heard, [32]this is the Messiah whom the Most High has kept until the end of days, who will arise from the posterity of David[c] and will come and speak to them; he will denounce them for their ungodliness and for their wickedness and will cast up before them their contemptuous dealings. [33]For first he will set them living before his judgment seat, and when he has reproved them, then he will destroy them. [34]But he will deliver in mercy the remnant of my people, those who have been saved throughout my borders, and he will make them joyful until the end comes, the day of judgment, of which I spoke to you at the beginning. [35]This is the dream that you saw, and this is its interpretation.

a. This verse and 12:32 reflect the typical viewpoint of the apocalyptist who believes that he is living at the end of the age.
b. Cf. Dan 7:11.
c. Cf. Gen 49:9; Rev 5:5.

In Ezra's vision the Messiah's function is to indict the eagle for its crimes. This indictment of the empire is a parody on the celebrated "Pax Romana" and Roman justice. It is most closely paralleled in our literature by Revelation 18, which is part of another, contemporary reinterpretation of the fourth beast of Daniel's vision. In the interpretation of Ezra's vision, the Messiah not only indicts but also destroys the Roman rulers. Thus he assumes a function attributed to God in Daniel 7 and to the Messiah in Psalms of Solomon 17.

The Eschatological Priest

Testament of Levi 18

Although the Testaments of the Twelve Patriarchs are in their present form an early Christian document, they are based on earlier Jewish traditions and documents. One of these documents is an Aramaic text concerning the patriarch Levi. In a fragment of this text, the royal blessing of Judah (Gen 49:10) is interpreted to refer to Kohath, the son of Levi, the founder of the high-priestly line.[1] Similarly, in the Greek Testament of Levi, the patriarch draws on the language of the royal messianic oracle in Isaiah 11 (v. 2) to describe both his own heavenly commissioning as high priest (4:5)[2] and his eschatological counterpart (18:7). Chapters 14–18 of the Greek Testament, which were present in some form in the Aramaic text,[3] are an apocalypse that describes the progressive disintegration of the Jerusalem priesthood (chaps. 14–17) and the appearance of the eschatological priest in the likeness of Levi (chap. 18). Although we cannot be certain of the original shape of the Jewish form of this chapter, the Greek text is interesting as a bridge between Jewish speculations about the eschatological priest and early Christian views about Jesus as that priest.[4]

When the Jerusalem priesthood has failed,

2Then the Lord will raise up a new priest,
   to whom all the words of the Lord will be revealed;
   and he will execute true judgment on the earth for a multitude of
      days.[a]
3And his star will arise in heaven as a king,[b]
   lighting up the light of knowledge as the day's sun;[c]
   and he will be magnified in the world until he is taken up.[d]
4He will shine as the sun on the earth,[e]
   and he will remove all darkness from under heaven;
   and there will be peace on all the earth.
5The heavens will exult in his days,[f]
   and the earth will be glad,
   and the clouds will rejoice.

And the knowledge of the Lord will be poured out upon the earth as
the water of the seas,[g]
and the angels of the glory of the presence of the Lord will be glad in
him.
[6]The heavens will be opened,
and from the temple of glory there will come upon him sanctification
together with the paternal voice,
as from Abraham, the father, to Isaac.[h]
[7]And the glory of the Most High will be uttered over him,
and the spirit of understanding and sanctification[i] will rest upon him
in the water.[j]
[8]He will give the majesty of the Lord to his sons in truth forever;
and he will have no successor for all generations forever.[k]
[9]And because of his priesthood,[l] the Gentiles will be multiplied in
knowledge upon the earth,
and they will be enlightened through the grace of the Lord.
But Israel will be diminished in ignorance,
and they will be darkened in grief.
With his priesthood[l] all sin will vanish,
and the lawless will cease to do evil,[m]
but the righteous will rest in him.
[10]Moreover, he will open the gates of paradise
and he will remove the threatening sword against Adam.
[11]And he will give the holy ones to eat from the tree of life,[n]
and the spirit of holiness will be upon them.
[12]And Beliar will be bound by him,
and he will give his children authority to tread on the evil spirits.[o]
[13]And the Lord will rejoice over his children,
and the Lord will be well pleased with his beloved ones forever.[p]
[14]Then Abraham and Isaac and Jacob will exult,
and I will be glad,
and all the holy ones will clothe themselves with joy.[q]

a. Cf. Isa 11:3–4.

b. Or "of a King." An allusion to Balaam's prophecy in Num 24:17, interpreted with reference to the royal Messiah in T. Judah 24:1 (see below, p. 171), and 4QTest 12–13 (see below, p. 176). Here the image of the star refers to the enlightenment provided by the priest's instruction.

c. Or "as the day (does) in the sun."

d. This last clause sounds Christian and contrasts with v. 8, where the continued presence of the priest is assumed.

e. Cf. the imagery of light and darkness in John 1:4, 5, 9, 14.

f. This imagery is drawn from Ps 96:11–13, which describes the cosmic response to God's epiphany as judge; on this motif, see above, v. 2.

g. Cf. Isa 11:9.

h. Or "to Isaac." The text of this line may be corrupt. One expects a reference to Gen 22:11–12, where the angel of the Lord speaks to Abraham.

i. Cf. Isa 11:2 and see n. *a*, above.

j. Although many scholars have bracketed "in the water" as a later Christian interpolation into an originally Jewish text, it is present in all mss., and must therefore be considered part of the text.

k. Perhaps an allusion to Ps 110:4 and the eternal priesthood.

l.–l. The enclosed words are missing in the best mss., undoubtedly omitted by a careless scribe.

m. The Greek verb for "will cease" is identical to the verb translated "will rest" in the next line.

n. These three lines allude to Gen 3:24.

o. Beliar is a common name for the chief demon in the Testaments, the Book of Jubilees, and the Qumran scrolls. Cf. also 2 Cor 6:15. The binding of a demon to render him inoperative is a common image. Cf., e.g., Tob 8:3; 1 Enoch 10:4, 11; Mark 3:27; Rev 20:2. On the last line, cf. Luke 10:18–19.

p. God's good pleasure in his people is a typical expression in Jewish and Christian literature; see Ernest Vogt, "Peace Among Men of God's Good Pleasure," in Krister Stendahl, ed., *The Scrolls and the New Testament* (New York: Harper & Row, 1957) 114–17. In Mark 1:11 it derives from Isa 42:1.

q. This is probably an allusion to Ps 132:9, 16, where reference is made to priests being clothed with salvation and the holy ones shouting for joy. However, the present verse as a whole may well be alluding to the resurrection of: the three patriarchs; the twelve patriarchs; the righteous. For these three groups, cf. T. Judah 25:1–3; and cf. also T. Benj. 10:6–8.

The language and imagery of this passage are highly appropriate to a description of the eschatological priest. This latter-day descendant of Levi is both the recipient and the dispenser of revealed, saving knowledge of God.[5] The light of this knowledge will disperse the darkness of sin and evil, the barrier that separates the Creator and his creatures. Holiness, the quality that distinguishes God from humanity, will rest both upon this eschatological priest and upon the redeemed—"the holy ones."

The Priestly and Royal Messiah(s)

Although the Testament of Levi depicts the eschatological priest as if he were the sole eschatological deliverer, who fulfilled hopes attributed to both king and priest, other texts in the Testaments and the Qumran scrolls make reference to salvation coming from Levi and Judah or Aaron and Israel.

Testament of Judah 21 and 24

This work, Christian in its present form, anticipates two eschatological figures. It is significant that Judah, the ancestor of David, asserts the superiority of the priest over the king.

21 [1]And now, my children, love Levi, that you may remain. And do not exalt yourselves against him, lest you be destroyed. [2]For to me the Lord gave the kingdom and to him, the priesthood; and he subjected the kingdom to the priesthood. [3]To me he gave the things upon earth, to him, the things in heaven. [4]As the heaven is higher than the earth, thus the priesthood of God is higher than kingdom over the earth (unless through sin it falls away from the Lord and is ruled over by the earthly kingdom).[a] [5]For the Lord chose him over you to draw near to him[b] to eat of his table and his first fruits, the delightful things of the sons of Israel. . . .

At the end of a lengthy prediction of Israel's future sin, punishment, and repentance, Judah describes their coming salvation. Part of this scenario includes the appearance of the royal descendant of Judah. The passage is remarkable both for its many allusions to biblical prophecies, especially about the Davidic Messiah, and for its similarity to the description of the eschatological priest in Testament of Levi 18.

24 [1]And after these things there will arise for you a star out of Jacob in peace;[c]
    and a man from my seed will arise like the sun of righteousness,[d]
    walking among the sons of men in meekness and righteousness;
    and no sin will be found in him.[e]
[2]And the heavens will be opened over him,
    pouring out from the spirit the blessing of the holy Father.[f]
And he will pour the spirit of grace upon you;[g]
[3] and you will be his sons in truth,
    and you will walk in his commandments, the first and the last.
[4]This (is the) branch of the Most High God,[h]
    and this fountain for the life of all flesh.[i]
[5]Then the scepter of my kingdom will shine,[j]
    and from your root will arise a stem.[k]
And in him[l] will grow a rod of righteousness for the Gentiles,
    to judge[m] and save all who call upon the Lord.

a. This parenthetical sentence appears to be an addition which interrupts the continuity between the first part of v. 4 and v. 5.

b. "To draw near" is a technical term for priestly activity.

c. An allusion to Num 24:17. See n. *b* on T. Levi 18 and see 4QTest 12–13, below, p. 176.

d. See Mal 4:2 and see n. *c*, below, p. 172.

e. Cf. Ps. Sol. 17:36, above, p. 164.

f. Cf. T. Levi 18:6–7, above, p. 169.

g. Cf. T. Levi 18:9, above, p. 169.

h. Cf. Isa 11:1.

i. Although the language of this line could be drawn straight from the Jewish wisdom tradition, it has a Johannine ring and may well reflect the Fourth Gospel; cf., e.g., John 4:14.

j. Cf. Jacob's prophecy about Judah in Gen 49:10.

k. Cf. Isa 11:1.

l. Or "from it."

m. Cf. Isa 11:3–4 and T. Levi 18:2.

Testament of Dan 5:10–13

In this passage, clearly Christian in its present form, salvation from Levi and Judah will come in *one person*. The imagery of the passage is reminiscent of Testament of Levi 18, but it is also drawn from Malachi's prophecy of the coming messenger, who is identified as the returning Elijah.

10 And there will arise[a] for you from the tribe of Judah and Levi the
  salvation of the Lord;
  and he will make war against Beliar,
  and he will give victorious vengeance to our fathers.
[11]And he will take the captivity from Beliar,[b] the souls of the holy ones;
  and he will turn disobedient hearts to the Lord,[c]
  and he will give eternal peace to those who call upon him.
[12]And the holy ones will rest in Eden,[d]
  and over the new Jerusalem the righteous will rejoice,
  which is for the glorification of God forever.
[13]And no longer will Jerusalem endure desolation,
    nor will Israel be captive;
  for the Lord will be in the midst of her, associating with men,[e]
and the Holy One of Israel rules over them in humility and poverty;[f]
  and he who believes in him will rule in truth in the heavens.

a. An allusion to Num 24:17; the same Greek verb occurs in T. Levi 18:3 and T. Judah 24:1.

b. Cf. Mark 3:23–27.

c. Cf. Mal 4:6. The next line here may allude to Mal 3:16.

d. Cf. T. Levi 18:10–11.

e. The passage sounds Christian, although the idea of God's eschatological presence among his people can be found in Jewish texts.

f. Surely this is an allusion to the incarnation.

Expectations of the Qumran Community

Although the texts just presented are Christian in their present form, the idea of two Messiahs or of a messianic figure of both priestly and royal lineage is Jewish in origin. We may trace this to the Book of Zechariah, which anticipates the leadership of postexilic Judah in the hands of Joshua the high priest and Zerubbabel the descendant of David (chaps. 3–4), who are called "sons of oil," that is, anointed ones.

The idea was an integral part of the eschatological expectations of the Qumran community and is alluded to or expounded in a number of texts found in the community's library.

Damascus Document 19:34—20:1

Two texts in this document mention the coming of the Messiah of Aaron and Israel. Many scholars emend the texts from singular to plural, interpreting it to refer to two Messiahs.[6]

None of the men who enter the New Covenant in the land of Damascus, and who again betray it and depart from the fountain of living waters,[a] shall be reckoned with the council of the people or inscribed in its book from the day of the gathering in of the Teacher of the Community until the coming of the Messiah out of Aaron and Israel.[b]

a. An allusion to the Torah as interpreted in the community.

b. For Aaron and Israel as designations of priesthood and laity, see Ps 115:12; 118:23; 135:19. Here the coming of the Messiah ends the period begun with the formation of the New Covenant community in "the land of Damascus."

Damascus Document 12:23—13:2

Those who follow these statutes in the age of wickedness until the coming of the Messiah of Aaron and Israel[a] shall form groups of at least ten men, by thousands, hundreds, fifties, and tens. And where the ten are, there shall never be lacking a priest learned in the Book of Meditation; they shall all be ruled by him.[b]

a. Here the coming of the Messiah ends the "age of wickedness."

b. As in the previous passage, the present time is marked by the existence of the community of the New Covenant and its interpretation of the Torah. Here, in the age of wickedness, members of the community gather to hear the instruction in the Torah as supervised by the Priest, the community's leader.

These two texts make only passing reference to the belief in the Messiah of Aaron and Israel, as to a known concept and to his coming as an event that marks a terminus in the present age. Other texts tell us a little about the expected functions of the twin rulers expected in the future.

Florilegium 1:10–13, 18–19

This text is mainly an exposition of the royal oracle in 2 Samuel 7. After interpreting 2 Samuel 7:10 to refer to the Qumran community as the "house" that would replace the sanctuary of Israel that was laid waste, the author interprets 2 Samuel 7:11 and its reference to the Davidic house.

10 "The Lord declares to you that he will build you a house" (2 Sam 7:11). "I will raise up your seed after you" (2 Sam 7:12). "I will establish the throne of his kingdom [forever]" (2 Sam 7:13). "I [will be] his father and he shall be my son" (2 Sam 7:14). He is the Branch of David,[a] who shall arise with the Interpreter of the Law [to rule] in Zion [at the end] of time. As it is written, "I will raise up the tent of David that is fallen" (Amos 9:11). That is to say, the fallen "tent of David" is he who shall arise to save Israel.

a. Cf. Jer 23:5.

Along with the Davidic Messiah, who will "save" Israel from its enemies, will come the Priest, whose function is indicated by his name, "The Interpreter of the Law."[7] The function of the Davidic Messiah is further alluded to in an interpretation of Psalm 2:1.

18 "[Why] do the nations [rage] and the peoples meditate [vanity, the kings of the earth] rise up, [and the] princes take counsel together against the Lord and against [his Messiah]?" (Ps 2:1). Interpreted, this saying concerns [the kings of the nations] who shall [rage against] the elect of Israel in the last days.

The choice of Psalm 2 is significant. Not only does the psalmist call the king God's "son" (v. 7), as he is named in 2 Samuel 7:14, but he also depicts him subjecting and destroying the nations, that is, the enemies of Israel. It is significant that Psalm 2 is also quoted in the messianic Psalm of Solomon 17:22–25 with reference to the Messiah's defeat of the nations (see above, p. 163).

The Messianic Rule 2:11–22

This badly damaged passage anticipates the appearance of the two Messiahs at the end-time. With the Priest having the preeminent position, they will preside over the meal of the community, the true Israel. Sitting before them will be, respectively, the priests and the lay leaders of Israel.[8]

11 "[This shall be the ass]embly of the men of renown [called] to the meeting of the council of the community when [the Priest-] Messiah shall summon them."

He shall come [at] the head of the whole congregation of Israel with all [his brethren, the sons] of Aaron the priests, [those called] to the assembly, the men of renown; and they shall sit [before him, each man] in the order of his dignity. And then [the Mess]iah of Israel shall [come], and the chiefs [15]of the [clans of Israel] shall sit before him, [each] in the order of his dignity, according to [his place] in their camps and marches. And before them shall sit all the heads of [family of the congreg]ation, and the wise men of [the holy congregation], each in the order of his dignity.

And [when] they shall gather for the common [tab]le, to eat and [to drink] new wine, when the common table shall be set for eating and the new wine [poured] for drinking, let no man extend his hand over the first fruits of bread and wine before the Priest, for [it is he] who shall bless the first fruits of bread [20]and wine, and shall be the first [to extend] his hand over the bread. Thereafter, the Messiah of Israel shall extend his hand over the bread, [and] all the congregation of the community [shall utter a] blessing, [each man in the order] of his dignity.

It is according to this statute that they shall proceed at every me[al at which] at least ten men are gathered together.

The final paragraph of the passage suggests that the messianic meal previously described was anticipated in the regular meals of the community, in which the priestly and lay leaders of the community played the roles of the priestly and royal messiahs. This eschatological, anticipatory dimension of a communal meal was present also in early Christian celebrations of the Eucharist (cf. 1 Cor 11:26).

The Two Messiahs and the Prophet

Qumran expectations were not limited to two eschatological figures. In a passage reminiscent of the two texts quoted above from the Damascus Document, the author mentions as a terminus to the present time the coming of the two Messiahs and "the Prophet," doubtless the prophet like Moses mentioned in Deuteronomy 18:18–19.[9]

The Rule of the Community 9:8–11

As for the property of the men of holiness who walk in perfection, it shall not be merged with that of the men of falsehood who have not purified their life by separating themselves from iniquity and walking in the way of perfection. They shall depart from none of the counsels of the law to walk in the stubbornness of their hearts, but shall be ruled by the primitive precepts in which the men of the community were first instructed until there shall come the Prophet and the Messiahs of Aaron and Israel.

The Testimonia

The trio—Prophet, Davidic Messiah, Priestly Messiah—is also presupposed in another Qumran writing. The document assembles four biblical texts which imply four eschatological figures.

THE PROPHET LIKE MOSES

1 And (the Lord) said to Moses,
"You have heard the words of this people, which they have spoken to you; they have rightly said all that they have spoken. Oh that they had such a mind as this always, to fear me and to keep all my commandments, that it might go well with them and their children forever!" (Deut 5:28–29). [5]"I will raise up for them a prophet like you from among their brethren; and I will put my words in his mouth, and he will speak to them all that I command him. And whoever will not give heed to my words which the prophet will speak in my name, I myself will require it of him" (Deut 18:18–19).

THE DAVIDIC MESSIAH

And he took up his discourse and said,
"The oracle of Balaam, the son of Beor, the oracle of the man [10]whose eye is opened, the oracle of him who hears the words of God and knows the knowledge of the Most High, who sees the vision of the Almighty, falling down, but having his eyes uncovered: I see him, but not now; I beheld him, but not nigh: a star shall come forth out of Jacob, and a scepter shall rise out of Israel; it shall crush the forehead of Moab, and break down all the sons of Sheth" (Num 24:15–17).[a]

THE PRIESTLY MESSIAH

To Levi he said,
"Give to Levi your Thummin, and your Urim to your godly one, whom [15]you tested at Massah, with whom you strove at the waters of Meribah; who said of his father and mother, 'I regard them not'; he disowned his brothers and ignored his children. For he observed your word and kept your covenant. They will teach Jacob your ordinances, and Israel your law; they will put incense before you, and whole burnt offering upon your altar. Bless (the Lord), his substance, and accept the work of his hands; crush the loins of his adversaries, of those that hate him, [20]that they rise not again" (Deut 33:8–11).

THE ENEMY OF THE COMMUNITY[b]

When Joshua had finished offering praise and thanksgiving with his psalms, he said,

"Cursed be the man who rebuilds this city. At the cost of his firstborn shall he lay its foundation, and at the cost of his youngest son shall he set its gates" (Josh 6:26). "And behold, cursed is the man of Belial who comes to power to be a trapper's snare to his people and ruin to all his neighbors. And he rose to power [25]and [his sons] . . . [with him], the two of them becoming violent instruments, and they rebuilt again the [city?] . . . and set up a wall and towers for it to make a stronghold of wickedness [   ] . . . horrors in Ephraim and Judah [   ] . . . [and they] committed sacrilege in the land . . . [bl]ood like water [shall] [flow?] on the battlements of the daughter of Zion and in the district of Jerusalem."

a. Cf. T. Judah 24:1, above p. 171.
b. This passage is excerpted from a sectarian work entitled "The Psalms of Joshua;" see J. T. Milik, *Ten Years of Discovery in the Wilderness of Judaea*, Studies in Biblical Theology 26 (London: SCM Press, 1959) 61–62.

TRANSCENDENT AGENTS

The Son of Man

1 Enoch 37–71

Running through the so-called Parables of Enoch is a series of heavenly vignettes or tableaux that portray the unfolding drama of salvation. The main characters are, on the one side, God, his angels, the righteous and chosen, and a transcendent figure designated variously as "the Chosen One," a "son of man," "the righteous one," and "the Anointed of the Lord," and, on the other side, the chief demon, Azazel, and his angels, and their human agents "the kings and the mighty," who persecute the righteous and deny the Lord and the heavenly realm. The book is presented as a revelation of that realm, where the events of the imminent judgment and deliverance are already in process.

From the titles and descriptions of the protagonist, it is clear that the author has conflated and modified at least three major streams of Jewish tradition. Like the "one like a son of man" in Daniel 7, he is the heavenly patron of the persecuted righteous; however, different from Daniel 7, he appears not after the judgment but in order to be the judge. At the same time he is identified as Second Isaiah's servant of the Lord, especially as that servant is interpreted in Wisdom of Solomon 5; nonetheless, different from both Second Isaiah and the Wisdom of Solomon, he is not a suffering human figure, but the heavenly deliverer and judge of the suffering righteous. Finally, language used of the Davidic Messiah is also applied to him even though he is not thought of as a human figure.

Although scholars debate the date of the composition of the Parables and disagree about whether they are a Jewish or a Christian composition, it seems best to consider the work as a Jewish writing from the decades around the turn of the era.[10]

The extracts that follow focus on the figure of the son of man, his characteristics and functions, and illustrate their biblical roots.

I. THE SON OF MAN
IS INTRODUCED[a]

Enoch's Vision (cf. Dan 7:13)

46 [1]And there I saw one who had a head of days;[b]
   and his head was like white wool.
And with him was another, whose face was like the appearance of a man;[c]
   and his face was full of graciousness like one of the holy angels.

The Identification of One Like a Man

[2]And I asked the angel of peace,[d] who went with me and showed me all the hidden things, about that son of man[e]—who he was and where he was from, and why he went with the Head of Days.

[3]And he answered me and said to me,
   "This is the son of man who has righteousness,
   and righteousness dwells with him.
And all the treasuries of what is hidden he will reveal;[f]
   for the Lord of Spirits has chosen him,[g]
   and his lot has surpassed all before the Lord of Spirits in truth forever.

*Description Anticipating
His Role as Judge[h]*

[4]And this son of man whom you have seen—
   he will raise the kings and the mighty from their couches,
      and the strong from their thrones.
   And he will loosen the reins of the strong,
      and he will crush the teeth of the sinners.

[5]And he will overturn the kings from their thrones and their kingdoms;[i]
   because they do not exalt him or praise him,
   or humbly acknowledge whence the kingdom was given to them.[j]

[6]And the face of the strong he will turn aside,
  and he will fill them with shame.[k]
And darkness will be their dwelling,[l]
  and worms will be their couch.[m]
And they will have no hope to rise from their couches,[n]
  because they do not exalt the name of the Lord of Spirits."

[Chapter 47 relates how the prayers of the righteous and the angels set the stage for the judgment.]

II. THE SON OF MAN
IS NAMED (cf. Isa 49)[o]

Enoch's Vision

48 [1]And in that place I saw the spring of righteousness, and it was inexhaustible;
  and many springs of wisdom surrounded it.
And all the thirsty drank from them and were filled with wisdom;[p]
  and their dwelling places were with the righteous and the holy and the chosen.

[2]And in that hour that son of man was named in the presence of the Lord of Spirits;
  and his name, before the Head of Days.
[3]Even before the sun and the constellations were created,
  before the stars of heaven were made,
  his name was named before the Lord of Spirits.[q]

*The Son of Man as
a Deliverer*

[4]He will be a staff for the righteous,[r]
  that they may lean on him and not fall;
And he will be a light of the nations,[s]
  and he will be a hope for those who grieve in their hearts.

[5]All who dwell on the dry land will fall down and worship before him,
  and they will glorify and bless and sing hymns to the name of the Lord of Spirits.[t]
[6]For this (reason) he was chosen and hidden in his presence,[u]
  before the age was created and forever.
[7]And the wisdom of the Lord of Spirits has revealed him to the holy and the righteous;
  for he has preserved the portion of the righteous.[v]

For they have hated and despised this age of unrighteousness;
  yea, all its deeds and its way they have hated
  in the name of the Lord of Spirits.[w]

For in his name they are saved,
and he is the vindicator of their lives.

*Anticipation of the Judgment of
the Kings (cf. Ps 2)ˣ*

⁸And in those days, downcast will be the faces of the kings of the earth,ʸ
and the strong who possess the dry land, because of the deeds of
their hands.
For on the day of their tribulation and distress they will not save
themselves;
9   and into the hand of my chosen ones I shall cast them.ᶻ

As straw in the fire and as lead in the water,
they will burn before the face of the holy,
and they will sink before the face of the righteous;
and no trace of them will be found.ᵃᵃ

¹⁰And before them they will fall and not rise,ᵇᵇ
and there will be no one to take them with his hand and raise them.
For they have denied the Lord of Spirits and his Anointed One.ᶜᶜ
And blessed be the name of the Lord of Spirits.

*The Wisdom of the
Chosen One (cf. Isa 11:2; 42:1)*

49 ¹For wisdom has been poured out like water,
and glory will not fail in his presence forever and ever.
²For he is mighty in all the secrets of righteousness;
and unrighteousness will vanish like a shadow,
and will have no place to stand.
For the Chosen One has taken his stand in the presence of the Lord of
Spirits;
and his glory is forever and ever,
and his might, to all generations.
³And in him dwell the spirit of wisdom and the spirit of insight,
and the spirit of instruction and might,
and the spirit of those who have fallen asleep in righteousness.ᵈᵈ
⁴And he will judge the things that are secret,
and no one will be able to speak a lying word in his presence;ᵉᵉ
for he is the Chosen One in the presence of the Lord of Spirits
according to his good pleasure.ᶠᶠ

III. THE SON OF MAN
IS ENTHRONED AS JUDGE (cf. Wis 5)ᵍᵍ

62 ¹And thus the Lord commanded the kings and the mighty and the
exalted and those who inhabit the earth, and he said,

"Open your eyes and lift up your horns,[hh]
if you are able to recognize the Chosen One."[ii]
[2]And the Lord of Spirits seated him[jj] upon the throne of his glory;
and the spirit of righteousness was poured upon him.[kk]
And the word of his mouth will slay all the sinners,[ll]
and all the unrighteous will perish from his presence.

[There follows a lengthy description of the judgment and its consequences (62:3—63:11). The chosen ones are saved and anticipate eternal fellowship with the Lord of Spirits and their champion, the son of man. The kings and the mighty petition for mercy and confess their sins, but the angels of punishment drive them from the presence of God to eternal darkness and damnation.]

a. The form of this section is typical of apocalyptic literature: vision; seer's question; angelic interpretation.

b. Cf. Dan 7:13, one ancient of days with hair like pure wool. With the present verse the author makes it immediately clear that he identifies his protagonist with the one like a son of man in Dan 7.

c. Angels may have the appearance of, or even be called, men (cf. Dan 8:15; 9:21). Here and in the next line this traditional usage and the statement that his face was angelic in appearance are set in antithetical or at least complementary parallelism with one another.

d. This title is typically used of the accompanying angel in the parables, but is found in this verse in only one ms. Others read "one of the holy angels."

e. Although "son of man" almost verges on a title in the Parables, it almost never appears without qualification (i.e., the son of man); thus "this/that son of man" or "the son of man who has righteousness" (46:3).

f. Cf. 49:1–2.

g. An allusion to his title, "the Chosen One." The title "the Lord of Spirits" is probably derived from the biblical title "Lord of Hosts" (cf. 39:12 and Isa 6:3), reformulated in line with Num 16:22.

h. This is the first of a number of passages that anticipate the judgment scene in chaps. 62–63.

i. Cf. Wis 5:23.

j. This acknowledgment will be made in chaps. 62–63—all too late.

k. An allusion to 62:10 and 63:11.

l. Cf. 63:11.

m. Cf. Isa 14:11. On the influence of this Isaianic chapter on the judgment tradition in the Parables, see George W. E. Nickelsburg, *Resurrection, Immortality, and Eternal Life in Intertestamental Judaism,* Harvard Theological Studies 26 (Cambridge: Harvard University Press, 1972) 74–75; cf. also Isa 66:24.

n. On the loss of hope, cf. 62:9; 63:7–8.

o. This passage is based on the call of the servant of the Lord in Isa 49.

p. The language of this passage suggests the popular idea of Torah as the fountain or spring of wisdom, but there is no indication that this author implies Torah here.

q. Cf. Isa 49:1. On the preexistence of the name of the Messiah, cf. Genesis Rabba 1:1. Whether the present passage and 48:6 teach the preexistence of the son of man himself or of God's plan for the son of man is uncertain.

r. Cf. Isa 49:6ab.

s. Cf. Isa 49:6d.

t. Anticipating chaps. 62–63.

u. Cf. 62:7 and Isa 49:2.

v. Cf. Isa 49:6c.

w. These lines reflect a typical apocalyptic view toward the present evil age.

x. This section and the next one use biblical language about the Davidic king.

y. For this expression cf. Ps 2:2, and for another allusion see below, n. cc. Although the kings are often said to possess the earth, here alone in the parables are they called "the kings of the earth."

z. That the righteous will participate in the judgment of their enemies is a common idea. Cf. Wis 2 and 5, and 1 Enoch 91:12; 95:3; 96:1.

aa. Cf. Exod 15:7, 10; Wis 5:9–12.

bb. Cf. Ps. Sol. 3:10 and contrast above, 1 Enoch 48:4.

cc. I.e., "his Messiah." Cf. Ps 2:2: "against the Lord and his anointed." See also above, 48:8.

dd. Cf. Isa 11:2, continuing the use of traditional royal language; anticipating 62:2.

ee. Anticipating 62:3.

ff. A clear allusion to Isa 42:1—the presentation of the servant of the Lord—and the source of the title "the Chosen One." Note also in that verse, as in vv. 3 and 4 here, the references to the servant as the executor of justice and the one on whom the Spirit dwells.

gg. On the complex relationship between this section and the interpretation of the last servant song (Isa 52:13—53:12) in Wis 5 (see above, pp. 134–35), see Nickelsburg, *Resurrection*, 70–74.

hh. The meaning is uncertain. Perhaps there is an allusion to Dan 7 and the representation of kings as horns of the fourth beast.

ii. The kings and the mighty are to recognize in the Chosen One the chosen ones whom they have persecuted. Cf. below, pp. 195–96, on Matt 25:31–46.

jj. Mss. read "sat."

kk. Cf. Isa 11:2 and above, 1 Enoch 49:3.

ll. Cf. Isa 11:4 and its reuse in Ps. Sol. 17:24 (above, p. 163). Cf. also 4 Ezra 13:4, 10, below, pp. 183.

4 Ezra 13

As we have seen in previous sections, the vision in Daniel 7 was an important source of Jewish speculations about God's eschatological deliverance. In 4 Ezra 11–12 the last of the four beasts in the Danielic vision was interpreted to refer to the Roman Empire—soon to be judged and destroyed by the Davidic Messiah (see above, pp. 166–68). In the Parables of Enoch, the son of man, who is the angelic patron of Israel in Daniel 7, was identified as a transcendent savior figure who would judge the enemies of the righteous and elect (see previous section). This tradition of interpreting Daniel 7 appears to be reflected in 4 Ezra 13, which recounts a vision that is based on Daniel 7.

1 After seven days I dreamed a dream in the night; ²and behold, a wind arose from the sea and stirred up all its waves.ª ³And I looked, and

behold, this wind made something like the figure of a man come up out of the heart of the sea.[b] And I looked, and behold, that man flew with the clouds of heaven;[c] and wherever he turned his face to look, everything under his gaze trembled, [4]and whenever his voice issued from his mouth, all who heard his voice melted as wax melts when it feels the fire.[d]

[5]After this I looked, and behold, an innumerable multitude of men were gathered together from the four winds of heaven to make war against the man who came up out of the sea. [6]And I looked, and behold, he carved out for himself a great mountain, and flew up upon it. [7]And I tried to see the region or place from which the mountain was carved, but I could not.

[8]After this I looked, and behold, all who had gathered together against him, to wage war with him, were much afraid, yet dared to fight. [9]And behold, when he saw the onrush of the approaching multitude, he neither lifted his hand nor held a spear or any weapon of war; [10]but I saw only how he sent forth from his mouth as it were a stream of fire, and from his lips a flaming breath, and from his tongue he shot forth a storm of sparks.[e] [11]All these were mingled together, the stream of fire and the flaming breath and the great storm, and fell on the onrushing multitude which was prepared to fight, and burned them all up, so that suddenly nothing was seen of the innumerable multitude but only the dust of ashes and the smell of smoke. When I saw it, I was amazed.

[12]After this I saw the same man come down from the mountain and call to him another multitude which was peaceable. [13]Then many people came to him, some of whom were joyful and some sorrowful; some of them were bound, and some were bringing others as offerings.

a. Cf. Dan 7:2.
b. Cf. Dan 7:3.
c. Cf. Dan 7:13.
d. Cf. Mic 1:4 and its use in 1 Enoch 1:6 (above, p. 122), and 52:6 of cosmic reactions to the epiphany of God and the son of man, respectively.
e. Cf. the similar image used of the Davidic king in Isa 11:4 and its reuse of the Davidic Messiah in Ps. Sol. 17:35 (see above, p. 164) and of the son of man in 1 Enoch 62:2.

The transcendent character of the "man" in this vision is difficult to overlook: his mysterious origin in the heart of the sea; his flying with the clouds of heaven; the terror that he evokes; the lethal fire that issues from his mouth. This imagery notwithstanding, the interest of the author of 4 Ezra is elsewhere. Although he is transmitting a traditional vision, his interests and emphases are reflected in the seer's comments (vv. 14–20, 51) and the interpreting angel's response (vv. 21–50, 52).[11]

For this author, the "man" is God's "servant," the Davidic Messiah (v. 37; cf. 7:28–29; 12:32). His origin in the heart of the sea relates to his being hidden until the end-time (vv. 26, 52; cf. 12:32). As in 12:32–34, his functions as judge and deliverer are stressed (vv. 26, 29, 37–38), although these are not explicit in the vision. In keeping with this interpretation, the fire from his mouth is interpreted as the Torah, the criterion of judgment that will condemn the wicked. Evidently also of interest to the author are the miracles wrought by the Messiah and the companions who will attend him (vv. 50, 52), neither of which is mentioned in the vision.[12] Thus in vision and interpretation we see this author's creative reuse of the eschatological traditions he had received.

Melchizedek

The figure of Melchizedek, "the priest of the Most High God," to whom Abraham offered tithes (Gen 14:18–20), is the subject of a number of Jewish and Christian texts which heighten the mystery of his sudden appearance and disappearance in Genesis by attributing to him a miraculous birth and divine characteristics.

The Qumran Melchizedek Document[13]

This fragmentary text takes its point of departure from the biblical commandments about the release of debts and slaves every fiftieth, or jubilee, year (Lev 25:8–17). The author speaks of "the last jubilee" or "tenth jubilee," evidently identifying it with the end of the 490 years mentioned in Daniel 9:24–27 and with the time of liberation spoken of in Isa 61:1. It is the end-time, when special atonement will be made for God's people and they will be the recipients of peace, good, and salvation. The chief agent of God's judgment and perhaps of this atonement will be Melchizedek, who is here described in angelic terms as the opponent of the arch-demon Belial and as a high, or the highest, functionary in the divine court.

9 . . . For he has decreed a year of good favor[a] for Melchize[dek] . . . and the holy ones of God for a re[ig]n of judgment. As it is written about it in the songs of David, who said, "Elohim has [ta]ken his stand in the as[sembly of 'El], in the midst of gods[b] he gives judgment" (Ps 82:1). And about it he sa[id, "A]bove it take your throne in the heights; let God judge (the) peoples" (Ps 7:7–8). And he s[aid, "How long] shall you judge unjustly and li[ft up] the face of (the) wic[ke]d? [Se]lah" (Ps 82:2). Its interpretation concerns Belial and concerns the spir[it]s of his lot

wh[ich . . .] . . . And Melchizedek shall exact the ven[ge]ance of the
jud[g]ments of God [from the hand of Be]lial and from the hand(s) of all
[the spirits of] his [lot]. And all the [eternal] gods are for his help . . .
[15]. . . This is the day of the [. . . (about) wh]ich he said [for the end of
days through Isai]ah the prophet who sai[d, "How] beautiful upon the
mountains are the feet [of] the heral[d proclaiming peace; the herald of
good, proclaiming salvat]ion (and) saying to Zion, 'Your God [is king' "]
(Isa 52:7).

> a. Cf. Isa 61:2.
> b. "Gods" here refers to the angels.

In his role as a judicial agent and opponent of Belial, Melchizedek
assumes functions ascribed elsewhere to Michael the archangel and
the Enochic Son of Man. The references to atonement suggest a
priestly role, as we might expect of Melchizedek. The quotation of
Isaiah 52:7 may indicate that Melchizedek is also identified or associated with the herald of good tidings, who later in the text appears to
be identified with "the anointed one" mentioned in Daniel 9:25.
This blending of several traditional figures into one is paralleled in
the Enochic portrayal of the Son of Man and Christian formulations
about Jesus.

2 Enoch, Appendix

Cultic activities are a special concern for the author of 2 Enoch.
When Enoch is taken to heaven, his son Methuselah erects an altar
and offers sacrifice on the spot. The main part of the book is then
followed by a narrative that describes how the priestly succession
survives from Methuselah until after the flood.

When Methuselah is about to die, he appoints as his successor
Nir, the son of his son Lamech and the brother of Noah. Nir's wife,
Sopanima, is barren, and in their old age husband and wife remain
celibate. Then one day Sopanima finds herself pregnant without
benefit of a consort. When Nir discovers her condition, he suspects
her of adultery, and his angry tirade strikes her dead on the spot. Nir
rushes out to find Noah, so that they can bury Sopanima secretly.[14]

3 [17]And then came an infant from the dead Sopanima, and sat on the
bed at her right hand. And Noah and Nir entered and saw the infant
sitting by the dead Sopanima and wiping its clothes. [18]And Noah and Nir
were tempted with a great fear, for the child was complete in its body,
like one of three years old; and it spoke with its lips, and blessed the

Lord. ¹⁹And Noah and Nir gazed upon it; and behold, the seal of the priesthood was on its breast, and it was glorious in countenance. ²⁰And Noah and Nir said, "See, the Lord renews the consecration according to our blood, as he desires." ²¹And Noah and Nir hastened and washed the child, and clothed it in priestly vestments, and gave it the blessed bread. And it ate. And they called its name Melchizedek.

Nir becomes concerned with the fate of the child because of the growing lawlessness of the generation that precedes the flood. God then appears to him in a vision.

²⁸"But do not trouble yourself about the child, Nir, for in a short time I will send my chief captain Michael, and he shall take the child and place him in the paradise of Eden, in the garden where Adam was formerly during a period of seven years, having the heaven always open until the time of his sin. ²⁹And this child shall not perish with those who perish in this generation, as I have shown, but shall be a holy priest in all things, Melchizedek, and I will appoint him that he may be the chief of the priests who were before."

In due time, Michael appears to Nir and identifies himself.

4 ⁵"Be not afraid, Nir, I am the chief captain of the Lord. The Lord has sent me, and behold, I will take your child today and will go with him, and will place him in the paradise of Eden, and there shall he be forever. ⁶And when the twelfth generation shall be, and a thousand and seventy years shall be, in that generation a just man shall be born (i.e., Abraham), and the Lord shall tell him to come out upon that mountain where the ark of your brother Noah shall stand, and he shall find there another Melchizedek who has lived there seven years, concealing himself from the people who worship idols, so that they should not slay him, and he shall lead him forth and he shall be priest, and the first king in the town of Salem after the fashion of this Melchizedek, the commencement of the priests. And 3,432 years shall be fulfilled till that time from the beginning and creation of Adam. ⁷And from that Melchizedek there shall be twelve priests in number till the great Igumen, that is to say leader, who shall bring forth all things visible and invisible.ᵃ

a. Perhaps a reference to a kind of reincarnation.

This story is typical of the genre of narratives that ascribes the birth of great figures to direct divine intervention (e.g., Abraham, Isaac, Samson). Its position at the end of 2 Enoch parallels the placement of the story of the wondrous birth of Noah in 1 Enoch 106–7. The conception without benefit of a human father reflects a very close relationship to the stories of Jesus' conception, and Nir's suspicion parallels the suspicion of Joseph in Matthew 1:19 and that of Lamech in the story of Noah's birth in the Qumran Genesis Apocryphon 2.

Although the story in its present form stands in a document transmitted in Christian circles, there is no reason to deny its Jewish origins. Its emphasis on the miraculous conception appears to reflect the same milieu of speculation that produced the Melchizedek traditions in the Epistle to the Hebrews (see below, p. 192).[15]

PARALLEL DEVELOPMENTS

The New Testament

Early Christian theology was in large part Christology. That is, its point of departure was Jesus of Nazareth, and its central concerns were informed by the church's understanding of who and what he was. In expressing itself on this matter, the church ascribed to Jesus the full array of titles and functions that contemporary Judaism attributed to agents of divine deliverance.

THE WISDOM OF GOD

In Chapter 6 we shall discuss Jewish speculations about the heavenly Wisdom, the agent of creation, who is sometimes identified with the Torah. A number of New Testament texts identify Jesus as the incarnation of divine Wisdom. Important here are those elements in the New Testament texts that describe Jesus as a savior figure.

In the Gospel according to John, Jesus' title par excellence is "Son of God," a title that denotes his divine status as Wisdom. For this evangelist, salvation is revelation.[16] Jesus is the revealer who descends from heaven to make the Father known to humanity, and those who believe in Jesus as the divine envoy have eternal life. As a prologue to his book, the author employs a poem that summarizes the message of the book (see below, p. 227). The eternal Wisdom, here called the *Logos* (God's "Word"), becomes flesh in order to reveal and mediate divine grace and truth, so that those who believe may become "children of God."

In both John 1:3 and Colossians 1:15–20, Jesus is identified as the agent of creation. The point appears to be that the Creator has intervened to deliver his wayward creatures.

Philippians 2:6–11 also expresses a Wisdom christology. Here the fact of salvation is Jesus' exaltation as "Lord," which was the result of his obedience unto death. This death, in turn, was made possible by the humility that led him to empty himself of his divine status and to take the form of a man. Thus incarnation does not function to facilitate revelation, but is the first step in the humiliation of the divine Wisdom, who becomes the suffering servant of God. Of Wisdom's role in creation we hear nothing.

THE DAVIDIC MESSIAH

Jesus' status as the Davidic Messiah is acclaimed in the earliest strata of the New Testament.

Romans 1:3–4

The apostle Paul quotes a creed:

. . . concerning his son—
born of the seed of David
   according to the flesh;
designated powerful Son of God
   according to the spirit of holiness by the resurrection of the dead
—Jesus Christ our Lord.

The creed contrasts Jesus' human origin as a descendant of David with his "spiritual" status as Son of God. The Greek is ambiguous about whether Jesus becomes (is "appointed") Son of God or is shown to have been (is "declared") Son of God by virtue of the resurrection. In the latter case, we may have combined in one text Jesus' status as Davidic Messiah and his identity as the divine Wisdom. According to either interpretation, however, his status as Davidic Messiah is superseded by his identity as God's Son. Moreover, the messianic title "Christ" is taken for granted and has become a part of the name of Jesus, whose title is "our Lord."

Matthew 21:1–11

For Matthew, Jesus' status as Davidic Messiah is central. The Gospel begins with a genealogy that legitimates Jesus as "son of David, son of Abraham" (1:1). The story of the Magi (chap. 2) identifies him as "King of the Jews." In recounting Jesus' entry into Jerusalem, Matthew, different from Mark,[17] explicitly identifies him as "son of David" and quotes Zechariah 9:9, on which the story is based.

[Handwritten margin notes: "Jesus was just a God the Son, he could have chosen not to die on the cross, but would have still been God's Son. He didn't do anything to earn the title."]

1 And when they drew near to Jerusalem and came to Bethphage, to the Mount of Olives, then Jesus sent two disciples, ²saying to them, "Go into the village opposite you, and immediately you will find an ass tied, and a colt with her; untie them and bring them to me. ³If anyone says anything to you, you shall say, 'The Lord has need of them,' and he will send them immediately."

4 This took place to fulfill what was spoken by the prophet, saying,
⁵"'Tell the daughter of Zion,
Behold, your king is coming to you,
  humble, and mounted on an ass,
  and on a colt, the foal of an ass.'"
⁶The disciples went and did as Jesus had directed them; ⁷they brought the ass and the colt, and put their garments on them, and he sat thereon. ⁸Most of the crowd spread their garments on the road, and others cut branches from the trees and spread them on the road. ⁹And the crowds that went before him and that followed him shouted, "Hosanna to the Son of David! Blessed is he who comes in the name of the Lord! Hosanna in the highest!" ¹⁰And when he entered Jerusalem, all the city was stirred, saying, "Who is this?" ¹¹And the crowds said, "This is the prophet Jesus from Nazareth of Galilee."

Verse 9 offers a hint as to Jesus' messianic function. He "comes in the name of the Lord," as God's agent. In the present context the acclamation "Hosanna" appears to be a word of praise. The Hebrew word, however, means "Save us," suggesting that in an earlier form of the story the crowd saw Jesus as the messianic agent by which God would deliver his people Israel. Thus, a view of the Davidic Messiah like that in Psalms of Solomon 17 appears to have been in the background. For Matthew, Jesus the Son of David is also a prophet (v. 11), though perhaps not the expected eschatological prophet (see above, p. 176).

Matthew 16:13–19

Matthew's emphasis on Jesus as the Davidic Messiah comes to focus in chapter 16.

13 Now when Jesus came into the district of Caesarea Philippi, he asked his disciples, "Who do men say that the Son of Man is?" ¹⁴And they said, "Some say John the Baptist, others say Elijah, and others Jeremiah or one of the prophets." ¹⁵He said to them, "But who do you say that I am?" ¹⁶Simon Peter replied, "You are the Christ, the Son of the living God."

[17] And Jesus answered him, *Son of Jonah*

"Blessed are you, Simon bar Jona!
  For flesh and blood has not revealed this to you,
  but my Father who is in heaven.
[18] And I tell you, you are Peter,
  and on this rock I will build my church,
  and the gates of Hades shall not prevail against it.
[19] And I will give you the keys of the kingdom of heaven,
  and whatever you bind on earth shall be bound in heaven,
  and whatever you loose on earth shall be loosed in heaven."

The disciples' answer to Jesus' question (vv. 13–14) recalls Jewish speculations about the return of Elijah and the eschatological prophet. However, Peter, responding to divine revelation, identifies him as the Messiah. Jesus responds, in turn, with language drawn from Isaiah 22:15–25, where Eliakim is appointed as major-domo of "the house of David." Here, however, Simon Peter is given the keys to the kingdom of heaven, and Jesus' authority as Lord (cf. Matt. 28:16–20) allows him to speak of the congregation of the true Israel as "my church." However one interprets v. 19, it is clear that for Matthew, Jesus' status as Messiah includes the authority—here delegated to Peter—to grant or to bar entry into the kingdom of heaven. Elsewhere, his status as "son of David" brings with it the expectation that he can heal the sick (Matt. 9:27; 12:23; 15:22; 20:30–31).

NO, No,   No,   No,
Jesus gives Peter the Authority to bind + cast out spirits. Spiritual authority, not an authority over salvation. This is a

THE HIGH PRIEST

The Epistle to the Hebrews

Jesus' office as high priest is most clearly described in the Epistle to the Hebrews. The book's Christology, however, is complex, ascribing to Jesus a number of titles and functions. Most of them are summarized in the opening lines of the book.

Hebrews 1:1–5

1 In many and various ways God spoke of old to our fathers by the prophets; [2] but in these last days he has spoken to us by a Son, whom he appointed the heir of all things, through whom also he created the world. [3] He reflects the glory of God and bears the very stamp of his nature, upholding the universe by his word of power. When he had made purification for sins, he sat down at the right hand of the Majesty on high, [4] having become as much superior to angels as the name he has

obtained is more excellent than theirs. [5]For to what angel did God ever say,

"You are my Son,
today I have begotten you"? (Ps 2:7)

Not a book that I've ever heard of. Not in agreement w/ mainline christianity

As the divine Wisdom, Jesus reflects God's glory (see the description of Wisdom in Wis 7:25–26 and cf. Col 1:15), he was the agent of creation, and he is the revealer, through whom God speaks (cf. John 1:1). Like Wisdom in Philippians 2, he descended, died, and has been exalted. Different from Philippians, his death is here understood as purification of sins, an idea consonant with his function as high priest; and his exaltation is described in the language of Psalm 110:1, where the Davidic king is called "a priest forever after the order of Melchizedek" (v. 4). As Wisdom, Jesus is God's Son, and this title is anchored in a quotation of Psalm 2:7, a royal psalm. Thus the introduction of the Epistle to the Hebrews presents Jesus as the Wisdom of God, called the "Son," the Davidic Messiah, and the great high priest. *aahh!! help these authors!!*

Hebrews 2:14–18; 4:14–16

Jesus' divine origins notwithstanding, he is the *incarnate* Wisdom, whose humanity was in the service of his high-priestly office.

2 [14]Since therefore the children share in flesh and blood, he himself likewise partook of the same nature, that through death he might destroy him who has the power of death, that is, the devil, [15]and deliver all those who through fear of death were subject to lifelong bondage. [16]For surely it is not with angels that he is concerned but with the descendants of Abraham. [17]Therefore he had to be made like his brethren in every respect, so that he might become a merciful and faithful high priest in the service of God, to make expiation for the sins of the people. [18]For because he himself has suffered and been tempted, he is able to help those who are tempted. . . .

4 [14]Since then we have a great high priest who has passed through the heavens, Jesus, the Son of God, let us hold fast our confession. [15]For we have not a high priest who is unable to sympathize with our weaknesses, but one who in every respect has been tempted as we are, yet without sinning. [16]Let us then with confidence draw near to the throne of grace, that we may receive mercy and find grace to help in time of need.

As high priest, Jesus made expiation for the people through his own death, when he passed through the veil of the heavens to the heavenly temple. Exalted in heaven, he is the helper of those who are weak, as he himself was in the days of his humanity. The use of the double negative in 4:15 ("do *not* have . . . *un*able") may indicate that this author is polemicizing against the belief that the heavenly high priest is an angel—perhaps Michael or Melchizedek—or that Jesus himself was really an angel who had the appearance of a man.

Hebrews 6:19—7:3

In chapters 6–7 the author compares Jesus' high priesthood with that of the mysterious Melchizedek.

6 ¹⁹We have this as a sure and steadfast anchor of the soul, a hope that enters into the inner shrine behind the curtain, ²⁰where Jesus has gone as a forerunner on our behalf, having become a high priest for ever after the order of Melchizedek.

7 ¹For this Melchizedek, king of Salem, priest of the Most High God, met Abraham returning from the slaughter of the kings and blessed him; ²and to him Abraham apportioned a tenth part of everything. He is first, by translation of his name, king of righteousness, and then he is also king of Salem, that is, king of peace. ³He is without father or mother or genealogy, and has neither beginning of days nor end of life, but resembling the Son of God he continues a priest forever.

That Melchizedek had no parents and that he had "neither beginning of days nor end of life" is not deduced here simply from the sudden appearance and disappearance of the priest in Genesis 14. This author may well be depending on traditions which spoke of Melchizedek's mysterious birth and of his transcendent heavenly status (see above, pp. 184–87). In any event, he makes clear in 7:3 that his description of the priest is preparing us for a comparison with Jesus.

In 7:4–10, the author asserts that Melchizedek was greater than Abraham, who paid him in tithes, and greater than Levi, his great-grandson, the founder of the Jewish priesthood. He concludes that Jesus, the priest after the order of Melchizedek, supersedes and replaces the imperfect Aaronitic priesthood (7:11–28).

Romans 8:31–34

There is some evidence that a high-priestly christology was not unique to the Epistle to the Hebrews. A well-known passage by the apostle Paul may reflect such a christology.

31 What then shall we say to this? If God is for us, who is against us? [32]He who did not spare his own Son but gave him up for us all, will he not also give us all things with him? [33]Who shall bring any charge against God's elect? It is God who justifies; [34]who is to condemn? Is it Christ Jesus, who died, yes, who was raised from the dead, who is at the right hand of God, who indeed intercedes for us?

In v. 33 Paul paraphrases Isaiah 50:8–9, a passage that describes the vindication of the suffering servant of the Lord (see pp. 150–51). In v. 34, however, he alludes to Psalm 110:1. That Jesus' exaltation at God's right hand puts him in a position to "intercede" suggests that Paul has in mind the priestly functions of the Messiah who is "a priest forever after the order of Melchizedek."

THE SON OF MAN

The title "Son of Man" occurs frequently in the Gospels and always on the lips of Jesus himself. Son of Man sayings in the Synoptic Gospels are of three kinds. The first group describes Jesus in his earthly existence. Here the term is used with its usual Semitic connotation (a human being). Some of these sayings stress Jesus' humility. For example,

Foxes have holes, and birds of the air have nests;
but the Son of Man has nowhere to lay his head (Matt 8:20).

In other cases the term appears to reflect a paradox:

". . . But that you may know that the Son of Man has authority on earth to forgive sins"—he said to the paralytic—"I say to you, rise, take up your pallet and go home" (Mark 2:10–11).

And he said to them,
"The sabbath was made for man, not man for the sabbath; so the Son of Man is lord even of the sabbath" (Mark 2:27).

In the stories in which these passages are found, Jesus is challenged because he has assumed divine prerogatives or has violated divine institutions. He responds by asserting that he—the Son of Man—has such divine authority, to forgive sins and to be lord of the Sabbath.

A second group of sayings about the Son of Man are predictions that Jesus, the Son of Man, will suffer and die and rise again. Again his humanity is in view, and his humility as the suffering one.

The third group of passages deal with a future, eschatological judicial figure, whose functions approximate those of the Enochic Son of Man.

Mark 14:61–62

One of these passages occurs in the account of Jesus' hearing before the Sanhedrin.

Again the high priest asked him, "Are you the Christ, the Son of the Blessed?" And Jesus said, "I am; and you will see the Son of Man sitting at the right hand of Power, and coming with the clouds of heaven."

The passage is remarkable for its blend of christological titles. The high priest asks whether Jesus is the Messiah, "the Son of the Blessed"—whatever that latter title may have connoted for the high priest. Jesus responds with reference to the Son of Man, using phraseology from Daniel 7:13 and the messianic Psalm 110 (v. 1). Here, as often in Mark, Jesus qualifies his messiahship by reference to his status as Son of Man. In the present passage, Jesus asserts the paradox that the man who stands before Caiaphas is "the Son of Man" whose future enthronement he will see with his own eyes. Jesus appears to be implying a threat. The future Son of Man is not simply the enthroned champion of the exalted Israel, whose enemies have been defeated, as in Daniel 7. He is the persecuted one, exalted as judge of those who persecuted him (see Wis 2–5, above, pp. 132–35). His function as judge is that of the Enochic Son of Man (see above, pp. 177–82).

[margin handwritten note: No, just stating his power]

Mark 8:38

Another passage attributes to the future Son of Man judicial functions that relate to the manner in which people have responded to Jesus.

For whoever is ashamed of me and of my words
   in this adulterous and sinful generation,
   of him will the Son of Man also be ashamed
   when he comes in the glory of his Father.

When originally formulated, this saying may have made a distinction between Jesus and the Son of Man; however, for Mark, the two figures are identical. The parallelism of the passage underscores the

[margin handwritten note: no distinction in any way whatsoever the two terms are identical]

Son of Man's judicial duties. At the judgment, he will vindicate Jesus by condemning in court those who opposed Jesus or, at least, would not side with him. This role of the Son of Man as eschatological champion and defender of the righteous is central to 1 Enoch 62–63 and to its reuse in Matthew 25 (see below, pp. 195–96).

Matthew 24:36–44

A typology between the flood and the last judgment is essential in the following passage:

36 But of that day and hour no one knows, not even the angels of heaven, nor the Son, but the Father only. [37]As were the days of Noah, so will be the coming of the Son of Man. [38]For as in those days before the flood they were eating and drinking, marrying and giving in marriage, until the day when Noah entered the ark, [39]and they did not know until the flood came and swept them all away, so will be the coming of the Son of Man. [40]Then two men will be in the field; one is taken, and one is left. [41]Two women will be grinding at the mill; one is taken and one is left. [42]Watch therefore, for you do not know on what day your Lord is coming. [43]But know this, that if the householder had known in what part of the night the thief was coming, he would have watched and would not have let his house be broken into. [44]Therefore you also must be ready; for the Son of Man is coming at an hour you do not expect.

Here the days of the Son of Man are seen as a time of disaster and judgment. This predominating element, together with the parallelism between flood and last judgment, indicates that the Son of Man imagery has here been influenced by the traditions found in 1 Enoch. The Son of Man is the judge who will pay the wicked their due reward.

Matthew 25:31–46

This is the fullest description of the judicial functions of the Son of Man. The form and conceptual structure of the passage appear to draw on the judgment scene in 1 Enoch 62–63.[18]

31 When the Son of Man comes in his glory, and all the angels with him, then he will sit on his glorious throne. [32]Before him will be gathered all the nations, and he will separate them one from another as a shepherd separates the sheep from the goats, [33]and he will place the sheep at his right hand, but the goats at the left. [34]Then the King will say to those at his right hand, "Come, O blessed of my Father, inherit the kingdom

prepared for you from the foundation of the world; [35]for I was hungry and you gave me food, I was thirsty and you gave me drink, I was a stranger and you welcomed me, [36]I was naked and you clothed me, I was sick and you visited me, I was in prison and you came to me." [37]Then the righteous will answer him, "Lord, when did we see you hungry and feed you, or thirsty and give you drink? [38]And when did we see you a stranger and welcome you or naked and clothe you? [39]And when did we see you sick or in prison and visit you?" [40]And the King will answer them, "Truly, I say to you, as you did it to one of the least of these my brethren, you did it to me." [41]Then he will say to those at his left hand, "Depart from me, you cursed, into the eternal fire prepared for the devil and his angels; [42]for I was hungry and you gave me no food, I was thirsty and you gave me no drink, [43]I was a stranger and you did not welcome me, naked and you did not clothe me, sick and in prison and you did not visit me." [44]Then they also will answer, "Lord, when did we see you hungry or thirsty or a stranger or naked or sick or in prison, and did not minister to you?" [45]Then he will answer them, "Truly, I say to you, as you did it not to one of the least of these, you did it not to me." [46]And they will go away into eternal punishment, but the righteous into eternal life.

Here, as in 1 Enoch, the heavenly Son of Man is closely associated with the oppressed righteous. He is, moreover, their eschatological vindicator. This vindication involves the condemnation of their oppressors, who now recognize that in maltreating the brethren they have maltreated the Judge.

The Rabbinic Writings

The hope of an eschatological deliverance continued to be part of the Jewish faith during the early centuries of the Common Era, although the lengthy descriptions that typified the earlier writings are not to be found in the writings of the rabbis.

THE DAVIDIC MESSIAH

The Weekday *Shemoneh Esreh*, Petitions 14–15

Jewish hopes for an eschatological deliverer focus mainly on the figure of the Davidic Messiah. This hope is evident in two petitions of the *Shemoneh Esreh* ("Eighteen Benedictions"), a prayer known to have been used already in the early decades after the destruction of Jerusalem in 70 C.E.

And to Jerusalem, your city, return in mercy, and dwell in it as you have spoken; rebuild it forever soon in our days and speedily establish in it the throne of David. Blessed are you, O Lord, who rebuild Jerusalem.

Speedily cause the offspring of your servant, David, to flourish, and let his horn be exalted by your salvation, because we wait for your salvation always. Blessed are you, O Lord, who cause the horn of salvation to flourish.

Hope for the restoration of Jerusalem is here tied to the hope that the Davidic dynasty will be revived. The messianic king will rule from the capital of the renewed Israel; he will bring salvation to his people by delivering them from their enemies, their Roman overlords.

Genesis Rabba 49:11

This is a commentary on part of Jacob's prophecy about the royal descendants of his son Judah.

Rabbi Hanin says, "Israel has no need of the teaching of the King, the Messiah, in the future. As it says, 'Nations will search him out' (Isa 11:10), not Israel. If so, why does the messianic king come, and what does he come to do? To gather the exiles of Israel and to give them (i.e., the nations) thirty commandments; as it says, 'And he will say to them, if it is good in your eyes, measure out for me my wages in thirty pieces of silver' " (Zech 11:12). Rab said, "These are thirty warriors." Rabbi Yoḥanan said, "These are thirty commandments."

Here the messianic king is depicted both as a teacher of the Gentiles and as the one who will gather the dispersion. The latter idea occurs in Psalms of Solomon 17. The passage from Zechariah is interpreted to refer to the Messiah's teaching function but also to his role as a military leader.

Babylonian Talmud *Sanhedrin* 97a–98a

Speculation about the time of the Messiah's advent did not cease with the end of the first century. This text from the Talmud attributes the delay in his appearance to Israel's sin, and it anticipates the time of his coming.

Just as the sabbatical year causes a one year's cessation for each seven years, so each seven thousand years the world rests for a thousand years, as it says, "And the Lord will be elevated by himself on that day" (Isa

2:11), and it says, "A Psalm: A Song for the Sabbath Day" (Ps 92:1), and it says, "For a thousand years in your eyes are like yesterday that it passes" (Ps 90:4).

A teaching from the academy of Elijah: The world will exist for six thousand years: two thousand years of confusion; two thousand years of Torah; and two thousand years of the days of the Messiah. And because of our sins which are many, we have already lost some of them (i.e., the days of the Messiah).[a]

Elijah said to Rabbi Judah, the brother of Rabbi Salah the Hasid, "The world exists for no less than eighty-five jubilees, and in the last jubilee the Son of David comes."[b] He said to him, "Is it at the beginning or at the end (of the jubilee)?" He said to him, "I do not know." He said to him, "Is it completed or not completed?" He said to him, "I do not know."

Rabbi Hanin the son of Tahlifa said to Rabbi Joseph, "I found a man who held a scroll written in the square script and in the holy tongue.[c] I said to him, 'Where have you got this from?' He said to me, 'I was a mercenary in the Roman army, and I found it in the archives of Rome.' And it was written in it, 'After 4,291 years of the creation of the world, it will come to an end. Some of them (i.e., the years) will be the wars between the dragons,[d] some of them will be the wars of Gog and Magog,[e] and the rest will be the days of the Messiah; and the Holy One, blessed be he, will renew his world only after seven thousand years.' "

a. I.e., the world has already moved into some of the time allotted for the days of the Messiah, without his having come.

b. The Son of David will come between the years 4200 and 4250 Anno Mundi. Cf. the last tradition below, which calculates 4,291 years.

c. It was written in Hebrew in square Aramaic characters. These were the requirements for a biblical book; see Louis Ginzberg, "Some Observations on the Attitude of the Synagogue towards Apocalyptic-Eschatological Writings," *JBL* 41 (1922) 119–20.

d. Cf. Add Esth 11:5–11 and 10:4–13.

e. See Ezek 38–39.

THE ROYAL AND PRIESTLY MESSIAHS

The hope for twin deliverers or leaders, expressed in the Qumran scrolls and the Testaments of the Twelve Patriarchs, does not die out in later Judaism.

Commentary on Psalm 43

"Why go I mourning under the oppression of the enemy?" (Ps 43:2). For from what did you redeem our fathers in Egypt? Was it not from the oppression wherewith the Egyptians oppressed them, of which God said, "Moreover, I have seen the oppression" (Exod 3:9)? For me too, life is nothing but oppression by an enemy. Then "Why must I go about by myself mourning under the oppression of the enemy?" Did you not send redemption at the hand of two redeemers to that generation, as is said, "He sent Moses his servant, and Aaron whom he had chosen" (Ps 105:26)? Send two redeemers like them to this generation. "O send out your light and your truth; let them lead me" (Ps 43:3), "your light" being the prophet Elijah of the house of Aaron, of which it is written, "The seven lamps shall give light in front of the candlestick" (Num 8:2); and "your truth" being the Messiah, son of David, as is written, "The Lord hath sworn in truth unto David; He will not turn from it: of the fruit of your body will I set upon thy throne" (Ps 132:11). Likewise Scripture says, "Behold, I will send you Elijah the prophet" (Mal 4:5) who is one redeemer, and speaks of the second redeemer in the verse, "Behold my servant whom I uphold" (Isa 42:1). Hence, "O send out your light and your truth."

The two leaders of ancient Israel, Moses and Aaron, are seen as prototypes of the royal and priestly deliverers of the future. The priestly figure will be the returning Elijah, promised by Malachi, who will be the light, the teacher of Israel. The Davidic Messiah embodies God's truth or faithfulness to his promises, here the promise to David. He is identified with the servant of the Lord in Second Isaiah. Since neither Elijah nor the Davidic Messiah is obviously referred to in the text of Psalm 43, it is evident that the compiler of the commentary had these two figures as part of his eschatological hope and that he found a suitable passage to which to attach this hope.

NOTES

1. Jonas C. Greenfield and Michael E. Stone, "Remarks on the Aramaic Testament of Levi from the Geniza," *RB* 86 (1979) 223–24.

2. The language of Isa 11:2 also appears in Levi's prayer, which is part of a lengthy addition at 2:3 in the Greek ms. e of T. Levi (v. 8) and which is contained in the Qumran Aramaic ms. 4QT Levi ara 1:14.

3. A fragment of T. Levi 14:3–4 is preserved in 4QT Levi ara 8 3:1–6. Correlations between Levi's prayer (see n. 2 immediately above), the description of his call (chap. 4), and chap. 18 suggest that this last passage in some form was the climax of the Aramaic text.

4. Especially noteworthy are those verses that fit better in a Christian setting than in a Jewish setting. Vv. 6–7 read like an interpretation of the story of Jesus' baptism (Mark 1:9–11), and they are paralleled by early Christian texts that interpret that event as the commissioning of Jesus as the anointed priest. See Tertullian, On Baptism 7.1; Cyril of Jerusalem, Catechetical Lectures 10.1; 21.5–6; de uno domine 11; Catechetical Lectures 21;

de sacro chrism. 5–6; Pseudo-Clement, Recognitions 1.44.6—48.6; Armenian Penitence of Adam 41–42 and Life of Adam and Eve 41–42. Vv. 10–12 could also be an interpretation of the story of Jesus' temptation (Mark 1:12–13). The contrast between the ignorance of Israel and the enlightenment of the Gentiles (v. 9) is typical of the Testaments of the Twelve Patriarchs and also fits well in a Christian context; cf. Jacob Jervell, "Ein Interpolator interpretiert," in Christoph Burchard, Jacob Jervell, and Johannes Thomas, *Studien zu den Testamenten der Zwölf Patriarchen,* Beiheft zur *Zeitschrift für die Neustestamentliche Wissenschaft* 36 (Berlin: Töpelmann, 1969) 30–61.

5. On the Testament of Levi and the teaching functions of the priests, see Greenfield and Stone, "Remarks," 226–27.

6. On this problem in particular and Qumran messianic belief in general, see Frank M. Cross, *The Ancient Library of Qumran,* 219–30; Geza Vermes, *The Dead Sea Scrolls* (Philadelphia: Fortress, 1981), 184–86, 194–97; and the bibliography cited by Joseph A. Fitzmyer, *The Dead Sea Scrolls: Major Publications and Tools for Study,* SBLSBS 8 (Missoula: Scholars Press, 1975) 114–18.

7. Cf. functions of the eschatological priest in T. Levi 18, above, pp. 168–70.

8. On the difficulties in reconstructing crucial parts of this passage, see the discussion in Cross, *Library,* 87–90.

9. For a similar lineup of possibilities, cf. Matt 16:13–16, above, p. 189.

10. See Jonas C. Greenfield and Michael E. Stone, "The Enochic Pentateuch and the Date of the Similitudes," *HTR* 70 (1977) 51–65; and George W. E. Nickelsburg, *Jewish Literature Between the Bible and the Mishnah* (Philadelphia: Fortress, 1981) 221–23. On the current discussion of the Parables, see David Winston Suter, "Weighed in the Balance: The Similitudes of Enoch in Recent Discussion," *RelSRev* 7 (1981) 217–21.

11. For this explanation of 4 Ezra 13, see Michael Stone, "The Concept of the Messiah in IV Ezra," in Jacob Neusner, ed., *Religions in Antiquity,* Memorial Volume for E. R. Goodenough (Leiden: Brill, 1968) 303–10.

12. Other elements in the interpretation not represented in the vision reflect concerns of the author: the fate and deliverance of "those who are left" (vv. 26, 48–49; cf. vv. 16–19); the woes of the end-time (vv. 30–33; cf. 5:1–13; 6:20–24); the new Jerusalem (v. 36; cf. chap. 10); the tortures of the damned (v. 38; cf. 7:79–87).

13. The translation below is that of Joseph A. Fitzmyer, "Further Light on Melchizedek from Qumran Cave 11," in idem, *Essays on the Semitic Background of the New Testament,* 249–50. The commentary is also based on his notes.

14. The textual criticism of 2 Enoch is in a state of flux. For two different appraisals, see A. Vaillant, *Le Livre des Secrets d'Hénoch* (Paris: Institut d'Études Slaves, 1952), the Slavonic text with facing French translation; and Francis Andersen's English translation in James H. Charlesworth, ed., *The Old Testament Pseudepigrapha* (Garden City, N.Y.: Doubleday, forthcoming).

15. For an example of the Gnostic development of the figure of Melchizedek, see Birger A. Pearson and Søren Giverson, "Melchizedek," in

James M. Robinson, ed., *The Nag Hammadi Library* (New York: Harper & Row, 1977) 399–403; and the discussion by Pearson in *Nag Hammadi Codices IX and X,* Nag Hammadi Studies 15 (Leiden: Brill, 1981) 28–34.

16. See Wayne Meeks, "The Man from Heaven and Johannine Sectarianism," *JBL* 91 (1972): 44–72.

17. Mark is the source from which Matthew derives this material.

18. On this passage, see above, pp. 180–81. On the relationship of Matthew 25:31–46 to 1 Enoch 62–63, see David R. Catchpole, "The Poor on Earth and the Son of Man in Heaven," *Bulletin of the John Rylands Library of Manchester* 61 (1979) 378–83.

BIBLIOGRAPHY

PRIMARY SOURCES

The Bible (except for Romans 1) and 4 Ezra are quoted from the RSV; 2 Enoch from W. F. **Morfill** and R. H. **Charles,** *The Book of the Secrets of Enoch* (Oxford: Clarendon, 1896), with some adaptation; the Damascus Document, the Florilegium, the Messianic Rule, and The Rule of the Community from Geza **Vermes,** *The Dead Sea Scrolls in English,* 2d ed. (Harmondsworth: Penguin, 1975); the Testimonia from Frank M. **Cross,** *The Ancient Library of Qumran,* rev. ed. (Garden City, N.Y.: Doubleday, 1961) 148–49; the Qumran Melchizedek Document from Joseph A. **Fitzmyer,** *Essays on the Semitic Background of the New Testament,* SBLSBS 5 (Missoula: Scholars Press, 1974) 249–50; the Commentary on Psalm 43 from William G. **Braude,** *The Midrash on Psalms,* Yale Judaica Series 13:2 (New Haven: Yale University Press, 1959) 445.

SECONDARY SOURCES

THE MESSIAH(S)

Walter **Grundmann,** Franz **Hesse,** Adam S. **van der Woude,** and Marinus **de Jonge,** "Chriō, etc.," *TDNT* 9 (1974) 492–580.

THE SON OF MAN

Carsten **Colpe,** *"Ho huios tou anthropou,"* *TDNT* 8 (1972) 400–477. David Winston **Suter,** "Weighed in the Balance: The Similitudes of Enoch in Recent Discussion," *RelSRev* 7 (1981) 217–21. Heinz E. **Tödt,** *The Son of Man in the Synoptic Tradition* (Philadelphia: Westminster, 1965).

MELCHIZEDEK

Joseph A. **Fitzmyer,** "Now This Melchizedek . . .' (Heb 7:1) and "New Light on Melchizedek," in idem, *Essays on the Semitic Background of the New Testament,* SBLSBS 5 (Missoula: Scholars Press, 1974) 221–43, 245–67, a good discussion of this figure in Hebrews and the Qumran fragment, together with relevant bibliography. Paul J. **Kobelski,** *Melchizedek and Melchireša',* Catholic Biblical Quarterly Monograph Series 10 (Washington, D.C.: Catholic Biblical Association of America, 1981), a detailed study of Qumran texts and their relationships to the New Testament.

6
Lady Wisdom
and Israel

Wise proverbs and pithy sayings embodying the experience of life are of immemorial antiquity and common to all human cultures. In the ancient Near East, however, the teaching of such wisdom became the particular responsibility of scribal schools which prepared clerks and high officials to serve in the royal bureaucracies of Egypt and Mesopotamia and other kingdoms. When we recall the complexities not only of the empires but even of the systems of writing (hieroglyphs and cuneiform) of these cultures, we can see that this was a specialized training.

In ancient Israel there was popular wisdom, of course; the parable of Jotham (Judg 9) and the traditions that clustered around the figure of King Solomon (1 Kgs 3; 4:29–34; 10:1–10) are examples of this. Some scholars would maintain, however, that stories of Solomon's wisdom reflect the existence and activity of a school of wisdom at the royal court. In any case, the figure of King Solomon became central in the books of collected wisdom sayings which became part of the Hebrew Bible. Solomon is the reputed author of Proverbs and Qoheleth (Ecclesiastes). Other wisdom writings in the Hebrew Bible include Job and certain psalms.

Of all the types of literature in Hebrew Scriptures, the wisdom literature makes least reference to the particular historical traditions which constituted the world view and self-understanding of the people of Israel. It does not mention the Exodus or Sinai or the Mosaic covenant. This silence is due to the ancient, international character of the wisdom tradition. Some parts of Proverbs, for example, are an adaptation of an Egyptian wisdom writing known already in the second millennium B.C.E.[1]

In the postbiblical wisdom literature, two related developments occur. First, wisdom is "Judaized"; the national and historical traditions of Israel are introduced into the wisdom literature. Consequently wisdom is identified with the Torah, and life in conformity with its teachings is that of the truly wise man. This development reflects the situation in which the Torah had become the common cultural and religious axiom of the whole Jewish people. The postbiblical wisdom traditions, and the social or religious institutions that transmitted them, are permeated by the Torah.

The second development in the wisdom tradition appears already in parts of Job and later sections of Proverbs. Wisdom emerges as a heavenly person. Sometimes Wisdom is God's, yet it is regarded as an independent entity; it is no longer merely the sum of the teachings of the wisdom schools, the collection of wise maxims for the conduct of men or even of court officials. In these later texts, Wisdom was associated with God in the act of creation, or at least existed before creation. It is hidden from men and often said to be revealed to them by God himself. This divine Wisdom is identified with the Torah, the special revelation of God to Israel, and it is thus particularized in it. At the same time, Torah develops from being the concrete revelation to Moses on Sinai and all that flows from it— although it never ceases to be that—and it becomes that in accordance with which the world is constituted.

There is a disjunction between the personified Wisdom and wisdom in the sense usually found in the wisdom writings of Israel and of the ancient Near East. The different passages in which personified Wisdom most clearly emerges seem to share certain features. Perhaps a common ancient mythological structure lies behind the figure of Wisdom as it appears in these passages. One possible piece of evidence for this is to be found in the Wisdom of Aḥikar, a pagan writing the earliest witness to which is a fifth-century B.C.E. papyrus in the Aramaic language from Egypt. The relevant text is fragmentary, but the following reading has been suggested: "[Wi]sdom is [from] the gods, and to the gods she is precious; for[ever] her kingdom is fixed in heav[en], for the lord of the holy ones (i.e., the gods of heaven) has raised her."[2] If this interpretation is accepted, the text talks of the heavenly origin of Wisdom, her celestial abode, and perhaps the theme of her search for a place in which to live.

The idea of Wisdom might have mythological origins or background, but its development owes much to the prominence of the concept of intermediary beings between God and the world in the second temple period. Angels were mentioned often in the Hebrew

Bible, but the extensive role they play in the period of the second temple is notable. Hellenistic Jewry, bringing Greek and Jewish modes of thought together, developed various intermediary beings, one of whom was *Sophia*, or Wisdom, and another, *Logos*, or the Divine Reason or Word. The Dead Sea Scrolls talk often of angelic or demonic spirits. The development of the figure of Wisdom must be seen in the same context.

WISDOM PERSONIFIED

Job 28:12–28

This passage forms part of Job's response to Bildad, which commences in 26:1. The first part of chapter 28 continues the discourse starting in 27:13, which emphasizes the pointlessness of the wealth and achievements of wicked men, including mining and precious metals, jewels, and the like.

WISDOM CANNOT BE FOUND ON EARTH

12 But where shall wisdom be found?
And where is the place of understanding?
[13]Man does not know the way to it,[a]
and it is not found in the land of the living.
[14]The deep says, "It is not in me,"
and the sea says, "It is not with me."

WISDOM CANNOT BE BOUGHT

[15]It cannot be gotten for gold,
and silver cannot be weighed as its price.
[16]It cannot be valued in the gold of Ophir,
in precious onyx or sapphire.[b]
[17]Gold and glass cannot equal it,
nor can it be exchanged for jewels of fine gold.
[18]No mention shall be made of coral or of crystal;
the price of wisdom is above pearls.
[19]The topaz of Ethiopia cannot compare with it,
nor can it be valued in pure gold.

WISDOM CANNOT BE FOUND IN
THE UNDERWORLD

[20]Whence then comes wisdom?
And where is the place of understanding?

²¹It is hid from the eyes of all living,
    and concealed from the birds of the air.
²²Abaddon and Death^c say,
    "We have heard a rumor of it with our ears."

GOD ALONE KNOWS WISDOM'S PLACE,
AND HE ESTABLISHED IT IN CREATION

²³God understands the way to it,
    and he knows its place.
²⁴For he looks to the ends of the earth,
    and sees everything under the heavens.
²⁵When^d he gave to the wind its weight,
    and meted out the waters by measure;
²⁶When he made a decree for the rain,
    and a way for the lightning of the thunder;
²⁷Then he saw it and declared it;
    he established it and searched it out.^e

GOD GRANTS WISDOM TO MEN

²⁸And^f he said to man,
    "Behold the fear of the Lord, that is wisdom;
    and to depart from evil is understanding."

a. Gk; Heb "its price."
b. Or "lapis lazuli."
c. Two synonymous terms for the underworld or Sheol.
d. When he created the world. Cf. esp. Isa 40:12–14.
e. Cf. Sir 24:28–29.
f. Is this verse deliberately anticlimatic? The wisdom God can reveal to men is simple to understand. Is this the wisdom which cannot be found, which was present at Creation and which God alone knows? Many have suggested that the verse is a later addition to the chapter, yet the idea that Wisdom is the fear of the Lord is found frequently in contexts like this; cf. Prov 8:13 (see note on this verse below); Sir 1:11–18. If these latter verses depend on Job, then the interpolation in Job is ancient. Observe that in Job 38–39 God poses Job an almost sarcastic series of questions. The first is, "Where were you when I laid the foundation of the earth?" implying that God alone is Creator and Lord of the forces of nature and the world. In 38:36–37 Job is asked, "Who has put wisdom in the clouds, or given understanding to the mists? Who can number the clouds by wisdom?" and in 39:26, "Is it by your wisdom that the hawk soars . . . ?" These verses imply that it is by God's wisdom, not Job's, that these things happen; thus these verses add some support to a possible contrast of divine and human wisdom implied by Job 28:28. For other earlier sources for God's wisdom in creation, see below, note a to Wis 9.

The Book of Proverbs

The first nine chapters of Proverbs are commonly regarded as a

literary unity. Throughout these chapters wisdom is often personified as a woman. Thus, by way of example, 1:20–21:

> Wisdom cries aloud in the street;
>> in the markets she raises her voice;
> on the top of the walls she cries out;
>> at the entrance of the city gates she speaks.

In apposite contrast, foolishness (or, according to some views, false
wisdom) is represented by the evil woman, the whore who is such a
sustained theme in these chapters. She is "the loose woman," the

> adventuress with her smooth words
>> who forsakes the companion of her youth
>> and forgets the covenant of her God;
> for her house sinks down to death,
>> and her paths to the shades;
> none who go to her come back
>> nor do they regain the paths of life.[3]

Proverbs 2:1–11 reads almost as a commentary on Job 28. If a man
seeks Wisdom more diligently than treasures, he "will understand
the fear of the Lord and find the knowledge of God" (2:5). "Wisdom
is given by the Lord, knowledge and understanding come from his
mouth" (2:6). In chapter 2 the divine origin and character of Wisdom
are implied.

The Speech of Wisdom

Proverbs 8

In chapter 8, however, characterization of Wisdom is carried to its
furthest point in Proverbs, and a number of themes, already observed in Job, come to the fore once again. Wisdom opens the
chapter with a speech addressed to the sons of men. In it she relates
her own virtues. Verses 22–36 are a distinctive hymn, extolling Wisdom's role in creation.[4]

> 1 Does[a] not wisdom call,
>> does not understanding raise her voice?
> ²On the heights beside the way,
>> in the paths she takes her stand;
> ³beside the gates in front of the town,
>> at the entrance of the portals she cries aloud.

WISDOM CALLS TO THE SONS OF MEN
AND DESCRIBES HERSELF

[4]To you, O men, I call,
   and my cry is to the sons of men.
[5]O simple ones, learn prudence;
   O foolish men, pay attention.
[6]Hear, for I will speak noble things,
   and from my lips will come what is right;
[7]for my mouth will utter truth;
   wickedness is an abomination to my lips.
[8]All the words of my mouth are righteous;
   there is nothing twisted or crooked in them.
[9]They are all straight to him who understands
   and right to those who find knowledge.

WISDOM IS MORE VALUABLE THAN
GOLD AND SILVER

[10]Take my instruction instead of silver,[b]
   and knowledge rather than choice gold;
[11]for wisdom is better than jewels,
   and all that you may desire cannot compare with her.

WISDOM DESCRIBES HERSELF
AND HER ROLE AMONG MEN

[12]I, wisdom, dwell in prudence,[c]
   and I find knowledge and discretion.
[13]The fear of the Lord is hatred of evil.[d]
   Pride and arrogance and the way of evil and perverted speech I hate.
[14]I have counsel and sound wisdom,
   I have insight, I have strength.
[15]By me kings reign,
   and rulers decree what is just;
[16]by me princes rule,
   and nobles govern the earth.
[17]I love those who love me,
   and those who seek me diligently find me.

WISDOM IS MORE PRECIOUS THAN WEALTH
AND GIVES MEN RICHES

[18]Riches and honor are with me,
   enduring wealth and prosperity.
[19]My fruit is better than gold, even fine gold,
   and my yield than choice silver.

[20]I walk in the way of righteousness,
    in the paths of justice.
[21]Endowing with wealth those who love me,
    and filling their treasuries.

WISDOM WAS THE FIRST
CREATED BEING

[22]The Lord created[e] me at the beginning of his work,[f]
    the first of his acts of old.
[23]Ages ago I was set up,
    at the first, before the beginning of the earth.
[24]When there were no depths I was brought forth,[g]
    when there were no springs abounding with water.
[25]Before the mountains had been shaped,
    before the hills I was brought forth;
[26]before he had made the earth with its fields,[h]
    or the first of the dust of the world.

WISDOM WAS PRESENT WITH GOD IN
THE ACTS OF CREATION

[27]When he established the heavens I was there,[i]
    when he drew a circle on the face of the deep,[j]
[28]when he made firm the skies above,
    when he established the fountains of the deep,
[29]when he assigned to the sea its limit,[k]
    so that the waters might not transgress his command,
when he marked out the foundations of the earth,
[30]   then I was beside him, like a master workman;[l]
and I was daily his[m] delight
    rejoicing before him always.
[31]rejoicing in his inhabited world,
    and delighting in the sons of men.[n]

WISDOM'S FINAL CALL TO MEN

[32]And now, my sons, listen to me:
    happy are those who keep my ways.
[33]Hear instruction and be wise,
    and do not neglect it.
[34]Happy is the man who listens to me,
    watching daily at my gates,
    waiting beside my doors.
[35]For he who finds me finds life
    and obtains favor from the Lord;

[36]but he who misses me injures himself;
   all who hate me love death.[o]

a. For the theme of Wisdom crying aloud in the city streets, cf. also 1:20–21 (quoted above) and elsewhere in chaps. 1–8.
b. Cf. Job 28:15–19 and Prov 8:18–21.
c. Heb obscure.
d. Cf. Job 28:28; Prov 1:7; 2:1–14; Sir 1:11–20. The last two share themes with the present passage.
e. Or "possessed."
f. Heb "way." Albright suggests a meaning analogous to ancient Canaanite DRKTH ("dominion").
g. Cf. Gen 1:1; 7:11.
h. Heb uncertain.
i. Cf. Gen 1:6–7.
j. Cf. Gen 1:9–10.
k. Cf. Job 38:8, 10–11; Ps 104:9; Jer 5:22.
l. Or "little child." Cf. Prov 3:19 for the translation accepted here.
m. Gk; Heb lacks "his."
n. Note that the self-praise of wisdom concludes with the relationship of wisdom to the world.
o. W. F. Albright ("Some Canaanite-Phoenician Sources of Hebrew Wisdom," Supplement to *Vetus Testamentum* 3 [1955] 1–15), following on his own earlier papers, has argued for a preexilic date of all of Proverbs, including these chapters, and for the Canaanite affinities of Israelite wisdom literature.

WISDOM IN
THE RIGHTEOUS PEOPLE

Apocryphal Psalms, col. 18

This composition is found in the Psalm Scroll from Cave 11 at Qumran, and its first two verses are extant only in a Syriac translation. The psalm probably stems from the third century or early second century B.C.E. In it Wisdom is said to have the function of telling the multitude of God's works, of making known God's glory.

WISDOM IS THE GLORIFICATION
OF GOD

1 [With a loud voice glorify God;
   in the congregation of the many proclaim his majesty. . . .]

[4]Form an assembly to proclaim his salvation,
   and be not lax in making known his might
   and his majesty to all simple folk.

[5]For to make known the glory of the Lord
   is Wisdom given,

[6]and for recounting his many deeds
    she is revealed to man:
[7]to make known to simple folk his might
    and to explain to senseless folk his greatness,
[8]those far from her gates,
    those remote from her portals.[a] . . .

WISDOM IN THE COMMUNITY
OF THE RIGHTEOUS

[12]From the gates of the righteous is heard her voice,
    and from the assembly of the pious her song.
[13]When they eat with satiety she is cited,
    also when they drink in community together,
[14]Their meditation is on the law of the Most High,
    their words on making known his might.
[15]How far from the wicked is her word,
    from all haughty men to know her.

a. Or "paths."

Wisdom is invoked in a psalmodic context of communal praise to God, for this writing is a mixture of psalmodic themes and wisdom concepts and is addressed not to the individual student ("my son" of Proverbs, etc.) but to a community. In vv. 12–15 there seems to be an extension of this combination. Not only is Wisdom expressed in the communal praise of the mighty deeds of God (perhaps in creation); it is also heard in the assembly of the pious living their communal life. Verse 14 seems to be on the verge of identifying Wisdom with Torah. Wisdom has moved far from being the teaching of the wisdom schools.[5]

WISDOM AND
THE FEAR OF GOD

The themes detected so far are further developed in the Wisdom of ben Sira, also called Sirach or Ecclesiasticus, which was written in the first decade or two of the second century B.C.E.[6] In this book, Joshua ben Sira collected wisdom sayings, most of which are of the traditional type. The collections of such sayings are punctuated by a series of hymns to the wise man and wisdom, and in some of these the personified figure of Wisdom and its Judaization are to be observed.

Wisdom of ben Sira 1:1-20

WISDOM COMES FROM GOD AND
IS IMMEASURABLE

1 All wisdom comes from the Lord
  and is with him forever.
[2]The sand of the sea, the drops of rain,
  and the days of eternity—who can count them?
[3]The height of heaven, the breadth of the earth,
  and the abyss and wisdom—who can track them out?
[4]Wisdom was created before all things,
  and prudent understanding from eternity.[a]

GOD ALONE KNOWS WISDOM AND
HAS GIVEN HER TO MEN

[6]The root of wisdom—to whom has it been revealed?
  Her clever devices—who knows them? . . .

[8]There is but One who is wise, greatly to be feared,
  sitting upon his throne.
[9]The Lord himself created wisdom;[b]
  he saw her and apportioned her,[c]
  he poured her out upon all his works.[d]
[10]She dwells with all flesh according to his gift,
  and he supplied her to those who love him.

THE FEAR OF THE LORD

[11]The fear of the Lord is glory and exultation,[e]
  and gladness and a crown of rejoicing.
[12]The fear of the Lord delights the heart,
  and gives gladness and joy and long life.
[13]With him who fears the Lord it will go well at the end;
  on the day of his death he will be blessed.
[14]To fear the Lord is the beginning of wisdom;[f]
  she is created with the faithful in the womb.[g]
[15]She made[h] among men an eternal foundation,
  and among their descendants she will be trusted.
[16]To fear the Lord is wisdom's full measure;
  for she satisfies[i] men with her fruits.
[17]She fills their whole house with desirable goods,[j]
  and their storehouses with her produce.
[18]The fear of the Lord is the crown of wisdom,
  making peace and perfect health to flourish.
[19]He saw her and apportioned her;

he rained down knowledge and discerning comprehension,
and he exalted the glory of those who held her fast.
²⁰To fear the Lord is the root of wisdom,
and her branches are long life.

a. For the ideas of the divine origin and precreation of Wisdom, see also Prov 8:22–29 and Job 28:23–27.
b. Gk "her."
c. Cf. v. 19 below.
d. For the themes of this section, cf. Job 28:23, 27–28; contrast Prov 8.
e. This whole section seems to be a development of Job 28:28; Prov 8:13.
f. Cf. Prov 1:7; Ps 111:10; etc.
g. The eternity of Wisdom is expressed in human, not cosmogonic, terms.
h. Gk "made as nest."
i. Gk "intoxicates." Cf. Sir 24:21; Apocryphal Psalm 154 (11QPs³ 18:13).
j. Prov 8:18–21.

THE PRAISE OF WISDOM

Wisdom of ben Sira 24

This is the most remarkable of the Wisdom hymns in the book. It opens with Wisdom praising herself in the divine court, among the heavenly beings. Wisdom mentions her role in creation and her search for a place to dwell. She is told to dwell in Jacob and said to be the Torah. This is one of the oldest texts making this identification explicit.

THE SELF-PRAISE OF WISDOM
IN THE DIVINE COUNCIL

1 Wisdom will praise herself
and will glory in the midst of her people.
²In the assembly of the Most High she will open her mouth,
and in the presence of his host she will glory;ᵃ

THE ORIGIN OF WISDOM AND HER SEARCH
FOR A DWELLINGᵇ

³"I came forth from the mouth of the Most High,ᶜ
and covered the earth like a mist.
⁴I dwelt in high places,
and my throne was in a pillar of cloud.ᵈ
⁵Alone I have made the circuit of the vault of heaven,
and have walked in the depths of the abyss.ᵉ
⁶In the waves of the sea, in the whole earth,
and in every people and nation I have gotten a possession.ᶠ

[7]Among all these I sought a resting place;
  I sought in whose territory I might lodge.

GOD GRANTS WISDOM A DWELLING
IN ISRAEL

[8]"Then the Creator of all things gave me a commandment,
  and the one who created me assigned a place for my tent.[g]
And he said, 'Make your dwelling in Jacob,
  and in Israel receive your inheritance.'[h]

WISDOM IN THE HEAVENLY TABERNACLE
AND IN ZION

[9]"From eternity, in the beginning, he created me,
  and for eternity I shall not cease to exist.
[10]In the holy tabernacle I ministered before him,
  and so[i] I was established in Zion.
[11]In the beloved city likewise he gave me a resting place,
  and in Jerusalem was my dominion.
[12]So I took root in an honored people,
  and in the portion of the Lord, who is their inheritance.

WISDOM FLOURISHES LIKE A TREE
AND IS FRAGRANT LIKE SPICES

[13]"I grew tall like a cedar in Lebanon,
  and like a cypress on the heights of Hermon.
[14]I grew tall like a palm tree in En-Gedi,[j]
  and like rose plants in Jericho;
 like a beautiful olive tree in the field,
  and like a plane tree I grew tall.
[15]Like cassia and camel's thorn I gave forth the aroma of spices,
  and like choice myrrh I spread a pleasant odor,
 like galbanum, onycha, and stacte,
  and like the fragrance of frankincense in the tabernacle.
[16]Like a terebinth I spread out my branches,
  and my branches are glorious and graceful.
[17]Like a vine I caused loveliness to bud,
  and my blossoms became glorious and abundant fruit.

WISDOM CONCLUDES HER ADDRESS WITH
A SUMMONS TO RECEIVE HER

[19]"Come to me, you who desire me,
  and eat your fill of my produce.
[20]For the remembrance of me is sweeter than honey,
  and my inheritance sweeter than the honeycomb.

[21]Those who eat me will hunger for more,
   and those who drink me will thirst for more.[k]
[22]Whoever obeys me will not be put to shame,
   and those who work with my help will not sin."

WISDOM IS THE TORAH OF MOSES

[23]All this is the book of the covenant of the Most High God,[l]
   the law which Moses commanded us
   as an inheritance for the congregation of Jacob. . . .
[25]It fills men with wisdom, like the Pishon,
   and like the Tigris at the time of the first fruits.
[26]It makes them full of understanding, like the Euphrates,
   and like the Jordan at harvest time.
[27]It makes instruction shine forth like light,
   like the Gihon at the time of vintage.

WISDOM CANNOT BE FATHOMED

[28]Just as the first man did not know her perfectly,
   the last one has not fathomed her;
[29]for her thought is more abundant than the sea,
   and her counsel deeper than the great abyss.[m]

BEN SIRA'S WISDOM TEACHING
TAKES ON ASPECTS OF DIVINE WISDOM

[30]I went forth like a canal from a river
   and like a water channel into a garden.
[31]I said, "I will water my orchard
   and drench my garden plot";
 and lo, my canal became a river,
   and my river became a sea.
[32]I will again make instruction shine forth like the dawn,
   and I will make it shine afar;
[33]I will again pour out teaching like prophecy,[n]
   and leave it to all future generations.
[34]Observe that I have not labored for myself alone,
   but for all who seek instruction.

a. These verses imply that Wisdom's self-praise is pronounced in the assembly of the Divine Council; cf. the self-predication by Wisdom in Prov 8 and the praise of Wisdom in the congregation of the pious, Apocryphal Psalm 154. Cf. The Ahikar fragment, cited above, p. 204.

b. Cf. Ahikar, quoted above, p. 204, and contrast the previous passage, which stresses the inaccessibility of wisdom; see also Job 28. Hans Conzelmann ("The Mother of Wisdom," in James M. Robinson, ed., *The Future of Our Religious Past*

[London: SCM Press, 1971] 230–43) and others, taking up a view formulated long ago by Wilfred L. Knox ("The Divine Wisdom," *Journal of Theological Studies* 38 [1937] 230–37), argue that the figure of Wisdom in vv. 3–7 derives from that of Isis. This is by no means a certainty.

c. Cf. Prov 2:6; creation in Genesis is by divine speech.

d. That is, the seat of Wisdom is in the heavens; see note *b*.

e. See 1:3 and cf. also Job 38:16.

f. The phrase "gotten a possession" is difficult. Most naturally v. 6b might be expected to announce Wisdom's inability to find a dwelling among the nations. Then that which follows in vv. 7–8 would be most easily comprehended. As it stands, however, v. 6 must be related to the widely ranging travels by Wisdom which form the subject of vv. 5–6a.

g. Is this a deliberate evocation of the tabernacle tent of the sanctuary? Compare v. 10 and Wis 9:8, below. The same verb describes the incarnation of the *Logos* in John 1:14.

h. Cf. Deut 32:9; Sir 17:17. This is the first of our texts identifying Wisdom and Torah; cf. Apocryphal Psalm 154 (18:14).

i. That is, Wisdom is established in Zion because she served God in the (apparently heavenly) tabernacle; cf. also Wis 9:8, below, p. 222.

j. A fertile oasis on the western shore of the Dead Sea. Note the carefully structured imagery of this lyrical passage, which moves from one type of comparison to another.

k. See 1:16.

l. Cf. Deut 4:6; the idea might have been heightened and stressed in deliberate opposition to the ideals of Hellenistic culture.

m. The statements above that God alone can search out Wisdom should be viewed in light of statements like these. Cf. also Job 28:27; Sir 1:3.

n. Observe the importance that the Sage attributes to his own teaching. Cf. also vv. 30–31 with vv. 25–27; 38:34; 39:1. These attributes are also reflected by the prologue to the Greek translation of the book, written by ben Sira's grandson. For the term "prophecy," see also Wis 7:27.

ISRAEL'S QUEST FOR WISDOM

Baruch 3:9—4:4

Certain standard elements of the Wisdom poems are to be observed in this passage: the quest for Wisdom (3:15, 28ff.); her value is above gold; God alone, who created the wonders of Nature and the world, has known her and he has given her not to men in general but to Israel. Even though it was probably composed in Greek in the second or first century B.C.E., it shows no discernible influence of Hellenistic ways of thought.

ISRAEL IS REPROACHED FOR
ABANDONING WISDOM

3 ⁹Hear the commandments of life, O Israel;
    give ear, and learn Wisdom!
¹⁰Why is it, O Israel, why is it

that you are in the land of your enemies,
that you are growing old in a foreign country,[a]
that you are defiled with the dead,
11   that you are counted among those in Hades?
12You have forsaken the fountain of Wisdom.
13If you had walked in the way of God,
   you would be dwelling in peace forever.

14Learn where there is Wisdom,
   where there is strength,
   where there is understanding,
  that you may at the same time discern
   where there is length of days, and life,
   where there is light for the eyes, and peace.

WHERE IS WISDOM?

15Who has found her place?[b]
and who has entered her storehouses?

THE POWERFUL, WEALTHY, AND STRONG
HAVE NOT FOUND HER

16Where are the princes of the nations,
   and those who rule over the beasts on the earth;
17those who have sport with the birds of the air,
   and who hoard up the silver and gold, in which men trust,
   and there is no end to their getting;
18those who scheme to get silver, and are anxious,
   whose labors are beyond measure?
19They have vanished and gone down to Hades,
   and others have arisen in their place.[c]

20Young men have seen the light of day,
   and have dwelt upon the earth;
  but they have not learned the way to knowledge,
   nor understand her paths,
   nor laid hold of her.
21Their sons have strayed far from her way.

THE PROVERBIAL WISE MEN OF THE NATIONS
DO NOT HAVE WISDOM

22She has not been heard of in Canaan,
   nor seen in Teman;
23the sons of Hagar, who seek for understanding on the earth,
   the merchants of Merran and Teman,[d]

the storytellers and the seekers for understanding,
have not learned the way to Wisdom
     nor given thought to her paths.

THE MIGHTY MEN OF OLD
DO NOT HAVE WISDOM

²⁴O Israel, how great is the house of God!
     and how great the territory that he possesses!
²⁵It is great and has no bounds;
     it is high and immeasurable.
²⁶The giants were born there, who were famous of old,^e
     great in stature, expert in war.
²⁷God did not choose them,
     nor give them the way to knowledge;
²⁸so they perished because they had no wisdom,
     they perished through their folly.

WISDOM IS HIDDEN AND
ONLY GOD THE CREATOR KNOWS HER PLACE

²⁹Who has gone up into heaven, and taken her,
     and brought her down from the clouds?
³⁰Who has gone over the sea, and found her,^f
     and will buy her for pure gold?
³¹No one knows the way to her,
     or is concerned about the path to her.

³²But he who knows all things knows her,
     he found her by his understanding.
He who prepared the earth for all time
     filled it with four-footed creatures;
³³he who sends forth the light, and it goes,
     called it and it obeyed him in fear;
³⁴the stars shone in their watches and were glad;
     he called them, and they said, "Here we are!"
They shone with gladness for him who made them.
³⁵This is our God;
     none other can be compared to him!^g

WISDOM IS TORAH

³⁶He found the whole way to knowledge,
     and gave her to Jacob his servant
     and to Israel whom he loved.
³⁷Afterward she appeared upon earth
     and lived among men.

4 ¹She is the book of the commandment of God,
  and the law that endures forever.
All who hold her fast will live,
  and those who forsake her will die.

²Turn, O Jacob, and take her;
  walk toward the shining of her light,
³Do not give your glory to another,
  or your advantages to an alien people.

⁴Happy are we, O Israel,
  for we know what is pleasing to God.

  a. In earlier sources, exile is a punishment for breaking the commandments of the Torah, not for abandoning wisdom.
  b. Cf., e.g., Job 28:12.
  c. Cf., in apocalyptic perspective, 1 Enoch 98:2–3.
  d. The proverbial wisdom of the Canaanites and particularly of the Arab tribes is here referred to; cf. 1 Kgs 4:30–31; Prov 30:1; 31:1.
  e. Cf. Gen 6:4; Num 13:33.
  f. Deut 30:11–14 is the source from which these rhetorical questions are drawn. There they are answered positively: the Torah is close to you, it is in your heart. Contrast Baruch's use of these biblical verses with that in Rom 10:5–7, where the same verses are used of the search after Christ.
  g. Vv. 33–35 seem to be inspired by Isa 40:22–26.

In this poem certain of the implications of the coming together of Torah and Wisdom are worked out. Wisdom teaching had traditionally been directed to the individual student. Once Torah and Wisdom were identified, the call to observe the ways of Wisdom became equally the call to observe the commandments of the Torah. If so, the addressee might be not just the single disciple, but the nation of Israel, which as a whole was bound by the Torah. Reproach for not following the way of Wisdom addressed to the whole of Israel resembles the prophets' censure of Israel for not observing the commandments of God. The idea already observed in the Wisdom of ben Sira 24—that Wisdom-Torah is the peculiar inheritance of Israel—here comes to the fore.

JEWISH HELLENISTIC WISDOM

Of quite different character is the Wisdom of Solomon. This is an example of the way wisdom teaching developed in Jewish Hellenistic circles.[7] In the second of the three parts into which this book is divided (6:12–16 and 6:21—10:21), there is a sustained hymn of praise to Wisdom. In it Wisdom's relationship to God is expressed in a most daring way; she is divine and is spoken of in highly exalted terms, yet God granted her to Solomon, and he bestows her upon all men. This poetic section is deeply influenced by Hellenistic culture. In particular, the hymns in praise of Isis, an Egyptian goddess of Wisdom whose Hellenized cult spread throughout the Greco-Roman world, have left traces in it.[8]

Solomon Discusses Wisdom

Wisdom of Solomon 7:15—8:1

INVOCATION TO GOD, THE GIVER OF WISDOM

7 [15]May God grant that I speak with judgment
    and have thoughts worthy of what I have received,
  for he is the guide even of wisdom
    and the corrector of the wise.
[16]For both we and our words are in his hand,
    as are all understanding and skill in crafts.

THE CONTENT OF SOLOMON'S WISDOM

[17]For it is he who gave me unerring knowledge of what exists,[a]
    to know the structure of the world and the activity of the elements;
[18]the beginning and end and middle of times,
    the alternations of the solstices and the changes of the seasons,
[19]the cycles of the year and the constellations of the stars,[b]
[20] the natures of animals and the tempers of wild beasts,
  the powers of spirits[c] and the reasonings of men,
    the varieties of plants and the virtues of roots;[d]
[21]I learned both what is secret and what is manifest,
[22] for wisdom, the fashioner of all things, taught me.

Observe that the range of Wisdom's teaching in this passage may be determined as much by Solomon's reputation as arch-magician as by the extent of knowledge usually attributed to teachers of wisdom. It has also been seen as reflecting the encyclopedic range of Hellenistic learning.[9]

THE NATURE OF WISDOM

[22b]For in her there is a spirit that is intelligent,[e] holy, unique, manifold,
    subtle,
  mobile, clear, unpolluted,
  distinct, invulnerable, loving the good, keen,

23   irresistible, beneficent, humane,
       steadfast, sure, free from anxiety,
       all-powerful, overseeing all,
       and penetrating through all spirits that are
       intelligent and pure and most subtle.
24For wisdom is more mobile than any motion;
       because of her pureness she pervades and penetrates all things.

WISDOM AND GOD[f]

25For she is a breath of the power of God,
       and a pure emanation[g] of the glory of the Almighty;
       therefore nothing defiled gains entrance into her.
26For she is a reflection[h] of eternal light,
       a spotless mirror of the working of God,
       and an image of his goodness.

WISDOM IN THE WORLD

27Though she is but one, she can do all things,
       and while remaining in herself, she renews all things;
   in every generation she passes into[i] holy souls
       and makes them friends of God,[j] and prophets;[k]
28for God loves nothing so much as the man who lives with wisdom.

CONCLUDING PRAISE OF WISDOM

29For she is more beautiful than the sun,
       and excels every constellation of the stars.
   Compared with the light she is found to be superior,
30for it is succeeded by the night,
       but against wisdom evil does not prevail.
8 1She reaches mightily from one end of the earth to the other,
       and she orders all things well.[l]

a. The range of subjects this passage presents has no parallel in other Jewish wisdom books.

b. That is, calendar, astronomy, and astrology—three intimately related branches of learning in the Hellenistic period.

c. Probably a reference to Solomon's famous ability to control demons.

d. Medical and magical knowledge are intended here.

e. This list of the characteristics of Wisdom exhibits much influence of Greek (particularly Stoic) philosophy and psychology. James M. Reese (*Hellenistic Influence on the Book of Wisdom*, 13–15) gives a detailed account of this.

f. These verses clearly depict Wisdom as an emanation of God.

g. A Greek philosophical and religious idea.

h. Or "radiance," a Hellenistic religious term.

i. The term used by Pythagorean philosophy for metempsychosis.

j. An expression not encountered in the Hebrew Bible but common in Hellenistic usage.

k. In these verses, Wisdom is described as omnipotent and entering the souls of the holy to make them prophets. With the latter, cf. Sir 24:33.

l. Note the role of Wisdom in the created world.

Solomon's Prayer

Wisdom of Solomon 9

SOLOMON PRAYS TO GOD TO GRANT
HIM WISDOM

1 O God of my fathers and Lord of mercy,
    who has made all things by your word,
[2]and by your wisdom has formed man,[a]
    to have dominion over the creatures you have made,
[3]and rule the world in holiness and righteousness,
    and pronounce judgment in uprightness of soul,
[4]give me the wisdom that sits by your throne,[b]
    and do not reject me from among your servants.
[5]For I am your slave and the son of your maidservant,
    a man who is weak and short-lived,
    with little understanding of judgment and laws;
[6]for even if one is perfect among the sons of men,
    yet without the wisdom that comes from you he will be regarded as
        nothing.

GOD HAS CHOSEN SOLOMON AND
LAID HEAVY CHARGES ON HIM

[7]You have chosen me to be king of your people
    and to be judge over your sons and daughters.
[8]You have given command to build a temple on your holy mountain,
    and an altar in the city of your habitation,
    a copy of the holy tent which you prepared from the beginning.[c]

THEREFORE LET GOD
SEND WISDOM TO HIM

[9]With you is Wisdom, who knows your works
    and was present when you made the world,[d]
  and who understands what is pleasing in your sight
    and what is right according to your commandments.
[10]Send her forth from the holy heavens,
    and from the throne of your glory[e] send her,
  that she may be with me and toil,
    and that I may learn what is pleasing to you.
[11]For she knows and understands all things,
    and she will guide me wisely in my actions
    and guard me with her glory.

[12]Then my works will be acceptable,
  and I shall judge your people justly,
  and shall be worthy of the throne of my father.

MAN CAN KNOW WISDOM ONLY
IF GOD GRANTS IT

[13]For what man can learn the counsel of God?
  Or who can discern what the Lord wills?
[14]For the reasoning of mortals is worthless,[f]
  and our designs are likely to fail,
[15]for a perishable body weighs down the soul,
  and this earthly tent burdens the thoughtful mind.
[16]We can hardly guess at what is on earth,
  and what is at hand we find with labor;
  but who has traced out what is in the heavens?
[17]Who has learned your counsel, unless you have given wisdom,
  and sent your holy spirit from on high?
[18]And thus the paths of those on earth were set right,
  and men were taught what pleases you,
  and were saved by wisdom.

a. Man is created by God's Wisdom. Is this an exegesis of Gen 1:27? For the role of Wisdom in creation, cf. also Jer 51:15; Ps 104:24; Prov 3:19; cf. also Ps 136:5; Apocryphal Psalms 26:9–15.
b. The term is also used of Isis. Cf. below, v. 10, and 1 Enoch 84:3.
c. Cf. also Sir 24:10.
d. Wisdom is present in creation.
e. Cf. v. 4, above.
f. This and the following verses are founded upon Greek views of man and his psychology.

In Wisdom of Solomon 9 the same central themes are expressed as in the other Wisdom poems, including Wisdom's role in creation, the quest for her, and God's bestowal of Wisdom upon men. The personal yearning for the experience of Wisdom expressed in this passage is more intense than in the poems discussed previously in the Wisdom of ben Sira, the Book of Baruch, and so forth. Perhaps this reflects the Hellenistic emphasis upon personal religious experience.

FURTHER OBSERVATIONS

The poems we have presented are central texts illustrating the development of the concept of wisdom in the second temple period. As we have seen, they reflect two themes. According to the first of these, wisdom comes to be identified with the Torah revealed to Israel through Moses. The second theme is the emergence of personified Wisdom, which becomes an attribute of God closely associated with him and is construed as an instrument by which his action in creation can be described.

As we shall see in the next section, the intermingling of these two themes undergoes further development in both Jewish and Christian texts. On the one hand, Wisdom is understood in a specific sense as God's revelation first and foremost to Israel. On the other hand, Torah as Wisdom gains a cosmic dimension; it was the plan by which the world was created. Moreover, as the writings of Philo of Alexandria and the prologue of the Gospel according to John show, Wisdom should be viewed in the broader context of other types of hypostases in the Greco-Roman period, for example, the Greek *Logos* ("word" or "reason"). For Christians, the divine creative Wisdom, or *Logos*, is revealed on earth not as Torah but in Jesus of Nazareth.

Before turning to these later texts, we shall take note of two other developments in the use of the language and imagery of Wisdom, which do not fit precisely our previous categories.

Wisdom Teaching Broadly Construed

A number of texts indicate the broad currency of wisdom terminology in the second temple period. Apocryphal Psalms col. 18 (see above, p. 20) applies the language of Wisdom to the study of Torah carried on in sectarian circles. Indeed, it came to be applied to various types of teaching, even those that had no necessary connection with the ordinary teaching of the wisdom books or with the developments of hypostatized Wisdom. For example, The Rule of the Community refers to the special doctrines and way of life of the Qumran sect in wisdom terms:

> And these are their (the spirits') ways in the world: to enlighten the heart of man and to make straight before him all the ways of true righteousness . . . and a spirit of . . . understanding and intelligence and the wisdom of might" (4:2–3; cf. Isa 11:2).

Later, the Rule speaks of those who "walk in wisdom or in foolishness" (4:24). Similarly, according to 4 Ezra 14, the seventy apocalyptic, secret writings which are revealed to the seer contain "the spring of understanding, the fountain of wisdom, and the stream of knowledge." In another dimension, some apocalypses talk of wisdom that will be revealed to the righteous at the end of days (1 Enoch 93:10; 91:11), and others refer to its disappearance as part of the upheavals that will precede the end (1 Enoch 93:8; 4 Ezra 5:10; 2 Bar 48:33, 36). This last theme is, perhaps, picked up in our next text.

Wisdom Withdraws from the World

1 Enoch 42

This passage is completely isolated from its context in 1 Enoch and is probably a fragment of a Wisdom writing.

1 Wisdom found no place where she might dwell;
  then a dwelling place was assigned to her in the heavens.
²Wisdom went forth to make her dwelling among the children of men,
  and found no dwelling place;
 Wisdom returned to her place,
  and took her seat among the angels.
³And unrighteousness went forth from her chambers;
  whom she sought not she found
  and dwelt with them,
 as rain in a desert
  and dew upon a thirsty land.

Here Wisdom is clearly a person. As in Wisdom of ben Sira 24 (see above, pp. 213–16), she is seated in heaven in the divine assembly (cf. also Aḥikar, above, p. 204) and she seeks a dwelling place on earth. However, the point of the present passage is that Wisdom has withdrawn from among humanity.[10]

DEVELOPMENTS AND PARALLELS

Philo of Alexandria

Jewish Hellenistic thinkers developed quite complex systems of hypostases. Wisdom, Greek *Sophia,* is one of them. Philo of Alexandria (ca. 25 B.C.E.–50 C.E.) describes her as God's virgin daughter and consort (see above, pp. 204–5).

On the Cherubim 49–50

I myself was initiated under Moses the God-beloved into his greater mysteries, yet when I saw the prophet Jeremiah and knew him to be not only himself enlightened but a worthy minister of the holy secrets, I was not slow to become his disciple. He out of his manifold inspiration gave forth an oracle spoken in the person of God to Virtue the all-peaceful. "Did you not call upon me as your house, your father and the husband of your virginity?" (Jer 3:4). Thus he implies clearly that God is a house, the incorporeal dwelling place of incorporeal ideas, that he is the father of all things, for he begat them, and the husband of Wisdom, dropping the seed of happiness for the race of mortals into good and virgin soil. For it is meet that God should hold converse with the truly virgin nature, that which is undefiled and free from impure touch; but it is the opposite with us. For the union of human beings that is made for the procreation of children turns virgins into women. But when God begins to consort with the soul, he makes what before was a woman into a virgin again, for he takes away the degenerate and emasculate passions which unmanned it and plants instead the native growth of unpolluted virtues. Thus he will not talk with Sarah till she has ceased from all that is after the manner of women (Gen 18:11) and is ranked once more as a pure virgin.

On Flight and Finding 50–51

For you shall find the house of wisdom a calm and fair haven, which will welcome you kindly as you come to your moorings in it; and it is wisdom's name that the holy oracles proclaim by "Bethuel," a name meaning, in our speech, "Daughter of God," yes, a true-born and ever-virgin daughter, who by reason alike of her own modesty and of the glory of him that begot her has obtained a nature free from every defiling touch.

He called Bethuel Rebecca's father. How, pray, can Wisdom, the daughter of God, be rightly spoken of as a father? Is it because, while Wisdom's name is feminine, her nature is manly? As indeed all the virtues have women's titles, but are powers and activities of consummate men. For that which comes after God, even though it were chiefest of all other things, occupies a second place, and therefore was termed feminine to express its contrast with the Maker of the Universe, who is masculine, and its affinity to everything else. For preeminence always pertains to the masculine, and the feminine always comes short of and is lesser than it.

Equally striking is Philo's language in his treatise On Drunkenness, where he states, "With his knowledge (i.e., his Wisdom) God had union, not as men have it, and begat created being" (30), and where he calls Wisdom "mother and nurse of all" (31; cf. Sir 4:11). Here and in the two texts quoted above, allegory and literary figure are involved, but a mythological structure probably lies behind these characterizations of Wisdom. It is not clear, however, what the relationship might have been between such a myth and the older mythical structure(s) very likely underlying the Wisdom of Aḥikar, Job, Proverbs, and Baruch (see above, pp. 204–5).

A development of the role of *Sophia* somewhat later than that in Philo appears in Gnostic cosmogonic and cosmological myths involving the descent (sometimes the fall) of *Sophia*. Most probably the figure of *Sophia* in these texts derived from Jewish sources.[11]

The New Testament

It is notable that the hypostasis of Wisdom plays little role in the New Testament, while that of the *Logos* became one of the terminologies used to describe Jesus' relationship to God.

John 1:1–14

1 In the beginning was the Word,
    and the Word was with God,
    and the Word was God.
[2]He was in the beginning with God;
[3]   all things were made through him,
    and without him was not anything made that was made.
[4]In him was life,
    and the life was the light of men.
[5]The light shines in the darkness,
    and the darkness has not overcome it.
[6]There was a man sent from God, whose name was John. [7]He came for
    testimony, to bear witness to the light, that all might believe
    through him. [8]He was not the light, but came to bear witness to
    the light. [9]The true light that enlightens every man was coming
    into the world. [10]He was in the world, and the world was made
    through him, yet the world knew him not.
[11]He came to his own home,
    and his own people received him not.
[12]But to all who received him, who believed in his name, he gave power
    to become children of God; [13]who were born, not of blood nor of
    the will of the flesh, nor of the will of man, but of God. [14]And the
    Word became flesh and dwelt among us, full of grace and truth; we
    have beheld his glory, glory as of the only Son from the Father.

1 Corinthians 1:18–25

Here Christ is called the Wisdom of God in the context of an argument designed to show how this is utterly different from human power and wisdom. The connection of Wisdom with the Greeks (vv. 22–24) is notable.

18 For the word of the cross is folly to those who are perishing, but to us who are being saved it is the power of God. [19]For it is written,

"I will destroy the wisdom of the wise,
   and the cleverness of the clever I will thwart."
[20]Where is the wise man? Where is the scribe? Where is the debater of this age? Has not God made foolish the wisdom of the world? [21]For since, in the wisdom of God, the world did not know God through wisdom, it pleased God through the folly of what we preach to save those who believe. [22]For Jews demand signs and Greeks seek wisdom, [23]but we preach Christ crucified, a stumbling block to Jews and folly to Gentiles, [24]but to those who are called, both Jews and Greeks, Christ, the power of God and the wisdom of God. [25]For the foolishness of God is wiser than men, and the weakness of God is stronger than men.

Other texts in the New Testament also use terminology and conceptions deriving from the wisdom tradition, but they do not use the term "wisdom" explicitly. Such texts, describing Jesus as the incarnate Wisdom, are, for example, Philippians 2:6–11, Colossians 1:15–20, and Hebrews 1:1–3.

Rabbinic Texts

In rabbinic literature the identification of Wisdom and Torah is self-evident, and Torah takes on cosmic functions which were previously those of Wisdom. The passage below interprets Genesis 1:1, applying to it verses from the Wisdom poem in Proverbs 8.

Genesis Rabba 1:1

"In the beginning God created" (Gen 1:1): R. Oshaya began the discourse:

" 'And I was beside him like a little child ('āmôn) and I was daily a delight' (Prov 8:30). . . . Another explanation is: 'āmôn (little child)— this means 'ûmān (craftsman). The Torah says, 'I was the Holy One's tool of craftsmanship.' Just as it is customary in the world, when a human king builds a palace he does not do so on his own counsel but on that of a craftsman. And the craftsman does not build it on his own counsel but has tablets and plans so as to know where he should make rooms and gateways. Thus the Holy One looked into the Torah and created the world. And the Torah says: 'In (or: with) the beginning God created . . .' (Gen 1:1). 'Beginning' is Torah just as it says, 'The Lord possessed me the beginning of his way' (Prov 8:22)."

Here the Torah is the cosmic plan according to which the world was created (cf. also Philo, On the Creation of the World, who uses the same image of the architect). The whole poem of Proverbs 8:22–31 is interpreted simply of Torah. There is no special role of the concept of Wisdom in rabbinic thought, but the cosmic dimension of Torah becomes central.

A Pagan Text

Praise of Isis

It has been suggested that the various inscriptions listing the praises of Isis are derived from a single archetype in Memphis (Egypt). This is by no means certain; there is, however, a clear resemblance between the self-predication of Isis in texts like the following and Wisdom poems, particularly in the Wisdom of Solomon (see also, above, on Sir 24, Wis 7).

Demetrius, son of Artemidorus, and Thraseas, the Magnesian from the Maeander, crave the blessing of Isis. The following was copied from the stele which is in Memphis, where it stands before the temple of Hephaestus:

I am Isis, the mistress of every land, and I was taught by Hermes, and with Hermes I devised letters, both the sacred (hieroglyphs) and the demotic, that all things might not be written with the same (letters).
I gave and ordained laws for men, which no one is able to change. . . .
I divided the earth from the heaven.
I showed the paths of the stars.
I ordered the course of the sun and the moon.
I devised business in the sea.
I made strong the right. . . .
I protect (or: honor) righteous guards.
With me the right prevails.
I am the Queen of rivers and winds and sea.
No one is held in honor without my knowing it.
I am the Queen of war.
I am the Queen of the thunderbolt.
I stir up the sea and I calm it.
I am in the rays of the sun.

I inspect the courses of the sun.
Whatever I please, this too shall come to an end.
With me everything is reasonable.
I set free those in bonds.
I am the Queen of seamanship.
I make the navigable unnavigable when it pleases me.
I created walls of cities.
I am called the Lawgiver.[a]
I brought up islands out of the depths into the light.
I am Lord[b] of rainstorms.
I overcome Fate.
Fate harkens to me.
Hail, O Egypt, that nourished me!

a. Thesmophoros, a classical epithet of Demeter.
b. Note masculine form.

NOTES

1. James Pritchard, *Ancient Near Eastern Texts* (Princeton: Princeton University Press, 1955) 421.

2. W. F. Albright, *From the Stone Age to Christianity* (Baltimore: Johns Hopkins Press, 1957) 368.

3. Prov 2:16–19; see also 5:1–23; 6:20–29; and chap. 7. This theme also comes to the fore in one of the Qumran documents, 4Q 184, as read by John Strugnell, "Notes en Marge . . . ," *Revue de Qumran* 26 (1970) 263–68. The interpretation of this figure has, however, been the subject of some debate.

4. Some scholars, such as W. F. Albright, have argued against the generally accepted late date of this passage, urging an ancient Canaanite or Ugaritic origin.

5. This is not the first "Wisdom Psalm," of course, and Psalms 1, 32, 49, 112, and 128 have the strongest claim to this title. They do not include the same themes as Apocryphal Psalm 154.

6. About two-thirds of the Wisdom of ben Sira survived in Hebrew, and it is completely preserved in Greek and Syriac translations, the Greek being the work of the author's grandson and dating some time soon after 132 B.C.E.

7. See also the Greek translation of Proverbs (particularly of 8:22ff.) and the fragments of the philosopher Aristobulus, Philo's predecessor (on Philo, see below).

8. James M. Reese, *Hellenistic Influence on the Book of Wisdom*, 46–48. Indeed, some would claim that this second part of the Wisdom of Solomon is partly intended to answer the challenge of the cult of Isis.

9. Michael E. Stone, "Lists of Revealed Things in Apocalyptic Literature," *Magnalia Dei*, ed. F. M. Cross et al. (Garden City, N.Y.: Doubleday, 1976) 436–38.

10. The withdrawal of wisdom could also be related to the sharp dualism of the apocalypses which regard the present world or age as bereft of divine guidance.

11. To illustrate this development in detail would lead beyond the confines of this presentation, but an excellent discussion of the matter is that by George W. MacRae, "The Jewish Background of the Gnostic Sophia Myth," *Essays on the Coptic Gnostic Library* (Leiden: Brill, 1970) 86–108.

BIBLIOGRAPHY

PRIMARY SOURCES

The Bible and Apocrypha are quoted from the RSV; the Pseudepigrapha from *APOT*, vol. 2; The Rule of the Community from A. Dupont-Sommer, *The Essene Writings from Qumran* (Cleveland: Meridian, 1962); Philo from LCL. The Cyme Isis inscription is cited from Frederick C. **Grant,** *Hellenistic Religions* (New York: Bobbs-Merrill, 1953) 131–33.

SECONDARY SOURCES

Burton L. **Mack,** "Imitatio Mosis: Patterns of Cosmology and Soteriology in the Hellenistic Synagogue," *Studia Philonica* 1 (1972) 27–55. George W. **MacRae,** "Sophia Myth," in *Essays on the Coptic Gnostic Library* (Leiden: Brill, 1970) 86–101. Roland E. **Murphy,** *Introduction to the Wisdom Literature of the Old Testament* (Collegeville: Liturgical Press, 1956). Gerhard **von Rad,** *Wisdom in Israel* (London: SCM Press, 1972). James M. **Reese,** *Hellenistic Influence on the Book of Wisdom and Its Consequences,* Analecta Biblica 41 (Rome: Biblical Institute, 1970). Ulrich **Wilckens** and Georg **Fohrer,** "Sophia," in *TDNT* 7:465–526, with extensive further bibliography.

Index of
Passages Quoted